MW00811586

# The Zero Percent

*Secrets of the United States,*
*the Power of Trust, Nationality,*
*Banking & ZERO TAXES!*

**Written By:**

**Du'Vaul Dey**

THE ZERO PERCENT

Copyright © 2021 by Imago Dei Publishing, Inc.

All rights reserved. Printed in the United States of America. No part of this book may be used or reproduced in any manner whatsoever without the prior written permission of the copyright owner except in the case of brief quotations or references embodied in critical articles or reviews.

This book is a work of non-fiction. Names, individuals, businesses, organizations, places, events, incidents and laws are strictly used to express information made available to the public. The information contained in this book is provided for informational purposes only, and should not be construed as legal advice on any subject matter but considered a lawful guide in common law. Proper counsel from a private lawyer or private professional advice is advised from acting on the basis of any and all content included in this book. The author and its associated persons (whether natural or artificial) may freely, write and publish their sentiments on all subjects, being responsible for the abuse of that right; and no law shall be passed to restrain or abridge the liberty of speech or of the press – Section Nine, 1849 California Constitution. No bill of attainder, ex post facto law, or law impairing the obligation of contracts, shall ever be passed. Section Sixteen, 1849 California Constitution. He who takes with notice of an equity takes subject to that equity.

For information contact:
imagodeipublishing@swissmail.com
Book and Cover design by Rasel Khondokar
Copyright Number: 00071692-1
Edited by: Du'Vaul Dey
Cover Art by: Rasel Khondokar
Formatted: Rasel Khondokar

# CONTENTS

# Introduction

M ost people are not entirely sure what they want to do or how to go about accomplishing it. So, they resort to getting an education, as if that's the cure-all to one's wealth aspiration. Graduating high school or college can be a huge accomplishment for most citizens, permanent residents, and foreign nationals in the United States, especially if it means being the first to graduate in the family! Being led to believe that the world's treasures are within arm's reach and so many options for success are now available; however, selecting the right path can be a course in itself.

After all, time is short, and time is money! Just as all people have an innate existential drive to understand who they are and why they are here, they also desire to create generational wealth. Some will be fortunate enough to locate a reputable firm, put in their time, and reach retirement or even learn a trade to one day run a successful business, but for some, not so much. Others have been in the work field with or without secondary education, creating one financial plan after another, renewing paying off student loans and credit card debt repeatedly. For some reason, the debt doesn't go away fast enough to see a difference in life. Life feels stagnant! If only wages covered enough monthly expenses to save enough money to eventually fire the boss and start the right business to earn money needed to pay off debts and finally experience freedom.

So how does one start a business? There are two types of classes in the world; the one-percenters or the ninety-nine percenters. Indeed, it is no secret that the best Fortune 500 companies have high-end attorneys who manage the step-by-step setup process for their client's businesses and at a hefty service charge that most people may not immediately be fortunate enough to afford at first. However, vigilance and a never-ending studious mindset position the individuals into the one percenters' realm. Many have the investor mentality and have thought long and hard about joining the 90% of the world's millionaires, who earned their wealth through real estate investing. Overall, people are just tired of the 9 to 5, Monday through

Friday, or what has become a more desirable work schedule, the four-tens.

Certainly, time is something that cannot be refunded, and every second deserves to be spent efficiently and by choice. Again time is short, and time is money! Everyone has either thought about going to the banks for cash to consolidate or invest. How the cash is managed with the attached interest is very important. Either borrowers pay the debt and have fun, or borrow to spend for a profit, which in turn pays the debt and a good life. This is what intelligent investors would call "good debt." Everyone who has prepared to enter into a repayment agreement has planned financial strategies before the loan application is approved. Although FICO scores may not be at their best, with high hopes, it should be good enough for the bank to provide funding, right?

Going into the bank can be nerve-racking, whether it's in person with a local banker or via an online application. So many people have experienced bankers explain credit denials with comments such as,

"It looks like Transunion and Equifax scores are exceptional; however, the Experian score does not meet our requirements. If a co-signer is available, we may be able to move forward!"

Sounds familiar, right? The uneasy feeling of credit rejection from the bank is a terrible experience. Having to involve a family member or a trustworthy friend to provide their creditworthiness is even worse. If traditional funding fails, then what else is there for a real estate investment deal? Indeed, all beginner real estate investors have scoured online to find many methods of "No Money No Credit" investment strategies from an endless list of real estate gurus. After all, the great Robert Kiyosaki had explained in his writings that real teachers are defined as teachers who practice what they teach. Unlike general public school teachers, their multi-layered degrees qualify them to teach the theory of the subject. In all actuality, generating profits from practical experience is lacking from the public school system teachers and professors. The truth is, no teacher or professor in the secondary or post-secondary education sector will tell their students that they can take today's lesson in class and go out into the world and make a successful profit.

Several real estate gurus charge an arm and a leg for their seminars, and worst of all, the reviews from their students alert many people to be aware of a scam or brilliant Ponzi Scheme. The only profit the students have made is a whopping zero. Simultaneously, the appetite for freedom and wealth still grows, while seeing and hearing more millionaires displaying their lavish life or introducing a "buy my money-making course" ad on YouTube, Tic-Tok, Facebook, Twitter, and Instagram. Their success is attractive, but the frustration from the due diligence process can be daunting! In America, the public schools have taught Americans, go to school, get a job, save money in a 401k, live within their means, finance a house, and pay taxes. And what exactly does that model produce? Anyone who has followed that model or knows someone who has certainly knows it most assuredly leads to more debt, on account of the financial banking system that has been in place in the United States ever since the enactment of the Federal Reserve Act in 1913. That system is known as a central banking operation that functions from a fractional reserve system, which does nothing for the economy but increases the national debt and inflates the U.S. dollar, raising the cost of everyday goods and services.

What happens when a college degree allows a salary cap that finally reaches a threshold and cannot sustain everyday expenses due to inflation? The answer is more debt and more time needed to continue education seeking another degree to earn an additional annual $20k to $35k. Suppose an employee continues school and completes the extra training and successfully obtains that salary increase and reaches retirement, living off a fixed income. The cost of everyday goods and services continues to rise, surpassing that fixed income. What happens when the retiree's property tax becomes too expensive because of the surrounding neighborhood's increase in property value due to gentrification? What other options are there at the age of retirement? As scary as it sounds, the reality is that the elderly community is working past the age of 65 at local retail stores and offices. It would easily make sense to increase current wage earnings and reduce the current tax bracket to as low as Zero Percent to encourage significant savings for other entrepreneurial endeavors. What if Federal, State, Social Security, and Medicare taxes were not withheld from employee earnings and did not have to be paid during tax season? What if that were the case for self-employment 1099 information filings as well? How much of that could be saved in the right asset-building account for the future?

There are precisely seven tax brackets for most ordinary incomes in the United States; 10 percent tax, 12 percent tax, 22 percent tax, 24 percent tax, 32 percent tax, 35 percent tax, and 37 percent tax, and believe it or not, tax is voluntary. Many people here in the United States live beyond the American Dream, whether they are United States citizens, United States nationals, or Nationals.

Many of them understand life is not a journey but instead a process. The life of a journey goes up and down, not knowing when or where the goal is nigh. A process is tested time and time again with successful results, no matter the environment, and has a foreseeable end before it begins. The wealthy understand the necessary process of obtaining generational wealth from a simple truth, which is understanding how the United States truthfully came into existence, how it operates commercially, and how it applies to its inhabitants.

The United States Constitution speaks of three different classes of people. The people, the subjects, and the citizens! What type are the majority today, and is one better than the other? It is a fact that there are approximately 11 million millionaires since 2017 and 788 billionaires in the United States since 2019, and most of them do not pay any taxes despite the famous saying, "The more you make, the more they take." Believe it or not, it has nothing to do with illegal tax evasion or hiding money in shell companies in tax haven countries. What exactly do the millionaires and billionaires know, and why does it seem like the educated alumni are the first to complete an unemployment application during a government financial crisis? How are the wealthy fairly procuring extreme amounts of money? Don't the tax bracket rules eat up most of their profits? How do they maintain good credit for 100% loan approvals several times a year? Does it take years to save substantial amounts of money to start a tax-exempt business? The answers to these meaningful questions have always been at the forefront, but knowing where to look and applying the information is another thing. Each chapter in The Zero Percent will provide the hidden answers many financial titans keep within their fold.

To resolve most Americans' financial issues, one must evaluate the various strategies of real estate investing and banking, credit secrets based on the Fair Isaac Corporation (FICO), entering a new commercial status, all while comprehending the truth about the United States and its affiliates. All resources are provided for anyone to easily obtain certified copies of the undeniable evidence before the reconstruction of the united States of America (republic government). It's imperative to explain the step-by-step process to start any business the right way and obtaining federal and state recognition in their system to never be required to file not one tax return statement from day one! Instead, if it is the company owner's choice, a well-executed filing would provide a refund in the exact amount earned in the fiscal tax year. This is just one of the many trade-secrets kept by the one-percenters that operate under treaty law with the United States derived from God's ordinances. The Internal Revenue Service and the United States Treasury Department are in sync with Biblical Treaty Law. The commencement of business in the united States of America or anywhere in the world requires an understanding of biblical trade secrets regarding trust, which affects commerce; practiced by the wealthiest nations on earth, such as the Jews, Mennonites, Chinese, Saudi Arabians, Armenians, etc. Although the steps and procedures are subject to change over time, learning the commerce rules will lead to many untold truths about one's nationality and its importance to encourage all aspects of stronger and wiser families. Be prepared for the in depth legal jargon and it is recommended to repeatedly read the information until fully comprehended.

# CHAPTER ONE

# The United States Corporation

The United States is a what? It's widespread that the United States is short for saying the United States of America, but how exactly can an entire country be on the same playing field as Apple, Amazon, Facebook, or Microsoft corporations? It is accurate, and Congress does not hide the truth in their codes and statutes. It may sound awkward to the majority because the elected officials never refer to the country as a company. In Title 28 U.S. Code § 3002 section 15, "United States" means – (A) a Federal corporation. The United States Corporation's Articles of Incorporation, file number

100009, was filed with the Secretary of State of New York, July 15, 1925, with its principal office in the Centennial Building, Tallahassee, Leon County. Section three and four states,

The maximum number of shares, which this corporation is authorized to have outstanding at any time is ONE HUNDRED (100), each of which shares shall have a par value of ONE HUNDRED DOLLARS ($100).

(Section Three)

The amount of capital with which the corporation will begin business is FIVE HUNDRED DOLLARS ($500).

(Section Four)

A certified copy of this imperative historical document can be obtained in Florida, revealing that the corporation is perpetual, meaning everlasting. The certificate provides its directors as Chief Executive Officer, Chief Financial Officer, and Secretary of the United States Corporation. These individuals are the private officers; the public officers known as Donald Trump and Mike Pence or Joe Biden and Kamala Harris. However, this document is indeed not the origin of the United States of America. In March of 1861, Abraham Lincoln gave his first inaugural speech. Surprisingly, the address translated to the English language from the Arabic language and many other treaties the United States has with the Aboriginal and Indigenous people. They were here in North, South, and Central

America, long before Columbus. A straightforward search within the Library of Congress to find his speech titled Abraham Lincoln First Inaugural Address (1861), which the first paragraph cites,

> In compliance with a custom as old as the government itself, I appear before you to address you briefly and to take in your presence the oath prescribed by the Constitution of the United States to be taken by the President before he enters on the execution of this office. I do not consider it necessary at present for me to discuss those matters of administration about which there is no special anxiety or excitement. Apprehension seems to exist among the people of the Southern States that by the accession of a Republic Administration, their property and their peace and personal security are to be endangered. There has never been any reasonable cause for such apprehension. Indeed, the amplest evidence, to the contrary, has all the while existed and been open to their inspection. It is found in nearly all the published speeches of him who now addresses you. I do but quote from one of those speeches when I declare that—I have no purpose, directly or indirectly, to interfere with the institution of slavery in the States where it exists. I believe I have no
>
> lawful right to do so, and I have no inclination to do so.
>
> *(Abraham Lincoln First Inaugural Address, 1861)*

Some keynotes to address regarding the President's speech. First, they are high tensions coming from the southern states regarding their property (i.e., their slaves) and President Lincoln's policy regarding the subject matter. He states that he has no plans to interfere with the slave trade in those particular states. Anyone who has studied history on a general level understands that Lincoln is known as the Great Emancipator, who freed the "black" slaves from involuntary servitude in 1865. Yet, he states he does not want to get involved with the institution of slavery.

Secondly, the proof of a mistranslation from the Arabic language to the English language when Lincoln states, "It is found in nearly all the published speeches of "him" who now addresses you." If Lincoln is the one giving the speech, he would not address himself as "Him" in the third person but instead in the first person, such as, "It is found in nearly all the published speeches that I have addressed you." One could think, how can such a mistake happen within an undisputable lawful congressional record? A more accurate question would be, why is President Lincoln speaking in Arabic in his inaugural speech in North America in 1861? Surprisingly, Latin was the common language in the entire world. There are words in one language that do not exist in another language to describe it adequately. The congressional record continues to reveal that President Lincoln explains how the corporation became to be and quote,

Descending from these general principles, we find the proposition that in legal contemplation, the Union is perpetual confirmed by the history of the Union itself. The Union is much older than the Constitution. It was formed, in fact, by the Articles of Association, in 1774. It was matured and continued by the Declaration of Independence in 1776. It was further matured, and the faith of all the then thirteen States expressly plighted and engaged that it should be perpetual, by the Articles of Confederation in 1778. And finally, in 1787, one of the declared objects for ordaining and establishing the Constitution was to "form a more perfect Union."

(Abraham Lincoln First Inaugural Address, 1861)

According to President Lincoln, the United States Corporation found its existence from the Articles of Association in 1774. So what exactly are articles of association? The Articles is a document that specifies the regulations for a company's operation and defines its purpose. A company's articles of incorporation detail what the organization can and cannot do. Including appointing directors and handling financial records. Very similar to a select group of individuals who decide to start a corporation or LLC, and its articles of incorporation or organization must be approved by the state's Secretary of State because the corporation or LLC is seeking existence from the state in which it will transact business. The most obvious question is, if the individuals who seek to start a company must first obtain approval from the Secretary of State, then who approved the United States Corporation's articles? What authority permitted the

U.S. corporation to exist? After all, Abraham Lincoln did say that the Constitution did not come about until 1787. To answer this question, examining the Articles of Association, 1774 itself, should provide great insight. It reads,

> That from and after the first day of December next, we will not import, into British America, from Great-Britain or Ireland, any goods, wares, or merchandise whatsoever, or from any other place, any such goods, wares, or merchandise, as shall have been exported from Great-Britain or Ireland; nor will we, after that day, import any East-India tea from any part of the world; nor any molasses, syrups, paneles, coffee, or pimento, from the British plantations or from Dominica; nor wines from Madeira, or the Western Islands; nor foreign indigo.

> *(Article One)*

> We will neither import nor purchase, any slave imported after the first day of December next; after which time, we will wholly discontinue the slave trade, and will neither be concerned in it ourselves, nor will we hire our vessels, nor sell our commodities or manufactures to those who are concerned in it.

> *(Article Two)*

The first article tells us that commerce took place under British America, and various merchandise would cease importation from Great Britain to East-India. A more important fact is found in the second article, that no slave of any kind, meaning voluntary or involuntary servitude, would be allowed due to the slave trade being discontinued. How is it that slavery was allowed within the Southern States as Lincoln addressed and then abolished in North America in 1865 if slavery was never intended to occur as per the initial document that created the United States in 1774? Another fair question is, who exactly were the slaves involved in the slave trade during that time? A lot of attention and condemnation is directed towards the African slave trade tragedy. The 16th and 19th century is when this took place. However, another equally despicable trading of humans was taking place around the same time in the Mediterranean's proximity. The Barbary pirates enslaved approximately 1.25 million Europeans, and their lives were just as pitiful as the Africans. They were referred to as the white slaves of the Barbary Slave Trade. Slavery is one of the oldest transactions known to man, and the records of the slave trade date back to The Code of Hammurabi in Babylon in the 18th century, are available. People from virtually every significant culture, civilization, and religious background have made slaves of their own and enslaved other peoples. However, comparatively little attention is focused on the prolific slave trade carried out by the pirates of corsairs along the Barbary coast (as the Europeans called it in that period) in what is now the empire of Morocco, Algeria, Tunisia, and Libya beginning around 1600 AD. In the 13th and 14th centuries, Christian pirates were primarily from Catalonia and Sicily, which conquered all admiralty seas, posing a constant threat to merchants. It was not until the Ottoman Empire's expansion in the 15th century that the Barbary corsairs started to become an irritable problem to Christian vessels. While the Barbary slave trade is depicted as Muslim corsairs capturing white Christian victims, the pirates were not concerned with the ethnicity or religious orientation of those held in captivity. Slaves in Barbary could be of any color with multiple backgrounds: black, brown or white, Catholic, Protestant, Orthodox, Jewish, or Muslim. It was all about their class of commercial status, which dictated slavery or not. The pirates were not only Muslim; however, English privateers and Dutch captains of the Dutch India Trading Company also exploited the ever-changing loyalties of how neighboring friends could quickly become enemies and enemies' could become colleagues with the stroke of a pen as per private contracts.

The captive slaves by the Barbary pirates faced a dark and horrible future. Many perished on the ships during the long voyage back to North Africa (North America, at this time) due to disease or lack of sustenance and hydration. Those who survived were taken to slave markets where they would stand for hours while buyers inspected them before selling at public or private auctions. Once slaves were purchased, they were immediately forced to work in several ways. Men were assigned to hard manual labor using their strength, such as working the quarries or heavy strenuous construction, while women and children were used for housework or sexual servitude. At night, the slaves were placed into prisons called bagnios that were uncomfortably hot and overcrowded. However, the worst fate for a Barbary slave could endure working the oars of galleys. Rowers were shackled together, seated, and never allowed to stand or leave their post. No form of privacy was allowed in the oars, only sleeping, eating, defecation, and urination at the oars' seat. Managing overseers would crack the whip over the bare backs of any slaves considered not to be working hard enough. As previously stated, Dutch captains were working alongside the Barbary pirates, who were associated with a significant Atlantic Slave Trade company named the Dutch West India Company, whose native name is Geoctrooieerde Westindische Compagnie. It was a Chartered West India Company founded on June 3, 1621, by Willem Usselincx and Jesse de Forest and other Dutch merchants and foreign investors. The company was permitted a charter for a trade monopoly founded within the Dutch West Indies. It is known that the Republic of the Seven United Netherlands granted this permission under the empire of Morocco and gave jurisdiction over Dutch participation in the Atlantic Slave Trade, Brazil, the Caribbean, and North America. Looking back at Walt Disney's Pirates of the Caribbean's film franchise, British America always displayed their Dutch West or East India Company flag while at sail, fighting against the pirates (i.e., Barbary pirates). All slaves within the company were classified as the Dutch West India Company employees and took on the identity, Indian! This is where the term Indian originates. The trading company could operate in West Africa and the Americas, which further included what is known today as the United States' outlying possessions.

There were slaves of all skin tones coming to the Americas, not just from Africa, contrary to popular belief, as told in public school textbooks. To refer back to the original question, who played the Secretary of State's role authorizing the Articles of Association of 1774 permitting the British America Corporation to transact agricultural and merchandise business on North American lands? The great Moor, the Sultan, in connection with his Majesty's King George, governed many dominions and permitted the Anglo-Saxon traders from Great Britain to begin their agricultural conquest on the east of North America (ancient Egypt – Mehomitan Nation), which developed into the Thirteen Colonies, which led to the development of the Department of Agriculture in 1862. The Atlantic Slave Trade aligned with the Dutch West India Trading Company, on the colonies' territories, found its way into the Southern States of America. Now, what exactly is a Moor? A Moor is currently known today as a Black or African American, with a complexion formerly known as swarthy (dark olive-skinned) or tawny (yellowish, red, golden-skinned). The term Moor is throughout the 1599 Geneva Bible, describing everyone to be swarthy and tawney complexion. The newer translated bibles purposely replace the Moors with Phoenicians, Ethiopians, Greeks, or Hebrews. Intermarrying took place between the Moors and the less-melanated slaves, referred to as quadroons, a person who is one-quarter Moor ancestry, and octoroons, a person who is one-eighth

Moor ancestry, or hexadecaroons, which is a person who has one-sixteenth Moor ancestry. Intermarrying led to mulatto's (a person mixed white and Moor ancestry, especially a person with one white and one Moor parent).

The Sultan, also referred to as the Imperial Majesty, permitted the Articles of Association of 1774 for the British America Corporation. That very document stated that no slavery of any kind would take place within North America. The Anglo-Saxons of Great Britain were under slavery themselves, controlled by the British Moors (i.e., Brutish Moors), including the European Slavic's (slaves), and others were being mistreated and brought to North America; all while under the reign of King George III (a Moor). The European Slavic's, the Africans, the Octoroons, etc., and other highly "melanated" people were branded Negro, Colored, Indian, Black remained as slaves except for the Anglo-Saxon peoples. The others were considered a rebel group and promoted insurrection against the Brutish Moors. King George III was a Moor, who possessed plenipotentiary action, ruled Britain as a Dominion of Morocco (Mehomitan Nation) under the Sultan, and authorized the Declaration of Independence of 1776, freeing the Anglo-Saxons from the Brutish Moors, to inhabit the available territories of incorporated British America within the colonies.

For a certified photograph of "His Most Sacred Majesty King George III," write the following mailing address: "Science Museum of London Exhibition Rd London SW7 2DD, United Kingdom" and request an authenticated copy, as seen on the following page.

His Most Sacred Majesty George III, King of Great Britain

Although the Declaration of Independence of 1776 freed the slaves, slavery was still oppressive throughout the thirteen colonial territories. It was repackaged and sold in a new form known as debtor camps of debtor prisons. Before diving into the debtor camps, Abraham Lincoln stated it was the Articles of Confederation of 1778 to follow the Declaration of Independence. The former British America Corporation would later be known as the United States of America in Congress Assembled. The Articles of Confederation kindly addresses all in the onset,

"To all to whom these presents shall come, We, the undersigned, Delegates of the States affixed to our Names, send greeting: Whereas the Delegates of the United States of America in Congress assembled, did on November 15, in the year of our Lord one thousand seven hundred and seventy-seven, and in the second year of the Independence of America, agree to certain Articles of Confederation and Perpetual Union between the states of New Hampshire, Massachusetts bay, Rhode Island and Providence Plantations, Connecticut, New York, New Jersey, Pennsylvania, Delaware, Maryland, Virginia, North Carolina, South Carolina, and Georgia."

In 1787, the United States of America's Constitution was finalized to make a perfect union between all the states during a constitutional convention. It was all a republic in an attempt to bring together the Powhatan Confederacy and Iroquois Confederacy. In New York on December 1, 1789, George Washington of the Washitaw Tribe wrote a letter to his masonic brother, Emperor Sidi Mohammed. The letter is fascinating due to the unknown truth that the two confederacies (Powhatan and Iroquois) were at war with each other regarding matters of the right to leave the property in trust to their heirs who were Mulattos from the intermarrying with Indian women of the Dutch slave trade. It was against the Mehomidan Law to turn over the property from a creditor or one who held Title of Nobility over to one who had a debtor's status, which was not of full blood descent. Title of Nobility was the real issue that motivated the Civil War between the confederacies and the apprehension within the Southern States that Lincoln was referring to in his inaugural speech of 1861!

The letter from Washington to the Emperor can be found within the Library of Congress or on founders.archives.gov/documents. It reads,

> To Sidi Mohammed, Since the Date of the Letter, which the "late Congress," by "their President" (meaning previous republican Moor President), addressed to your Imperial Majesty, the United States of America have thought proper to "change their Government," (meaning the Moors of the Continental Congress Assembled) and to "institute a new one" (meaning from republic to democratic) agreeable to the Constitution, of which I have the Honor of, herewith, enclosing a Copy. The Time necessarily employed in this arduous Task, and the Derangements occasioned by so great, though "peaceable a Revolution" (meaning to peacefully change the political system of one's country), will apologize, and account for your Majesty's not having received those regular "Advices, and Marks of Attention" (meaning blackmail or tax payment for protected services), from the United States, which the Friendship and "Magnanimity" (meaning generous in forgiving an insult) of your Conduct, towards them, afforded reason to expect. The "United States" (meaning corporation), having unanimously appointed

me to the supreme "executive" (meaning having the power to put plans, actions, or laws into effect) authority, in this nation, your Majesty's Letter of the August 17, 1788, which, by Reason of the "Dissolution" (meaning the closing down or dismissal of a republic) of the late government, remained unanswered, has been delivered to me. I have also received the Letters which your Imperial Majesty has been so kind as to write, in Favor of the United States, to the Bashaws of Tunis and Tripoli, and I present to you the sincere acknowledgments, and Thanks of the United States, for this important Mark of your Friendship for them. We greatly regret that the hostile Disposition of those Regencies, towards this nation, who have never injured them, is not to be removed, on Terms in our power to comply with. Within our "Territories" (meaning thirteen colonies) there are no Mines, either of Gold, or Silver, and this young nation, just recovering from the "Waste and Desolation of a long War" (meaning the Civil War including the wars between Tunis, Tripoli, Iroquois and Powhatan), have not, as yet, had time to acquire Riches by Agriculture and Commerce. But our Soil is bountiful, and our People industrious; and we have reason to flatter ourselves, that we shall gradually become useful to our Friends. The Encouragement which your Majesty has been pleased, generously, to give to our commerce with your "Dominions" (meaning territory of the Mehomitan Nation) the Punctuality with which you have caused the treaty with us to be observed, and the just and generous Measures taken, in the Case of Captain Proctor, made a deep Impression on the United States, and confirm their Respect for, and Attachment to your Imperial Majesty. It gives me Pleasure to have this Opportunity of assuring your Majesty that, while I remain at the "Head of this Nation" (meaning United States Corporation), I shall not cease to promote every Measure that may conduce to the Friendship and Harmony, which so happily subsist between your Empire and them, and shall esteem myself happy in every Occasion of convincing your Majesty of the high Sense (which in common with the whole nation) I entertain of the Magnanimity, Wisdom, and "Benevolence" (meaning the quality of kindness) of your Majesty. In the Course of the approaching Winter, the national Legislature (which is called by the former Name of Congress) will assemble, and I shall take Care that Nothing be omitted that may be necessary to cause the Correspondence, between our Countries, to be maintained and conducted in a Manner agreeable to your Majesty, and satisfactory to all the Parties concerned in it. May the Almighty bless your Imperial Majesty, our great and magnanimous Friend, with his constant Guidance and Protection. Written at the City of New York the first Day of December 1789. –

Addressed to our great and magnanimous Friend, His imperial Majesty, the Emperor of Morocco.

*(From George Washington To Sidi Mohammed, December 1, 1789 – founders.archives.gov)*

Regarding the penal colonies, as mentioned, the former Moors, now known as the Negro, the Black, the Colored, the Octoroon, and even the Indian employee of the Dutch slave trade, would eventually accumulate great amounts of debt from the loss of Title of Nobility. Working in the thirteen colonies, debts were paid to the Department of Agriculture collections department, in contract with the Dutch East/West India Trading Company. The inhabitants of the debtor prisons were to work off their debt. As the Mehomidan Law was ignored by the Moors, intermingling their seed with foreigners and seeking to pass their inheritance to their offspring, the various wars continued, leaving the Sultan with no choice but to strip their title of nobility away to preserve the lands and the law. New trustees would emerge and control their inheritance in trust, placing the Moors' remnants to become indebted and to endure the Trials of Job. In the Bible and the Quran, Job experienced loss and hardship that no man has ever experienced.

The British (Anglo-Saxons, New Trustees) used colonial North America as a penal colony through indentured servitude. Merchants transported convicts and Indians, auctioned to plantation trustees upon arrival to the colonies. An estimated 50,000 British convicts (Indian employees) were delivered to colonial North America. Transported convicts represented perhaps a quarter of all British emigrants during the 18th century. For example, the colony of Georgia was founded by James Edward Oglethorpe, who originally intended to use prisoners taken largely from debtor prisons, creating a "Debtor Colony," where the prisoners could learn trades and work off their debts. Every photograph or paintings of a black slave adult or child working on the plantations was attributed to this purpose, a debtor prison or colony for nothing more than working off debts, not slaves brought to America from Africa alone. General James Edward Oglethorpe founded the Georgia Corporation, known today as the State of Georgia. The General, including other trustees such as Thomas Marriott (a forefather of JW Marriott) of the Colony of Georgia, agreed with the Creek Nation to become the land's trustees to collect debts owed to His Majesty, King George. The Creek Nation lands had become populated with Dutch India Trading Company employees (Indians) that assumed the land from the native Moors due to intermarrying and death from the many wars. The collection of debts to the Colony of Georgia was collected from the Indians, also known as Five Dollar Indians, to surrender their rebellion and insurrection against Great Britain. The trustee(s) of the Colony of Georgia would become the equitable owners in exchange for $300,000 as consideration, leaving the Creek Nation as "tenants in commons." The evidence of this trade can be reviewed within the Treaty of Savannah of 1733 and The Georgia Historical Quarterly, March 1920, Vol. 4, No. 1, pages 3-16, which reads,

To All to Whom these Presents shall come: I Stephen Theodore Janssen Lord Mayor of the City of London In pursuance of an act of Parliament made and passed in the fifth year of the Reign of our Sovereign Lord King George the Second Entitled an Act for the more easy recovery of Debts in His Majesty's Plantations and Colonies in America,

*(Page 4 - The Georgia Historical Quarterly, March 1920, Vol. 4, No. 1)*

And they do acknowledge the Grant they have already made to the Trustees for Establishing the Colony of Georgia in America all the Lands upon Savannah River as far as the Ogeechee and all the Lands along the Sea-Coast as far as the River St. John's and as high as the tyde flows and all the Islands as far as the said River Particularly the Islands of Frederica, Cumberland and Amelia to which they have given the names of his Majesty King George's Family out of gratitude to him. But they Declare that they did and do reserve to the Creek Nation the Lands from Pipe Maker's Bluff to Savannah and the Islands of Saint Catherines, Ossebaw, and Sapelo; and they further declare that all the said Lands are held by the Creek Nation as Tenants in Common –

*(Page 7 - The Georgia Historical Quarterly, March 1920, Vol. 4, No. 1)*

The Charter of Georgia of 1732 can be examined from the Lillian Goldman Law Library, The Avalon Project that reads,

And whereas we have been well assured, that if we will be most graciously pleased to erect and settle a corporation, for the receiving, managing and disposing of the contributions of our loving subjects; divers persons would be induced to contribute to the uses and purposes aforesaid-Know ye, therefore, that we have, for the considerations aforesaid, and for the better and more orderly carrying on the said good purposes; of our special grace, certain knowledge and mere motion, willed, ordained, constituted and appointed, and by these presents, for us, our heirs and successors, do will, ordain, constitute, declare and grant, that our right trusty and well-beloved John, lord-viscount Percival, of our kingdom of Ireland, our trusty and well-beloved Edward Digby, George Carpenter, James Oglethorpe, George Heathcote, Thomas Tower, Robert Moore, Robert Hucks, Roger Holland, William Sloper, Francis Eyles, John Laroche, James Vernon, William Beletha, esquires, A. M. John Burton, B. D. Richard Bundy, A. M. Arthur Bedford, A. M. Samuel Smith, A. M. Adam Anderson and Thomas Corane, gentlemen; and such other persons as shall be elected in the manner hereinafter mentioned, and their successors to be elected in the manner hereinafter directed; be, and shall be one body politic and corporate, in deed and in name, by the name of the Trustees for establishing the colony of Georgia in America. And we do hereby, for our heirs and successors, ordain, will and establish, that for and during the term of twenty-one years, to commence from the date of these our letters patent, the said corporation assembled for that purpose, shall and may form and prepare, laws, statutes, and ordinances, fit and necessary for and concerning the government of the said colony, and not repugnant to the laws and statutes of England.

The State of Georgia is a corporation like every other "State Of," within the United States of America Corporation. Its trustees listed above were the Anglo-Saxon peoples from Britain who were once property to the British (Brutish) Moors. Shortly after the Declaration of Independence, in 1776 and within the same year as the Articles of Confederation, in 1778, the thirteen colonies' trustees formed the United States. Of the thirteen colonies were the Delawares who are also recognized as the Delaware Nation and they instituted the six article Treaty With the Delawares, 1778. The Delaware Nation were Moors and were nationals. They are not to be mistaken as Indians. The treaty states,

> Articles of agreement and confederation, made and, entered; into by, Andrew and Thomas Lewis, Esquires, Commissioners for, and in Behalf of the United States of North-America of the one Part, and Capt. White Eyes, Capt. John Kill Buck, Junior, and Capt. Pipe, Deputies and Chief Men of the Delaware Nation of the other Part.

*Article V.*

Whereas the confederation entered into by the Delaware nation and the United States, renders the first dependent on the latter for all the articles of clothing, utensils and implements of war, and it is judged not only reasonable, but indispensably necessary, that the aforesaid Nation be supplied with such articles from time to time, as fas as the United States may have it in their power, by a well-regulated trade, under the conduct of an intelligent, candid agent, with an adequate salary, one more influenced by the love of his country, and a constant attention to the duties of his department by promoting the common interest, than the sinister purposes of converting and binding all the duties of his office to his private emolument: Convinced of the necessity of such measures, the Commissioners of the United States, at the earnest solicitation of the deputies aforesaid, have engaged in behalf of the United States, that such a trade shall be afforded said nation conducted on such principles of mutual interest as the wisdom of the United States in Congress assembled shall think most conducive to adopt for their mutual convenience.

*Article VI.*

Whereas the enemies of the United States have endeavoured, by every artifice in their power, to possess the Indians in general with an opinion, that it is the design of the States aforesaid, to extirpate the Indians and take possession of their country to obviate such false suggestion, the United States do engage to guarantee to the aforesaid nation of Delawares, and their heirs, all their territorial rights in fullest and most ample manner, as it hath been bounded by former treaties, as long as the said Delaware nation shall abide by, and hold fast the chain of friendship now entered into. And it is further agreed on between the contracting parties should it for the future be found conducive for the mutual interest of both parties to invite any other tribes who have been friends to the interest of the United States, to join the present confederation, and to form a state whereof the Delaware nation shall be the head, and have a representation in Congress: Provided, nothing contained in this article to be considered as conclusive until it meets with the approbation of Congress. And it is also the intent and meaning of this article, that no protection or countenance shall be afforded to any who are at present our enemies, by which they might escape the punishment they deserve.

The fifth article describes why the State of Delaware is known as the First State. The Delaware Nation provided an internal agreement to enter into trade markets with the United States. The sixth article provides that the United States had real enemies known as the southern States who wanted to eradicate or re-enslave all of the Indians from the slave trade with permission from the Moors of the Delaware Nation, including any other nations who agreed to aid the

United States. This treaty confirms that the Moors of the Delaware Nation, including other nations, are truly aboriginal to North America and are completely separate from the misnomer term Indian.

One of the most popular among the Anglo-Saxons was Benjamin (Ben' Yamin) Franklin, and he expressed who were present in not just the Americas but also the entire face of the earth. Franklin wrote many essays. One of his most important writings was sent to Peter Collinson and Richard Jackson, which appeared in the *Gentlemen's Magazine* for November 1755 and the *Scots Magazine* for April 1756. In 1760 and 1761, it was printed, with excisions, as an appendix to London, Dublin, Boston, and Philadelphia editions of Franklin's *Interest of Great Britain Considered*. It was reprinted in part in the London Chronicle, May 20, 1760. Franklin included it in the fourth edition of his *Experiments and Observations of Electricity*, 1769. His essay can also be found within the founders.archives.gov website; section twenty-three and twenty-four of the essay reads,

And since Detachments of English from Britain sent to America, will have their Places at Home so soon supply'd and increase so largely here; why should the "Palatine" (the meaning of an official or feudal lord having local authority that elsewhere belongs only to a sovereign) "Boors" (meaning ill-mannered persons) be suffered to swarm into our Settlements, and by herding together establish their Language and Manners to the Exclusion of ours? Why should Pennsylvania, founded by the English, become a Colony of Aliens, who will shortly be so numerous as to Germanize us instead of our Anglifying them, and will never adopt our Language or Customs, any more than they can acquire our Complexion, which leads me to add one Remark: That the Number of purely "white" (Anglo-Saxon) people in the world is proportionably very small. All Africa is black or "tawny" (yellowish, red, golden light-skinned). Asia is chiefly tawny! America (exclusive of the new Comers) wholly so! And in Europe, the Spaniards, Italians, French, Russians, and Swedes, are generally of what we call a "swarthy" (dark olive-skinned) Complexion; as are the Germans also, the Saxons only excepted, who with the English, make the principal Body of White People on the Face of the Earth. I could wish their Numbers were increased. And while we are, as I may call it, Scouring our Planet, by clearing America of Woods, and so making this Side of our Globe reflect a brighter Light to the Eyes of Inhabitants in Mars or Venus, why should we in the Sight of Superior Beings, darken its People? Why Increase the Sons of Africa by Planting them in America, where we have so fair an Opportunity, by excluding all Blacks and Tawneys, of increasing the lovely White and Red? But perhaps I am partial to the Complexion of my Country, for such Kind of Partiality is natural to Mankind.

(Observations Concerning The Increase of Mankind, 1751 – founders.archives.gov)

The main thing to take away from Mr. Franklin's words is that 269 years ago, people known today as "Blacks" or "African-Americans" were everywhere on the earth and people known as "Whites" are properly known as the Anglo-Saxons, are fairly new to inhabiting the earth. A large number of people referred to as either swarthy or tawny outnumbered them. Once the republican government of the United States of America Corporation was formed in 1787, its Constitution reformed to a democratic in 1789, as George Washington mentioned in his letter to the Emperor. It was necessary for the Moors within the First Continental Congress to establish a treaty for commerce with Morocco's other dominions (Mehomitan Nation). The Treaty – Between the United States of America, and His Imperial Majesty the Emperor of Morocco of January 1787, can be obtained through the Library of Congress. The Twenty-Six article treaty begins with a preface addressing its Ministers and Moroccan Ambassadors for his Majesty, the Emperor. Towards the end of the preface, before the seal of his Majesty, it reads,

> hath arranged articles for a treaty of amity and commerce between the United States of America, and his Majesty the Emperor of Morocco, which articles, written in the Arabic language, confirmed by his said Majesty the Emperor of Morocco, and sealed with his royal seal, being translated into the language of the said United States of America, together with the attestations thereto annexed, are in the following words, to wit: In the Name of Almighty God. This is a Treaty of Peace and Friendship established between us and the United States of America, which is confirmed, and which we have ordered to be written in this book, and sealed with our royal seal, at our court of Morocco, on the twenty-fifth day of the blessed month of Shaban, in the year one thousand two hundred, trusting in God it will remain permanent.

> (Treaty of Peace and Friendship – Treaties and Other International Acts of the United States of America. Edited by Hunter Miller, Volume 2, Documents 1-40: 1776-1818, Washington: Government Printing Office, 1931.)

Other evidence of the U.S. residing in Morocco (Mehomitan Nation) can be found in Public Law 857 – August 1, 1956, which reads,

Whereas the consuls of the United States in Morocco are permitted to exercise jurisdiction over American nationals under the treaty between the United States, and Morocco signed September 16, 1836, and the Act of Algeciras signed April 7, 1906.

(Public Law 857 – August 1, 1956, 70 STAT, page 774)

To further clarify P.L. 857, the consuls of the U.S. are located in North America (Morocco – Mehomitan Nation), and the U.S. is permitted jurisdiction over U.S. nationals, also known as U.S. citizens by the treaty of September 16, 1836; which is the Morocco – Treaty of Peace. Permission over American citizens can be found in articles twenty through twenty-three.

If any of the citizens of the United States, or any persons under their protection, shall have any disputes with each other, the Consul shall decide between the parties, and whenever the Consul shall require any aid or assistance from our government to enforce his decisions, it shall be immediately granted to him.

(*Morocco – Treaty of Peace: Article twenty*)

If a citizen of the United States should kill or wound a Moor, or on the contrary, if a Moor shall kill or wound a citizen of the United States, the law of the country shall take place, and equal justice shall be rendered, the Consul assisting at the trial; and if any delinquent makes his escape, the Consul shall not be answerable for him in any manner whatever.

(*Morocco – Treaty of Peace: Article twenty-one*)

If an American citizen shall die in our country, and no will shall appear, the Consul shall take possession of his effects; and if there shall be no consul, the effects shall be deposited in the hands of some person worthy of trust, until the party shall appear who has a right to demand them; but if the heir to the person deceased be present, the property shall be delivered to him without interruption; and if a will appears, the property shall descend agreeable to that will as soon as the Consul shall declare the validity thereof.

(*Morocco – Treaty of Peace: Article twenty-two*)

The consuls of the United States of America shall reside in any seaport of our dominion that they shall think proper, and they shall be respected, and enjoy all the privileges which the consuls of any other nation enjoy; and if any of the citizens of the United States shall contract any debts or engagements, the Consul shall not be in any manner accountable for them, unless he shall have given a promise in writing for the payment or fulfilling thereof, without which promise in writing, no application to him for any redress shall be made.

*(Morocco – Treaty of Peace: Article twenty-three - Treaties of Other International Acts of the United States of America, Edited by Hunter Miller, Volume 4, Documents 1-40: 1776-1818.)*

The democracy was further matured by establishing a separate city-state, a body corporate for the District of Columbia, formed on February 21, 1871. The 41st Congress, Session III, Chapter 61, 62, page 419, declares An Act to provide a Government for the District of Columbia, known as the Organic Act of 1871. It reads,

CHAP. LXII – An Act to provide a Government for the District of Columbia. Be it enacted by the Senate and House of Representatives of the United States of America in Congress assembled, That all that part of the territory of the United States included within the limits of the District of Columbia be, and the same is hereby, created into a government by the name of the District of Columbia, by which name it is hereby constituted a body corporate for municipal purposes, and may contract and be contracted with, sue and be sued, plead and be impleaded, have a seal, and exercise all other powers of a municipal corporation not inconsistent with the Constitution and laws of the United States and the provisions of this act.

*(Organic Act of 1871 – Section one, page 419)*

The Organic Act of 1871 is an Act of Congress that repealed the individual charters of the cities of Washington and Georgetown and established a new territorial government for the whole of D.C. The District of Columbia (controlling the world militarily) joined the other two city-states, Vatican City (controlling the world's religion) and London City (controlling the world's financial/law sector), to make up the three corporations, The Empire of the City, that runs the world. Due to the fourteenth amendment, many people, including the Moors who once had Title of Nobility and were creditors on their land (the Americas), lost their lawful status and nationality and became subject to the District of Columbia by way of the Sultan allying with the democratic United States. This truth can be found in the Library of Congress, titled Citizenship of the United States, Expatriation, etc.,

There are, strictly speaking, no Moroccan laws relating to citizenship of Moorish subjects in Morocco. The fundamental laws of this non-Christian country are based entirely upon the Islamitic code, no part of which treats the subject of citizenship. There are, however, numerous treaties and conventions between the various Christian countries and the Moorish Empire, by means of which citizenship in this country is defined; but, as I understand, from the above-acknowledged instructions, that it is not the desire of the Department to call for a report upon such lines, I will, therefore, confine these remarks to general conditions existing, which may possibly be of some use in connection with the information desired. (1) Citizenship in Morocco may be said to be governed by the laws pertaining to the same in other countries, with the exception that all persons residing in Morocco who cannot prove foreign citizenship or protection are considered ipso jure as Moorish subjects. (2 and 3) Moorish subjects lost their nationality only by becoming naturalized in or protected by another country having treaty relations with the Moorish Empire.

*(Citizenship of the United States, Expatriation, etc., Pages 459-460)*

The Moors lost their nationality after the Civil War by the fourteenth amendment to the United States constitution and other nationalities. Due to the several treaties connected with the U.S. and through naturalization and protection from the U.S., nationality is forfeited. The U.S. has maintained its position of power by utilizing deceiving contracts, in which U.S. citizens, U.S. nationals, and even foreign nationals unknowingly submit consent to several contracts. The deceptive contractual offers that promote protection and naturalization of the United States fall within the category of accepting benefits and privileges that the United States freely gives its citizens within the public sector. There is a difference between operating in public and in private. Such benefits and privileges of the United States consist of taking uncertificated securities, including everything related to the social security number, applications related to "driver's" licenses, and the so-called right to "vote." All of the above require the social security number to obtain a license or register to vote locally and nationally. The definition of a driver is,

> One employed in conducting a coach, carriage, wagon, or other vehicles, with horses, mules, or other animals, or a bicycle, tricycle, or motor car, though not a street railroad car.

> (See Davis v. Petrinovich, 112 Ala. 654, 21 South. 344, 36 L.R. A.615; Gen. St. Conn, 1902)

And the definition of vote is,

> Suffrage; the expression of his will, preference, or choice, formally manifested by a member of a legislative or deliberative body, or of a constituency or a body of qualified electors, in regard to the decision to be made by the body as a whole upon any proposed measure or proceeding, or the selection of an officer or representative. And the aggregate of the expressions of will or choice, thus manifested by individuals, is called tile "vote of the body."

> (See Maynard v. Board of Canvassers, 84 Midi. 228, 47 N.W. 756, 11 L. R. A. 332; Gillespie v. Palmer, 20 Wis. 546; Davis v. Brown, 46 W. Va. 716, 34 S. E. 839)

Upon comprehending the word driver's lawful definitions, the only person rightfully deserving of the title operates a motor vehicle as an employee with a registered employer. It doesn't stop there; there is more to the term driving that may come as a surprise. Per the United States Transportation Codebook, Title 49,

(4) "motor vehicle" means a vehicle, machine, tractor, trailer, or semitrailer propelled or drawn by mechanical power and used on public streets, roads, or highways, but does not include a vehicle operated only on a rail line.

*(Title 49, U.S.C. 31301 part four)*

(5) "motor vehicle operator's license" means a license issued by a State authorizing an individual to operate a motor vehicle on public streets,

roads, or highways.

(Title 49, U.S.C. 31301, part five)

In Title 49 the United States Code 31301, section six, seven, and eight, the definitions of driver's license, employee, and employer in the transportation codebook as follows,

(6) "driver's license" means a license issued by a State to an individual authorizing the individual to operate a motor vehicle on highways.

*(Title 49, U.S.C. 31301, part six)*

(7) "employee" means an operator of a commercial motor vehicle (including an independent contractor when operating a commercial motor vehicle) who is employed by an employer.

*(Title 49, U.S.C. 31301, part seven)*

(8) "employer" means a person (including the United States Government, a State, or a political subdivision of a State) that owns or leases a commercial motor vehicle or assigns employees to operate a commercial motor vehicle.

*(Title 49, U.S.C. 31301, part eight)*

And continuing in subsection 31301, part three and four, reads,

(3) A commercial driver's license means a license issued by a State to an individual authorizing the individual to operate a class of commercial motor vehicles.

*(Title 49 U.S. Code § 31301, part three)*

(4) commercial motor vehicle means a motor vehicle used in commerce to transport passengers or property that (A) has a gross vehicle weight rating or gross vehicle weight of at least 26,001 pounds, whichever is greater, or a lesser gross vehicle weight rating or gross vehicle weight the Secretary of Transportation prescribes by regulation, but not less than a gross vehicle weight rating of 10,001 pounds;

*(Title 49 U.S. Code § 31301, part four)*

This is the law dealing with motor vehicles, which requires a driver's license to operate. This is also describing what a commercial motor vehicle is in its weight class, which requires a commercial driver's license. But wait, the lawmakers have decided to move the true definition of a motor vehicle from Title 49, Transportation Codebook to Title 18, Crimes and Criminal Procedure. Title 18 U.S. Code 31 reads,

> (6) Motor Vehicles. – The term "motor vehicle" means every description of carriage or other contrivance propelled or drawn by mechanical power and used for commercial purposes on the highways in the transportation of passengers and property, or property or cargo.
>
> (*Title 49 U.S. Code § 31301, part six*)

The legal code and statute state a motor vehicle is for "commercial purposes only," carrying passengers or their property, which requires a driver's license or commercial driver's license. Many Americans drive small and large compact, midsize crossovers, S.U.V.s, and trucks throughout the united States of America with family, friends, and their furry friends. Question! Does the government consider all of the above to be legal passengers? Well, Title 49 U.S. Code subsection 32101, part 10 provides a clear understanding, which reads,

(10) "passenger motor vehicle" means a motor vehicle with motive power designed to carry not more than 12 individuals but does not include –

(A) a motorcycle; or

(B) a truck not designed primarily to carry its operator or passengers.

A passenger motor vehicle must be a motor vehicle that provides a commercial purpose and seats a maximum of 12 people. Any car sold among average families does not meet these standards. But what exactly does this law mean when it states "motive power" for passenger motor vehicles? Well, Merriam-Webster 1828 dictionary defines it as,

Definition of motive power –

1) an agency (such as water or steam) used to impart motion, especially to machinery
2) something (such as a locomotive or a motor) that provides motive power to a system

Anyone who holds a driver's license does not drive locomotive (cargo trains) vehicles to and from work or take their families on that annual road trip. If people are not drivers because they are not employees working for an employer going to the gym, grocery store, or to and from work and they're not operating a motor vehicle because they're not engaging in any action for commercial purposes, then why the need for a driver's license? The legal codes and statutes explain in the same 49th Title, subsection 32901, part 3, which reads,

> (3) except as provided in section 32908 of this title, "automobile" means a 4-wheeled vehicle that is propelled by fuel, or by alternative fuel, manufactured primarily for use on public streets, roads, and highways and rated at less than 10,000 pounds gross vehicle weight,

The truth is in plain sight! Regular everyday people do not operate motor vehicles; they operate automobiles on a non-commercial level, not needing a driver's license. Suppose one is not operating in a motor vehicle or passenger motor vehicle on behalf of an employer and the "automobile" weighs less than 10,000 pounds. In that case, that person is not "driving." They are simply traveling as a traveler on land and not as an employed driver. In the United States, all vehicle manufacturers have an average curb weight for compact cars at 2,919 pounds, midsize cars at 3,361 pounds, large cars at 3,882 pounds, compact trucks, or S.U.V's at 3,590 pounds, midsize trucks at 4,404 pounds, and large trucks or S.U.V's at 5,603 pounds. The current largest weighing truck or S.U.V. available for personal use and not for commercial use as an employee is the 2021 Ford F450 Super Duty Crew Cab, weighing 8,600 pounds. It is less than the minimum curb weight requirement to classify a traveler as a driver requiring a driver's license.

There is no code or statute within any State legislation or United States codebook that requires anyone to have a driver's license to operate an automobile but only for motor vehicles. Most of each state's citizens do not operate. Most Americans have experienced an unfortunate routine traffic stop by a policeman or state trooper and are always required to provide some identification. "License and registration, please!" Everyone has heard this demand and knows the consequences of not providing specific information when asked. So, if there is no "lawful" driver's license requirement for those operating an automobile, then what should one use as identification along with the registration and insurance documents? Many foreign nationals have a way around this, but for now, it is quite simple. If one is not an employed driver, then driving a motor vehicle is false, but instead, more correctly, a traveler traveling public roads and highways. A simple travel I.D. would suffice, such as a valid United States of America Passport Card.

> (e) Passport Card – A passport card is issued to a national of the United States on the same basis as a regular passport. It is valid only for departure from and entry to the United States through land and seaports of entry between the United States and Mexico, Canada, the Caribbean, and Bermuda. It is not a globally interoperable international travel document.

> *(Title 22 CFR 41.3 9(e))*

Passport means a travel document regardless of format issued under the authority of the Secretary of State attesting to the identity and nationality of the bearer.

*(Title 22 CFR 51.1)*

So, what should travelers say to any officer when pulled over on the roadside? If one does have a driver's license, it is best to keep it out of the officer's visibility and always have both hands on the steering wheel, displaying a calm demeanor. Keep in mind the driver's license is a contract, which permits the officer to issue an unlawful summons on a public easement. If the officer asks for the license and registration, ask the officer, "Are you seeking to identify my nationality properly? Or are you seeking a driver's license required for employees employed to operate a motor vehicle over 10,000 pounds for commercial purposes?" It may be wordy, but it is absolutely what the officer needs to hear from the traveler. The officer may try to pin the traveler into a corner, asking if the traveler is a resident of the state or if the automobile is properly registered with the Department of Motor Vehicles. To further entrap the traveler into the jurisdiction of the "STATE OF" whatever state ceded to the District of Columbia, the officer will proceed with persistence in obtaining a driver's license. It is up to the traveler to continue to stand their ground and provide the passport card, stating that the passport is valid for land, sea, and air travel. No driver's license is necessary for an automobile but only for motor vehicles over 10,000 pounds and employees operating on a commercial level. It is highly recommended that all travelers study and be well-versed in the subject of their state's Constitution. And not just any constitution but a state constitution before 1933 (the year of the United States Bankruptcy).

For example, if one lives in California State, an authenticated certified copy of the 1849 California Constitution can be obtained as an arsenal for any court case on the state level. If an officer continues to request a driver's license after the traveler has presented a valid U.S.A. Passport Card during a routine traffic stop, the traveler, should state the following,

"Sir or Ma'am, I have provided sufficient identification to a constitutional oath swearing officer. I would respectfully and lawfully request that you provide an affidavit of complaint, approved by a judge or clerk of the court, attached to your warrant to stop me and provide a search to my effects."

The statement alerts the officer that the traveler knows their God-given rights protected by the Constitution and confirms the officer's limits unless the traveler has physically harmed another citizen. Looking at the Declaration of Rights within the California State Constitution, it reads,

> The right of the "people" to be secure in their persons, houses, papers and "effects" against unreasonable seizures and searches, shall not be violated; and no warrant shall issue but on probable cause, "supported by oath or affirmation," particularly describing the place to be searched, and the persons and things to be seized.
>
> (1849 California State Constitution, Article One – Declaration of Rights – Section Nineteen)

Notice how section nineteen addresses the subject as "The People" of California and not the United States' citizens or subjects, pertaining to the District of Columbia. The people are the Californians, and if referring to the Nevada constitution, the people are the Nevadans or Oregonians or New Yorkers. According to this law, all officers who swear an oath to the Constitution to uphold the law must have a warrant based on probable cause supported by an approved attached affidavit (supported by oath or affirmation) from a competent judge or clerk of the court. So, how exactly is a routine traffic stop supposed to work if a traveler has not caused any harm to anyone? Well, simply put, suppose a traveler operating an automobile is speeding and runs a red light without injuring anyone in front of an officer. Constitutionally speaking, that officer is supposed to take down the travelers license plate, pull the traveler's information from their internal "motor vehicle" computer system, and begin the process of filing a complaint with the local superior or district court; awaiting approval from the clerk of court or the judge for a certified warrant, which is a summons. The Sheriff or a deputy within the traveler's county can then properly serve the traveler in person at their abode for a future court date. The law-breaking traveler could then present their case as innocent or guilty in front of their accuser before the court.

As mentioned before, foreign nationals have a way around using driver's licenses or passports. Driver licenses are valid within the local police department's system, and Passports only serve their purpose with State Trooper's registry system, so it is wise to understand which form of I.D. is necessary when dealing with specific law enforcement officers. However, foreign nationals and nationals of the republic of the united States of America utilize the laws provided in every state/country, allowing travelers to use a foreign driver's license without the need of the DMV. For example, in California Code, Vehicle Code – VEH § 12505 (f) states,

> Subject to Section 12504, a person over the age of 16 years who is a resident of a foreign jurisdiction other than a state, territory, or possession of the United States, the District of Columbia, the Commonwealth of Puerto Rico, or Canada, having a valid driver's license issued to him or her by any other foreign

jurisdiction may operate a motor vehicle in this state without obtaining a license from the department unless the department determines that the foreign jurisdiction does not meet the licensing standards imposed by this code.

In addition to California's foreign driver's license rule, Florida is the same in Title XXIII, Chapter 322, § 322.04 (c), which reads,

A nonresident who is at least 16 years of age and who has his or her immediate possession a valid noncommercial driver's license issued to the nonresident in his or her home state or country operating a motor vehicle of the type for which a Class E driver's license is required in this state.

A noncommercial driver's license issued from another county allows for foreign nationals and nationals of America, who are foreign to the "State" (Washington D.C.) falls in line with the Convention on International Road Traffic, signed into international law on September 19, 1949. This international treaty regulates automobile traffic, of which the United States of America became a member in 1952. Coupled with the foreign noncommercial driver's license is the International Driving Permit (IDP) issued from the driver's license country. It is valid in over 200 countries, and it obligates the traveler to follow all the traffic laws of the jurisdiction the traveler is operating the automobile. Some laws on the books are not designed for public safety but are mere excuses for the local authorities to check to see if the traveler has all documentation in order. With an IDP, an officer will generally treat the traveler with the utmost respect because the traveler is not in the officer's local computer system to engage in any form of a contract, such as a citation or a summons. IDP's can also be used to rent cars and trucks, cash checks, show proof of age, obtain a commercial airline or cruise ship admission ticket or general ID. It is also in the format of a passport book and must be given to any law enforcement officer with a foreign noncommercial driver's license. In regards to nationals living in the republic of the united States of America, who have personal effects (cars) as their everyday means of commuting, the IDP and the foreign noncommercial driver's license must be paired with the registration of the automobile with the DMV, but not in the traveler's name. Only in the name of a Trust! Suppose the traveler uses an IDP and foreign noncommercial driver's license with an automobile registered in their personal "ens legis" name with a domestic address. In that case, they are presenting a conflict of law, and the officer will most likely cite the traveler for "false identification."

Therefore, a Trust is a viable solution, registering the automobile in Trust, without any liens on the property. If there is a lien, it would be wise to utilize the Trust to lawfully challenge the creditor, questioning lawful consideration to remove the electronic lien holder with the Department of Motor Vehicles. The title must be at hand in the traveler's name as proof via a Bill of Sale before the DMV can transfer ownership to the Trust. The traveler must use a Trust name, which presents a significant presence, such as The Merovingian 0101 Trust, and the traveler must operate the automobile at all times as the beneficiary. A public trustee would be the person to register the automobile at the DMV on behalf of the beneficiary and obtain the Trust's insurance policy using their domestic driver's license. According to their private contract, the beneficiary would give the trustee the money to pay for the premium upfront or on monthly installments (Declaration of Trust and Minutes of Meeting). The public trustee would also provide the DMV with I.R.S. Form W-8BEN to prevent being obligated to annual registration fees. Like clockwork, the DMV will send the Trust its tags and registration without the need for franchise fees or smog checks. A foreign trust is not subject to the taxes owed by a domestic Trust ("State Of" or U.S.) In the upcoming chapters, a more in-depth explanation of proper I.R.S. forms will be provided. The beneficiary needs to obtain a new name and foreign address listed on their foreign noncommercial driver's license. For example, George Stuart, a New Yorker born in Manhattan, New York, could obtain a Panama or South Wales Australia driver's license along with the countries IDP, in the name George Duke or George Bey. This will ensure no cross-referencing of information should the officer perform a name search within the DMV database.

And lastly, to perfect the foreign noncommercial driver's license with an IDP and Trust registration process known as The Injunction Filing. Wealthy families and communities enforce their inalienable

God-given rights, protected by the Bill or Declaration of Rights of the State Constitution in the form of an injunction contract with the County Sheriff. The injunction is a three-step, First Notice, Notice to Cure, and Default Notice administration process sent via registered restricted mail to the County Sheriff, State Chief Justice, State Attorney General, and the State Governor's office. Once all three servings are complete, the traveler can rest assure they have been manually entered into a state of protection known as the "Do Not Detain" list for total protection and respect from local law enforcement against victimless crimes in the name of their Trust and a foreign new name. The injunction is such a powerful tool that can be used even if the traveler's automobile is not in Trust and they choose to list their original state driver's license name on the "Do Not Detain" list.

Regarding voting, the legislative members or qualified electors are the only persons required to select an officer or representative. There is no definition, no U.S. code, or any State code that includes citizens or subjects of the United States to vote for any President or Vice President. This is the reason for the existence of the Electoral College. Taking a look at the 1838 Florida Constitution, it reads,

> No special law shall be passed unless notice of intention to seek enactment thereof has been published in the manner provided by general law. Such notice shall not be necessary when the law, except the provision for referendum, is conditioned to become

effective only upon approval by a vote of the electors of the area affected.

*(1838 Florida Constitution – Article III Legislature – Section ten. Special laws)*

(c) QUALIFICATIONS. Each legislator shall be at least twenty-one years of age, an elector, and resident of the district from which elected and shall have resided in the state for a period of two years prior to the election. (*1838 Florida Constitution – Article III Legislature – Section fifteen. Terms and qualifications of legislators*)

The Department of Motor Vehicles has a role to play within voter registration in every state. All state constitutions provide information about those considered an elector's qualifications, electing high-ranking officials on behalf of the United States' citizens and subjects. Even the fourteenth amendment that caused the forfeiture of the Moors and other nationalities provides insight on who votes for the President and Vice President. As mentioned before, the uncertificated security known as the social security number or ITIN is a requirement for the driver's license application, at least for those who have an SSN from the Social Security Administration, which is a requirement to vote. Both applications play hand in hand per Title 52 of the United States codebook, which reads,

(a) In general

(1) Each State motor vehicle driver's license application (including any renewal application) submitted to the appropriate State motor vehicle authority under State law shall serve as an application for voter registration with respect to elections for Federal office unless the applicant fails to sign the voter registration application.

(2) An application for voter registration submitted under paragraph (1) shall be considered as updating any previous voter registration by the applicant.

(c) Forms and Procedures

(2) The voter registration application portion of an application for a State motor vehicle driver's license –

(c) shall include a statement that –

(i) states each eligibility requirement (including citizenship);

(ii) contains an attestation that the applicant meets each such requirement; and

(iii) requires the signature of the applicant, under penalty of perjury;

*(Title 52 U.S. Code § 20504. Simultaneous application for voter registration and application for motor vehicle driver's license)*

The applicant's free consent enters one into a special jurisdiction unknowingly unless the law in its entirety is read and understood. So, why exactly do these applications matter a great deal to the legislative officials? And what does the stripping of one's nationality mean? And why are the electors the only ones qualified to select certain officers and representatives? The answers are ultimately rooted in the fourteenth amendment mentioned in the latter half of this chapter. Before investigating this amendment, it is important to understand how the Department of Motor Vehicles and Voter Registration applications work together, determining citizens as debtors. It is accomplished through the Zone Improvement Plan, also known as the ZIP Codes. If one consents to reside in a ZIP Code, which is voluntary, that individual has automatically given jurisdiction to the District of Columbia and its agencies. The use of the ZIP Code is voluntary according to Domestic Mail Services Regulations, Section 122.32, and the United States Postal Service cannot discriminate against the non-use of the ZIP Code. According to the Postal Reorganization Act, Public Law 91-375 of August 12, 1970,

> (c) In providing services and in establishing classifications, rates, and fees under this title, the Postal Services shall not, except as specifically authorized in this title, make any undue or unreasonable discrimination among users of the mails, nor shall it grant any undue or unreasonable
>
> preferences to any such user.

*(Section 403, page 723)*

The federal government utilizes the ZIP Code program to validate citizens reside in a "federal district of the District of Columbia." The Internal Revenue Service and other similar agencies (STATE and FEDERAL) require a ZIP Code when they assert jurisdiction by sending its alleged citizens an official letter. The United States claims the need for a ZIP Code increases mail delivery speed and efficiency, but of course, this is a deceptive tactic. It is prima facie evidence that the alleged citizen is a "citizen of the District of Columbia" who is a "resident" in several States. The term resident is defined as,

> One who has his residence in a place; "Resident" and "Inhabitant" are distinguishable in meaning. The word "inhabitant" implies a more fixed and permanent abode than does "resident," and a resident may not be entitled to all the privileges or subject to all the duties of an inhabitant.
>
> [*Frost v. Brisbin, 19 Wend. (N.Y.) 11, 32 Am. Dec. 423.*]

The receiving of mail accompanying a ZIP Code is one of the requirements for the I.R.S. to have jurisdiction to send alleged citizens notices. The government cannot bill a non-citizen of the United States or a New Yorker national, for example, because they are not within the purview of the MUNICIPAL LAWS of the

*The Zero Percent*

District of Columbia (meaning the STATE OF NEW YORK or the STATE OF DELAWARE). The Internal Revenue Service has adopted ZIP Code areas as Internal Revenue Districts. According to the Federal Register Vol. 51, No. 53,

> Under the command of the President to establish and alter Internal Revenue Districts by section 7621 of the amended, and vested in me as Secretary of the Treasury by Executive Order 10289, approved September 17, 1951, as made applicable to the Internal Revenue Code of 1954 by Executive Order 10574, approved November 5, 1954, and according to the authority vested in me by section 321(b) of 31 U.S.C., and Reorganization Plan No. 1 of 1952 as made applicable to the Internal Revenue Code of 1954 by section 7804(a) of such code and by Executive Order 10574, the following Internal Revenue Districts continue as they existed before this order, with the changes noted below:
>
> 1. Designation of Internal Revenue Districts That Comprise an Entire State:
>
> Alabama, headquarters located in Birmingham, Alabama
>
> Alaska, headquarters located in Anchorage, Alaska
>
> Arizona, headquarters located in Phoenix, Arizona, etc.
>
> *(Federal Register/ Vol. 51, No. 53/ Wednesday, March 19, 1986, page 9571)*

60

The Postal Service is a private corporation, a quasi-governmental agency. It is no longer a full government agency during the days of the republic of the united States of America in Congress Assembled in 1787 before becoming a democracy in 1789. It is now like the Federal Reserve System, the Internal Revenue Service, and the United States Marshall Service. They are all outside the Federal Constitution's restrictions of 1789, as private corporations or, in other words, a business trust. They are all-powerful in their respective areas of responsibility to enforce collection for the federal debt. So, suppose a person uses a ZIP Code. In that case, that person is stating openly and notoriously that the person does not live in Nevada State, for example, but instead a "resident" in the Nevada Internal Revenue District (STATE OF NEVADA) of the District of Columbia (a federal district). Many citizens are familiar with addressing their address as JOHN DOE, 1234 Main Street, Denver, CO 80019. This structure notifies the federal government its citizens have yielded to its jurisdiction to adhere to all codes and statutes. The correct form of the same address would be Doe, John, care of [1234] Main Street, [Denver], Colorado Republic, Zip Code Exempt (DMM 122.32) [00000]. This is the form residing outside of the United States. No ZIP Code is needed for accurate delivery! Title 26 (The Internal Revenue Code) of the United States Codebook clearly describes how one is held responsible or not held responsible for filing a return, which reads,

(a) General Rule

When not otherwise provided for by this title, the Secretary shall by regulations prescribe the place for the filing of any return, declaration, statement, or other documents, or copies thereof, required by this title or by regulations.

(b) Tax Returns

In the case of returns of tax required under the authority of part II of this subchapter –

(1) Persons Other Than Corporations

(A) General Rule Except as provided in subparagraph (B), a return (other than a corporation return) shall be made to the Secretary –

(i) in the internal revenue district in which is located the legal residence or principal place of business of the person making the return, or

(ii) at a service center serving the internal revenue district referred to in clause (i), as the Secretary may by regulations designate.

(B) Exception Returns of –

(i) persons who have no legal residence or principal place of business in any internal revenue district,

(ii) citizens of the United States whose principal place of abode for the period with respect to which the return is filed is outside the United States,

*(Title 26 U.S. Code §6091. Place for filing returns or other documents)*

It should be notated from section (B) Exception Returns; any person or business not listed within any Internal Revenue District or any citizen whose primary place of living is "outside of the United States" are not subjected to filing a return to the IRS. But, where exactly is the United States located? It's no doubt a Federal Corporation, but where is its principal place of business? Many people and their families live in residential homes, multi-family tracts, apartments, condominiums, mobile homes, and businesses in several business center tracts within the 50 nation countries that became a confederation. They would automatically think that their abode or place of business qualifies as being within the United States. In all actuality, the United States, after 1789, is not the 50 nation-states of the united States of America. By using the ZIP Code classification, the alleged citizen falls in line with Article 9 – Secured Transactions of the Uniform Commercial Code as not being a creditor with a nation but instead a state-less debtor, which reads,

LOCATION OF DEBTOR

(a) ["Place of business."]

In this section, "place of business" means a place where a debtor conducts its affairs.

(b) [Debtor's location: general rules.]

Except as otherwise provided in this section, the following rules determine a debtor's location:

(1) A debtor who is an individual is located at the individual's principal residence.

(2) A debtor that is an organization and has only one place of business is located at its place of business.

(3) A debtor that is an organization and has more than one place of business is located at its chief executive officer.

(c) [Limitation of applicability of subsection (b)]

Subsection (b) applies only if a debtor's residence, place of business, or chief executive office, as applicable, is located in a jurisdiction whose law generally requires information concerning the existence of a nonpossessory security interest to be made generally available in a filing, recording, or registration system as a condition or result of the security interest's obtaining priority over the rights of a lien creditor with respect to the collateral. If subsection (b) does not apply, the Debtor is located in the District of Columbia.

(h) [Location of the United States]

The United States is located in the District of Columbia.

*(U.C.C. 9-307. Location of Debtor)*

The United States is located in the District of Columbia. Let that sink in once more, the United States is located in the District of Columbia, and it has Internal Revenue Districts in all of the 50 STATES as private corporations. If one consents to reside in any of the 50 STATES (federal districts), that person is liable for submitting tax returns to the Secretary of the I.R.S. Another viable question is, how exactly did all of the states become a part of the District of Columbia? After all, the 50 states existed within the united States of America's Constitution in 1787 before the new 1789 Constitution leading to the Organic Act of 1871, establishing Washington D.C. Article One of the United States constitution reveals the answer. It reads,

> To exercise exclusive Legislation in all Cases whatsoever, over such district (not exceeding ten Miles square) as may, by Cession of particular States, and the Acceptance of Congress, become the Seat of the Government of the United States, and to exercise like Authority over all Places purchased by the Consent of the Legislature of the State in which the Same shall be, for the Erection of Forts, Magazines, Arsenals, dock-Yard, and other needful Buildings;

(The Constitution of The United States, Article I, Section 8, Clause 17)

The keyword in this section of the Constitution is Cession. Each state has voluntarily participated in Cession (meaning the formal giving up of rights, property, or territory by a state), giving jurisdiction over to the District of Columbia. For example, the evidence in the preamble of the Tennessee Constitution of 1796,

> We the People of the territory of the United States south of the river Ohio, having the right of admission into the General Government as a Member State thereof, consistent with the Constitution of the United States and the act of Cession of the State of North Carolina, recognizing the ordinance for the government of the territory of the United States northwest of the river Ohio, do ordain and establish the following Constitution or form of government, and do mutually agree with each other to form ourselves into a free and independent State by the name of the "State of" Tennessee.

By Cession that the republic Tennessee State became the democratic STATE OF TENNESSEE (federal district) or the republic California state became the democratic STATE OF CALIFORNIA (federal district). All of the 50 states have become a part of the STATE OF's ceded to the District of Columbia, which is why the fourteenth amendment states,

No State shall make or enforce any law, which shall abridge the privileges or immunities of citizens of the United States;

(Constitution of United States of America 1789, 14th Amendment, Section One)

The fourteenth amendment was ratified in 1868, and when it mentions the United States, it refers to the ten square mile District of Columbia. Suppose one is identified as a U.S. citizen, a State citizen, a U.S. national, a Legal Permanent Resident, or State Resident authorized by the fourteenth amendment. In that case, such a one is liable for taxes, licenses, Real I.D.'s, state permits, and licenses. The following questions were asked in this chapter, what is the origin of the fourteenth Amendment? What type of person does it create, a citizen or a subject? What does it allow a person to do or not do? After all, isn't it an honor to be a United States citizen?

# CHAPTER TWO

# The 14th Amendment Citizen

The fourteenth amendment was officially ratified on July 9, 1868, granting citizenship to everyone born or naturalized in the United States, which included alleged slaves; or did it? By directly mentioning the states' role, the fourteenth amendment greatly expanded civil rights protections to all Americans and is cited in countless litigation cases than any other amendment.

It's interesting to read that the fourteenth amendment is the most cited litigation over any amendment to the Constitution. President Donald Trump spoke heavily about the removal of the amendment.

Why is that? Could the fourteenth amendment be illegal, fraudulent, and cause restrictions or all the above? Reading each section of the fourteenth amendment in its entirety for a complete understanding is paramount.

> All persons born or naturalized in the United States and subject to the jurisdiction thereof are citizens of the United States and of the State wherein they reside. No State shall make or enforce any law which shall abridge the privileges or immunities of citizens of the United States; nor shall any State deprive any person of life, liberty, or property, without due process of law; nor deny to any person within its jurisdiction the equal protection of the laws.

> *(1789 U.S. Constitution – 14th Amendment – Section one)*

Notice how the first sentence uses keywords such as born, naturalized, the United States, and jurisdiction thereof. Again, the United States is a federal corporation which, located in the District of Columbia. Looking at the word born and the definition of naturalized, it means to confer citizenship upon an alien, to make a foreigner the same, in respect to rights and privileges, as if he or she were a native citizen or subject per *Black's Law Dictionary, Second Edition*. It would raise the question of how can someone be born into a fictitious federal corporation, knowing the United States is in the District of Columbia, and one is naturally born in one of the 50 countries/states? Just from the first sentence, the fourteenth amendment does not make any lawful sense. Another fact to observe is the word "all persons." Exactly whom is the amendment referring to? It is an artificial person, defined as,

> It is a nonhuman entity created by law and is legally different from owning its rights and duties. Also known as a juristic person and legal person. Refer to a body corporate.
>
> (*Black's Law Dictionary* – *Second Edition* – *Artificial Person*)

A similar word is a juridical person, defined as,

> An entity, as a firm, that is not a single natural person, as a human being, authorized by law with duties and rights, recognized as a legal authority having a distinct identity, a legal personality. Also known as an artificial person, juridical entity, juristic person, or legal person. Also, refer to a body corporate.
>
> (*Black's Law Dictionary* – *Second Edition* – *Juridical Person*)

The fourteenth amendment is referring to a legally generated juridical person or fictitious artificial person. According to Black's Law Dictionary- Second Edition, a natural-born person is a human being, naturally born, versus a legally generated juridical person. An artificial person is created in the United States and subjected to its jurisdiction thereof and initially created through the Certificate of Live Birth by an elected official within the county government. This official is the Registrar-Recorder/County-Clerk!

The second part of section one explains, No State shall make or enforce any law which shall abridge the privileges or immunities of citizens of the United States; nor shall any State deprive any person of life, liberty, or property, without due process of law; nor deny to any person within its jurisdiction the equal protection of the laws. All states have ceded their power over to the District of Columbia so that no State can make any law against Washington D.C.'s alleged citizens. The only rules that govern the alleged citizens are any state constitution after 1933 and any code after the ratification of the fourteenth amendment. This is precisely where the District of Columbia wants their alleged citizen's rights and privileges to be derived. The second section of the fourteenth amendment dives more into the election process, which reads,

> Representatives shall be apportioned among the several States according to their respective numbers, counting the whole number of persons in each State, excluding Indians not taxed. But when the right to vote at any election for the choice of electors for President and Vice President of the United States, Representatives in Congress, the Executive and Judicial officers of a State, or the members of the Legislative thereof, is denied to any of the male inhabitants of such State, being twenty-one years of age, and citizens of the United States, or in any way abridged, except for participation in rebellion, or other crime, the basis of representation therein shall be reduced in the proportion which

the number of such male citizens shall bear to the whole number of male citizens twenty-one years of age in such State.

(1789 U.S. Constitution – 14th Amendment – Section two)

Notice how several States is used with a capital "S" and not a lower case "s" referring to the federal districts and not the several national country/states from the republic united States of America, 1787. Section two mentions the "Representatives," who are an entirely different group of individuals compared to the male inhabitants or U.S. citizens over the age of 21, the electors, the President or Vice President, and Congress members, including the Legislatures. The specific groups of Representatives are whom "We the People" select within local government. For example, in Riverside County of California, the Riverside County Organization Chart lists several departments and positions that run the county. Jobs such as County Executive Officer, County Counsel, Public Social Services, Economic Development Agency, Public Health, or Assistant CEO RUHS Health and Hospital Services. These are the positions that the people select to run their local government, and from these selected positions, they choose the principal electors, such as the Sheriff. The final electors have the opportunity to vote and elect the President and Congress members on behalf of the people. Bouvier's Law Dictionary, 1856 Edition defines Electors of President as,

Persons elected by the people, whose sole duty is to elect a president and vice president of the U.S.

Only a select few officials hold the electors' title within Riverside County, California, such as Sheriff-Coroner, District Attorney, Assessor-Clerk, Auditor-Controller Treasurer-Tax Collector. It is true; citizens choose to submit ballot tickets that allow them to place their votes for the Sheriff, Assessor, and others. Still, the real matter of concern is how exactly are the people's ballots considered per the fourteenth amendment's voting procedure?

The amendment states the Representatives shall be apportioned according to their respective numbers, counting the whole number of male inhabitants, excluding Indians who are not taxed. Remember that the Indians derive their name as an employee of the Dutch East or West India Trading Company; therefore, an Indian employee was not taxed by its third party employer (the U.S.), solely owing allegiance to the trading company. When the right to vote for any Representative for the choice of electors for the President and the like, is denied to any male inhabitant or citizen of the United States being over the age of 21, the whole number of Representatives shall be reduced according to the whole number of male inhabitants or citizens of the United States over the age of 21; "except" when a male inhabitant or citizen of the United States over the age of 21 has participated in rebellion or committed a crime, then the

Representatives respective numbers shall usurp the whole number of male inhabitants or citizens of the United States over the age of 21.

Many citizens of the United States would claim that they have not committed any crimes or engaged in any form of rebellion against the United States. And should meet the requirement of having the right to vote for a Representative for the choice of electors for the President and the like, let alone choose the President themselves if they could. It is essential to understand that after 1789 and under the Organic Act of 1871, the United States is located in D.C. and is not a country; it is a federal corporation consisting of Presidents, Chief Executive Officers, Chief Financial Officers, Chairman's and Secretary's. Countries have Kings, Queens, Princes, Grand Dukes, Emperors, Caesars, Khans, Sultans, and others. Therefore, a corporation is never to rely on the public to elect its Presidents or Chairmans. It would indeed be the responsibility of those who hold the highest number of shares in the company's certificates. It is beginning to make sense as to why this amendment has been the most talked-about amendment within every United States court.

If male inhabitants or citizens of the United States over the age of 21 participate in rebellion or commit crimes against the United States, their right to vote (abridged) would be forfeited against the number of Representatives within the local government. It would be their whole number to exceed the entire amount of the people they represent. How is this possible? What crime could have been committed unknowingly by the citizens of the United States? The answer has always been in plain sight, especially to the U.S. citizens who travel the world. To move across the earth, one must apply for a United States of America Passport. The actual application allows each applicant to voluntarily state that he or she is a criminal or not! From the use of federal and state forms, the United States federal government can reduce the number of male inhabitants or citizens of the United States over the age of 21 against the Representatives for electors' choice. Mostly, all Americans are familiar with the DS-11 passport application. Jumping to page 4 and focusing on the section titled "ACTS OR CONDITIONS," the federal government, in their crafty ways, has deemed U.S. citizens to be criminals and rebel against the United States if they are not careful in comprehending instructions. It reads,

> If any of the below-mentioned acts or conditions have been performed by or apply to the applicant, "the portion which applies should be lined out," and a "supplementary explanatory statement" under oath (or affirmation) by the applicant should be "attached and made a part of this application."

With full comprehension of the first sentence regarding instructions, how many Americans have drawn a line through select wording in the Acts or Conditions portion of the application and provided a supplementary explanatory statement in the form of an affidavit? It clearly says the part, which applies, should be "lined out" on the actual application. Everyone has been taught to cross out or line out sections whenever it "does not" apply, but here within the DS-11 passport application, it is the opposite. The next sentence reads,

> I have not, since acquiring United States citizenship/nationality, been naturalized as a citizen of a foreign state; taken an oath or made an affirmation or other formal declaration of allegiance to a foreign state; entered or served in the armed forces of a foreign state; accepted or performed the duties of any office, post, or employment under the government of a foreign state or political subdivision thereof; made a formal renunciation of nationality either in the United States, or before a diplomatic or consular officer of the United States in a foreign state; or been convicted by a court or court-martial of competent jurisdiction of committing any act of treason against, or attempting by force to overthrow, or bearing arms against, the United States, or conspiring to overthrow, put down, or to destroy by force, the government of the United States.

> Furthermore, I have not been convicted of a federal or state drug offense or convicted of a "sex tourism" crimes statute, and I am not the subject of an outstanding federal, state, or local warrant of arrest for a felony; a criminal court order forbidding my departure from the United States; a subpoena received from the United States in a matter involving federal prosecution for, or grand jury investigation of, a felony.

It's fascinating to see what Americans sign before understanding word for word and how it implies to them. This is one of many tactics the federal government entraps the people into voluntary participation in rebellion, which is considered a criminal offense. If one wanted to submit a correct DS-11 passport application with information on how to complete an explanatory statement, it is thoroughly detailed in the "Nationality" chapter of this book. The following is how to "line out" the portion, which applies to the applicant as a non-criminal. I have...taken an oath...made an affirmation...formal declaration of allegiance to a foreign state; made a formal renunciation of nationality...in the United States...Furthermore, I have not been convicted of a federal or state drug offense or convicted of a "sex tourism" crimes statute, and I am not the subject of an outstanding federal, state, or local warrant of arrest for a felony; a criminal court order forbidding my departure from the United States; a subpoena received from the United States in a matter involving federal prosecution for, or grand jury investigation of, a felony.

Simply line out the applicable words in the "ACTS OR CONDITIONS" section of the DS-11 Passport Application. By doing this, Americans have just prevented themselves from allegedly participating in rebellion or openly admitting to a federal or state criminal offense, which is on record with the Department of State that can be obtained as a Freedom Of Information Act request. Continuing with section three of the fourteenth amendment, reads,

> No person shall be a Senator or Representative in Congress, or elector of President and Vice President, or hold any office, civil or military, under the United States, or under any State, who, having previously taken an oath, as a member of Congress, or as an officer of the United States, or as a member of any State Legislature, or as an executive or judicial officer of any State, to support the Constitution of the United States, shall have engaged in insurrection or rebellion against the same, or given aid or comfort to the enemies thereof. But Congress may, by a vote of two-thirds of each House, remove such disability.

(1789 U.S. Constitution – 14th Amendment – Section three)

Section three gives more of a precise description that no fourteenth amendment citizen by way of section one can be a Senator, Representative of Congress, or, more importantly, "an elector of the President or Vice President." Senators, Representatives of Congress, Executive, Judicial or Legislative officers, or electors are not U.S. citizens or U.S. nationals. They hold a higher lawful status than the legal status of a citizen of the United States. They are nationals but NOT a U.S. citizen per Public Law 94-241 – March 24, 1976. Nationals are "the People." U.S. citizens do not select the United States President or Vice President. Their ballots are simply surveys informing the corporate leaders of the whereabouts of the people's opinions on specific political topics. Once again, it is the people, nationals, who can select their Representatives within local government, who then choose county electors, who then elect the Senators, Representatives in Congress, and the Presidents or Vice Presidents. According to section four of the amendment,

> The validity of the public debt of the United States, authorized by law, including debts incurred for payment of pensions and bounties for services in suppressing insurrection or rebellion, shall not be questioned. But neither the United States nor any State shall assume or pay any debt or obligation incurred in aid of insurrection or rebellion against the United States, or any claim for the loss or emancipation of any slave; but all such debts, obligations, and claims shall be held illegal and void.
>
> *(1789 U.S. Constitution – 14th Amendment – Section four)*

A community referred to as the Secured Party Creditor movement or the Patriot movement claims that there is no lawful money since 1933. The basis of this observation comes from the federal government demanding all citizens to turn in their precious metals in exchange for paper fiat currency. In fact, there is lawful money, and debts can be questioned for discharge, but it must be done through a particular vehicle known as a Trust, as a natural person. The federal government left the choice up to the people to have lawful money. They either expand the national public debt using fiat currency or utilize private treasury notes, which cancels interest; furthermore, section four states that no U.S. citizen, Naturalized citizen, or Legal Permanent Resident can question the public debt by way of the fourteenth amendment. And sadly, this section just admitted that a fourteenth amendment citizen is likened to an emancipated slave, just like the Anglo-Saxon slaves under the Brutish Moors of Great Britain, were freed by the Declaration of Independence of 1776. The word emancipation comes from the Latin word mancipatio, which means,

> A certain ceremony or formal process anciently required to be performed to perfect the sale or conveyance of res mancipi (land, houses, slaves, horses, or cattle). The parties were present (vendor and vendee) with five witnesses and a person called "libripens," who held a balance or scales. A set form of words repeated on either side, indicative of transfer of ownership, and certain prescribed gestures performed, and the vendee then struck the scales with a piece of copper, thereby symbolizing the payment, or weighing out, of the stipulated price.
>
> (*Black's Law Dictionary – Second Edition*)

To be emancipated is to transfer ownership of a property from one owner to another. Slaves of the Atlantic Slave Trade were transferred from involuntary servitude of penal colonies or debtor prisons, an old form of slavery, into a new, taxed-based voluntary servitude form of slavery controlled by the District of Columbia. People today are not transferred from one owner to another; they have voluntarily surrendered their God-given birthright as a national but not a citizen of the United States over to the District of Columbia's jurisdiction by way of the fourteenth amendment contract. Section four is why not everyone can use House Joint Resolution 192 to discharge the public debt. If one is a fourteenth amendment citizen attempting to offset public liability, it "will not" work unless a trust is used, as previously said. The last section of the fourteenth amendment states,

> The Congress shall have the power to enforce, by appropriate legislation, the provisions of this article.
>
> *(1789 U.S. Constitution – 14th Amendment – Section five)*

Section five gives the federal government the right to create any law, which controls every fourteenth amendment citizen even though every state's Constitution says, "No bill of attainder, ex post facto law, or law impairing the obligations of contracts, shall ever be passed." No law such as the entire fourteenth amendment shall usurp the state constitutional law. However, it is an individual's voluntary consent to surrender to the several fourteenth amendment contracts via social security forms, driver's license or state I.D. applications, insurance forms, passport applications, and voter registration forms. All of the above applications allow Congress to have the power to enforce any corporate code or statute over the corporate juridical person. Who are the juridical persons exactly? Unfortunately, the people of this beautiful land hold identification as U.S. citizens, U.S.

nationals, State citizens, Residents, or Legal Permanent Residents. It is the corporate name listed in their system in ALL CAPITAL LETTERS, such as FIRST MIDDLE LAST Name. This classification system is an ancient Roman law system known as Capitis Diminutio Law, which diminishes a person's personality or status. A person may lose his nature or legal capacity either in whole or in part. There are three stages of losing a person's personality—the first, Capitis diminutio minima consisting of losing someone's family relations. The right to liberty is unaltered in this stage; there is only a minimum loss of status. The second, Capitis diminutio media, includes losing one's citizenship and their family name. In capitis dimuntio minima, there is a medium loss of status. The third is Capitis diminutio maxima, consisting of the deprivation of freedom, citizenship, and family name. In this stage, a person's status is changed from freedom to bondage; this is the highest status loss. This is the status of all U.S. citizens, U.S. nationals, State citizens, Residents, and Legal Permanent Residents, and to correct it, it must be done on every level of government, beginning at the Department of State with the Passport Application, followed by the Social Security Administration, then the Department of Motor Vehicles. Each inhabitant's status should be a "national but not a citizen of the United States," which is naturally a creditor.

The fourteenth amendment's real motive comes from the words of Senator Benjamin R. "Pitchfork Ben" Tillman. On March 23, 1900, a speech was given before the U.S. Senate; Senator Benjamin

R. "Pitchfork Ben" Tillman of South Carolina defended his white constituents' actions who had murdered several black citizens of his home state. Tillman blamed the violence on the "hot-headedness" of Southern blacks and the misguided efforts of Republicans during the Reconstruction era after the Civil War to "put white necks under black heels." He also defended violence against black men, claiming that southern whites "will not submit to [the black man] gratifying his lust on our wives and daughters without lynching him" – an evocation of the deeply sexualized racist fantasies of many whites. He quotes,

> And he [Senator John C. Spooner, of Wisconsin] said we had taken their rights away from them. He asked me was it right to murder them in order to carry the elections. I never saw one murdered. I never saw one shot at an election. It was the riots before the elections precipitated by their own hot-headedness in attempting to hold the government that brought on conflicts between the races and caused the shotgun to be used. That is what I meant by saying we used the shotgun.

> I want to call the Senator's attention to one fact. He said that the Republican party gave the negroes the ballot in order to protect themselves against the indignities and wrongs that were attempted to be heaped upon them by the enactment of the black code. I say it was because the Republicans of that day, led by Thad Stevens, wanted to put white necks under black heels and

to get revenge. There is a difference of opinion. You have your opinion about it, and I have mine, and we can never agree.

I want to ask the Senator this proposition in arithmetic: In my State, there were 135,000 negro voters, or negroes of voting age, and some 90,000 or 95,000 white voters. General Canby set up a carpetbag government there and turned our State over to this majority. Now, I want to ask you, with a free vote and fair count, how are you going to beat 135,000 by 95,000? How are you going to do it? You had set us an impossible task. You had handcuffed us and thrown away the key, and you propped your carpetbag Negro government and bayonets. When it was necessary to sustain the government, you held it up by the Army.

Mr. President, I have not the facts and figures here, but I want the country to get the full view of the Southern side of this question and the justification for anything we did. We were sorry we had the necessity forced upon us, but we could not help it, and as white men, we are not sorry for it, and we do not propose to apologize for anything we have done in connection with it. We took the government away from them in 1876. We did take it. If no other Senator has come here previous to this time, who would acknowledge it, more is the pity. We have had no fraud in our elections in South Carolina in 1884. There has been no organized Republican party in the State.

We did not disfranchise the Negroes until 1895. Then we had a constitutional convention, which took the matter up calmly, deliberately, and avowedly with the purpose of disfranchising as many of them as we could under the "fourteenth and fifteenth" amendments. We adopted the educational qualification as the only means left to us, and the Negro is as contented and as prosperous and as well protected in South Carolina today as in any State of the Union south of the Potomac. He is not meddling with politics, for he found that the more he meddled with them, the worse off he got. As to his "rights", – I will not discuss them now. We of the South have never recognized the right of the Negro to govern white men, and we never will. We have never believed him to be equal to the white man, and we will not submit to his gratifying his lust on our wives and daughters without lynching him. I would to God the last one of them was in Africa and that none of them had ever been brought to our shores. But I will not pursue the subject further.

I want to ask permission in this connection to print a speech which I made in the constitutional convention of South Carolina when it convened in 1895, in which the whole carpetbag regime and the indignities and wrongs heaped upon our people, the robberies which we suffered, and all the facts and figures there brought out are incorporated, and let the whole of the facts go to the country. I am not ashamed to have those facts go to the country. They are our justification for the present situation in our State. If I can get it, I should like that permission; otherwise, I shall be forced to bring that speech here and read it when I can put my hand on it. I will then leave this matter and let the dead past bury its dead.

*("Speech of Senator Benjamin R. Tillman, March 23, 1900," Congressional Record, 56th Congress, 1st Session, 3223-3224)*

From the South Carolinian Senator, it is straightforward that the government in South Carolina and all southern states were governed by the Moors (swarthy and tawny men). They had voting rights and outnumbered the white (Anglo-Saxon) voters, 135,000 to 95,000. The Senator understood very well to make a difference; a constitutional convention would need to disenfranchise the Moors, meaning to deprive one's right to vote and strip them of their nationality, into the jurisdiction of the fourteenth amendment. Several important questions arise from reading the Senator's speech. He mentioned, they took the government away from the Moors who held Title of Nobility in 1876, and they did not disenfranchise the Moors until 1895. The most obvious question is how is it possible, Moors (black men) controlled all government until 1895, and why would white men be concerned with depriving their right to vote if they were enslaved and freed 30 years before abolishment in 1865? This is one of the many pieces of the puzzle the federal government did not expect the American people to uncover. Yet again, the federal government is found guilty in a deceptive detour of reconstructive history. It is undoubtedly impossible that in just 30 years, uneducated "African slaves" who were brought to the thirteen colonies could receive their freedom in 1865 and immediately run all of the southern states as a republican government, to lose it in 1876.

The 90th Congress of 1967 would also agree about the Moors' position, their government, and their power within the confederate United States of America Corporation. Per the United States of America Congressional Record, Volume 113 – Part 12 of June 12, 1967, to June 20, 1967,

## III. PROPOSED AMENDMENT NEVER RATIFIED BY THREE-FOURTHS OF THE STATES

1. Pretending the ineffectiveness of said resolution, as above, fifteen (15) States out of the then thirty-seven (37) States of the Union rejected the proposed fourteenth amendment between the date of its submission to the States by the Secretary of State on June 16, 1866, and March 24, 1868, thereby further nullifying said resolution and making it impossible for its ratification by the constitutionally required three-fourths of such States, as shown by the rejections thereof by the Legislatures of the following states:

Texas rejected the 14th Amendment on October 27, 1866.

Georgia rejected the 14th Amendment on November 9, 1866.

Florida rejected the 14th Amendment on December 6, 1866.

Alabama rejected the 14th Amendment on December 7, 1866.

North Carolina rejected the 14th Amendment on December 14, 1866.

Arkansas rejected the 14th Amendment on December 17, 1866.

South Carolina rejected the 14th Amendment on December 20, 1866.

Kentucky rejected the 14th Amendment on January 8, 1867.

Virginia rejected the 14th Amendment on January 9, 1867.

Louisiana rejected the 14th Amendment on February 6, 1867.

Delaware rejected the 14th Amendment on February 7, 1867.

Maryland rejected the 14th Amendment on March 23, 1867.

Mississippi rejected the 14th Amendment on January 31, 1867.

Ohio rejected the 14th Amendment on January 15, 1868.

New Jersey rejected the 14th Amendment on March 24, 1868.

(*Congressional Record, Volume 113 – Part 12, June 13, 1967, Page 15642*)

There was no question that all of the Southern states which rejected the 14th amendment had legally constituted governments, were fully recognized by the federal government, and were functioning as member states of the Union at the time of their rejection.

5. Faced with the positive failure of ratification of the 14th amendment, both Houses of Congress passed over the veto of the President three Acts known as Reconstruction Acts, between the dates of March 2 and July 19, 1867, especially the third of said Acts, 15 Stat. p. 14, etc., designed illegally to remove with "Military force" the lawfully constituted State Legislatures of the 10 Southern States of Virginia, North Carolina, South Carolina, Georgia, Florida, Alabama, Mississippi, Arkansas, Louisiana, and Texas. In President Andrew Johnson's veto message on the Reconstruction Act of March 2, 1867, he pointed out these unconstitutionalities:

"In all these States, there are existing constitutions, framed in the accustomed way by the people. Congress, however, declares that these constitutions are not 'loyal and republican' and requires the people to form them anew. What, then, in the opinion of Congress, is necessary to make the Constitution of a State' loyal and republican?' The original act answers the question: 'It is universal negro suffrage, a question which the federal Constitution leaves exclusively to the States themselves. All this legislative machinery of martial law, military coercion, and political disfranchisement is avowedly for that purpose and none other. The existing constitutions of the ten States conform to the acknowledged standards of loyalty and republicanism. Indeed, if there are degrees in republican forms of government, their constitutions are more republican now than when these States – four of which were members of the original thirteen – first became members of the Union."

*(Congressional Record, Volume 113 – Part 12, June 13, 1967, Page 15643)*

From all of the above documented historic facts, it is inescapable that the 14th amendment never was validly adopted as an article of the Constitution, that it has no legal effect, and it should be declared by the Courts to be unconstitutional, and therefore null, void and of no effect.

*(Congressional Record, Volume 113 – Part 12, June 13, 1967, Page 15645)*

The above undisputable record details the fourteenth amendment's very reason to raise many issues in the United States courts. Since the amendment was illegally ratified by military force, subduing all legislative Moors for the sole purpose of ending their republican government by way of universal negro suffrage or political deprivation of their right to vote. All southern states were against it, and therefore military coercion was necessary for the ratification of the amendment. Federal and State programs have utilized the fourteenth amendment's illegal ratification to entrap as many Americans as possible into the District of Columbia's jurisdiction. The

Social Security Administration requires the applicant to provide their race and ethnicity on questions six and seven of the SS-5 form. Interesting enough, these two sections are the only sections the Social Security Administration advises the applicant that any information provided is "voluntary." Section six asks the applicant to provide information on whether the applicant is Hispanic or Latino voluntarily, and section seven asks for race information. The applicant can select Native Hawaiian, Alaska Native, Asian, American Indian, Black/African American, Other Pacific Islander, and White. This is another deceptive tactic to voluntarily have the applicant admit to being a "franchisee" of the fourteenth amendment. There is only one race! The race of mankind comprised of many nationalities upon the earth. Suppose the question was asked, where is the nation of White, Latino, or Asian? What would be the answer? That fact is it doesn't exist! There is only Italian National, Californian National, Chinese National, Colombian National, Sudanese National, Irish National, etc. Section five of the application pertains to citizenship. The applicant can voluntarily select United States citizen, Legal Alien Allowed To Work, Legal Alien Not Allowed To Work, and Other. The obvious answer is "Other." Per the instructions of the SS-5 form, the applicant must provide a document from the U.S. Federal, State, or local government agency to support selecting others, which will be revealed.

Under The GPO Style Manual, 2016 – Section 5.23, Nationalities, etc., the correct information that all Americans born in the 50 national states should provide on all applications requesting race or nationality.

**5.23.** In designating the natives of the States, the following forms will be used.

| | |
|---|---|
| Alabamian | Alaskan |
| Arizonian | Arkansan |
| Californian | Coloradan |
| Delawarean | Floridian |
| Georgian | Hawaii resident |
| Hoosier (Indiana) | Idahoan |
| Illinoisan | Iowan |
| Kansan | Kentuckian |
| Louisianian | Mainer |
| Marylander | Massachusettsan |
| Michiganian | Minnesotan |
| Mississippian | Missourian |
| Montanan | Nebraskan |
| Nevadan | New Hampshirite |
| New Jersyan | New Mexican |
| New Yorker | North Carolinian |
| North Dakotan | Ohioan |
| Oklahoman | Pennsylvanian |
| Rhode Islander | South Carolinian |

| South Dakotan | Tennessean |
|---|---|
| Texan | Utahn |
| Vermonter | Virginian |
| Washingtonian | Wisconsinite |
| Wyomingite | |

(GPO Style Manual, 2016 – Section 5.23, Nationalities, etc., page 95)

The above nationalities are the actual native tribes of the Moors who inhabited the states under a republican government. The states are their own countries that form a confederation, which formed the United States of America in Congress Assembled. The definition of a state is,

> a nation or territory considered an organized political community under one government or concerned with a country's civil government.

*(Oxford Dictionary)*

The information is the same on all other government agency applications. One's country is one's rightful nationality. However, if one voluntarily elects to classify themselves as a franchise of the fourteenth amendment by identifying as Black, White, Asian, Hispanic, etc., it would allow a true national also to be classified as a United States citizen, which is also on par of an enemy of the State

(District of Columbia) per Trading With The Enemy Act of 1917. According to Title 50 – War and National Defense, Chapter 53 – Trading With The Enemy,

> The word "enemy," as used herein, shall be deemed to mean, for such trading and of this chapter –

> (a) Any individual, partnership, or other body of individuals, of any nationality, resident within the territory (including that occupied by the military and naval forces) of any nation with which the United States is at war, or resident outside the United States and doing business within such territory, and any corporation incorporated within such territory of any nation with which the United States is at war or incorporated within any country other than the United States and doing business within such territory

> (b) The government of any nation with which the United States is at war, or any political or municipal subdivision thereof, or any officer, official, agent, or agency thereof.

> (c) Such other individuals, or body or class of individuals, as may be natives, citizens, or subjects of any nation with which the United States is at war, other than citizens of the United States, wherever resident or wherever doing business, as the President, if he shall find the safety of the United States or the successful prosecution of the war shall so require,

may, by proclamation, include within the term "enemy."

*(Title 50 U.S. Code §4302 (a)(b)(c))*

Part C just verified that by Proclamation by the President, if in the best interest of the United States Corporation located in the District of Columbia, the President may deem United States citizens to be an enemy of the State (U.S.). Part C highlights citizens of the United States with the phrase "other than a citizen of the United States," which can be explained as,

> You use "other than" after a negative statement to say that the person, item, or thing that follows is the only exception to the statement.

*(Pursuant to Collins Dictionary)*

Further evidence of the type of control the President has over people classified as U.S. citizens on par with an enemy of the State can be read in

Senate Report No. 93-549 of the 93rd Congress, 1st Session, Titled: EMERGENCY POWERS STATUTES: Provisions Of Federal Law Now In Effect Delegating To The Executive Extraordinary Authority In Time Of National Emergency – November 19, 1973,

REPORT OF THE
SPECIAL COMMITTEE ON THE
TERMINATION OF THE
NATIONAL EMERGENCY
UNITED STATES SENATE,

**FOREWORD**

Since March 9, 1933, the United States has been in a state of declared national emergency. There are now in effect four presidentially proclaimed states of national emergency: In addition to the national emergency declared by President Roosevelt in 1933, there is also the national emergency proclaimed by President Truman on December 16, 1950, during the Korean conflict, and the states of national emergency declared by President Nixon on March 23, 1970, and August 15, 1971.

These proclamations give force to 470 provisions of Federal law. These hundreds of statutes delegate to the President extraordinary powers, ordinarily exercised by the Congress, which affect American citizens' lives in a host of all-encompassing manners. This vast range of powers, taken together, confer enough authority to rule the country without reference to normal constitutional processes.

Under the powers delegated by these statutes, the President may: seize property; organize and control the means of production;

seize commodities; assign military forces abroad; institute martial law; seize and control all transportation and communication; regulate the operation of private enterprise; restrict travel; and, in a plethora of particular ways, control the lives of all American citizens.

*(Senate Report No. 93-549 of the 93rd Congress, 1st Session, & Titled: EMERGENCY POWERS STATUTES, Nov. 19, 1973, page three)*

The President can control every aspect of the U.S. citizen, U.S. national, Resident, State citizen, and Legal Permanent Resident or Alien, and all forms of businesses registered under the Secretary of State utilizing a license or permit. However, the Trading With The Enemy Act does not bind nationals of their respective countries.

# CHAPTER THREE

# Existence of Life

The origin of the ALL CAPITAL LETTER fiction, the ens legis, that the United States created began in London in 1666. The ens legis is the same name as the natural physical person. It has a dual nature or two sides of the same coin. Very similar to the two sides of a standard checking account. A debit and credit side of the ledger. The all capital letter JOHN DOE SMITH is the legal fiction (corporation) debtor, and the all capital letter SMITH, JOHN DOE is the (natural physical person) creditor. In today's commercial system, the debtor side is utilized for every commercial transaction in public. The ens legis began during the Black plague and great fires of London; Parliament enacted an act behind closed doors, unknown to the people, called the Cestui Que Vie Act 1666. The year is by no accident being reminiscent of the Book of Revelations, Chapter 13 verse 16-18,

> And he causeth all, both small and great, rich and poor, free and bond, to receive a mark in their right hand, or in their foreheads: And that no man might buy or sell, save he that had the mark, or the name of the beast, or the number of his name. Here is wisdom. Let him that hath understanding count the number of the beast: for it is the number of a man, and his number is Six hundred threescore and six.
>
> (King James Version)

Six hundred threescore and six are the coded numbers the ruling governments will ultimately use to identify their citizens for total control. The act being debated was to subrogate men and women's rights, meaning all men and women were declared dead, lost at sea from the law of Admiralty Law. The State (London) took custody of everyone and their property into a trust. The State became the trustee/husband holding all titles to the people and property until a living man returns to reclaim those titles; he can also claim damages. The ALL CAPITAL LETTER legal fictitious name is owned by foreign governments, on the same footing with the likes of owning a share in the Stock Market, to own a percentage, but it is still a share of the Stock. Its Latin name, Ens Legis, meaning,

> A creature of the law, an artificial being, as contrasted with a natural person. Applied to corporations, considered as deriving their existence entirely from the law.

*(Blacks Law Dictionary — Second Edition)*

As of today, in the year 2021, all ens legis public debt is calculated at a staggering $22 Trillion, to which twelve countries own a share of the stock in the United States Corporation. Number one is China, at $1.11 Trillion, holding 17.3%. Second is Japan at $1.06 Trillion, holding 16.5%. Third is Brazil at $307 Billion, holding 4.8%. Fourth is the United Kingdom at $301 Billion at 4.7%. The fifth is Ireland at $270 Billion, holding 4.2%. Sixth is Switzerland at $227 Billion, holding 3.5%. Seventh is Luxembourg at $224 Billion, holding 3.5%. The Eighth is the Cayman Islands at $217 Billion, holding 3.4%. Ninth is Hong Kong at $206 Billion, holding 3.2%. The tenth is Belgium at $180 Billion, holding 2.8%, the eleventh is Saudi Arabia at $177 Billion, holding 2.8%, and the twelfth position is Taiwan at $171 Billion, holding 2.7% share of stock. All twelve countries are dominions of Morocco (Mehomitan Nation). Their stock shares are truthfully in the Sultan's hands, headquartered in the finance capital of the world, New York City, New York.

London is an Independent City State controlling the world's banking system. The Vatican is an Independent City State controlling the world's religious structure and corporate soles. Washington D.C. is also an Independent City State controlling the earth militarily, and the Crown is an unincorporated association to be private. The temple bar is in London, and every lawyer called to the "bar" swears allegiance to the temple bar. By becoming the executor of the fictitious name and collapsing the Cestui Que Vie trust, one can reclaim their property and compensation for damages. It takes a trust to collapse another trust in a court of equity or chancery. Until this process is complete within the court, citizens will always need representation when involved in legal matters because the fictitious name is pronounced dead and lost at sea. Legal fictions are a construct on paper, an estate in trust. When a legal person receives a summons from a court, it is always addressed to the fictitious person in the ALL CAPITAL LETTER sense as FIRST MIDDLE LAST or LAST, FIRST MIDDLE; similar to tombstones in graveyards. Capital letters signify death. A fictitious legal person is created when someone informed the government that a new vessel has arrived upon birth. Birth Certificates are issued to the government by the "Doc.," just as ships are given Berth Certificates at the "Dock." It's all about commerce! Newborns are delivered through their mother's water, a birth canal, just like a ship. The ship is moved by the "current," guided by the "river banks," and the "currency" moves the lives of all persons through the "banks." Parents register the birth of their babies, unknowingly entering them into the matrix of admiralty law. In 1837, the Births, Deaths, and the Marriages Act were formed in the UK, and the post of registrar general was established. His job was to collect all the data from the churches, which held the records of birth. Regis meaning from the Queen or Crown; all people are seen to be in the custody of "The Crown." This allows people to function in commerce and to accept the benefits provided by the State. A Cestui Que Vie Trust, known later as a "Fide Commissary Trust" and also referred to as "Secret Trust," is a fictional concept being a Temporary Testamentary Trust, first established during the reign of Henry VII of England through the Cestui Que Vie Act of 1540 and updated by Charles II through the Cestui Que Vie Act of 1666. Wherein an Estate may be affected for the benefit of one or more Persons presumed lost or abandoned at "sea" and therefore assumed/presumed "dead" after seven (7) years. Additional presumptions by which such a Trust was added in later statutes to include bankrupts, minors, incompetents, mortgages, and private companies. The original purpose and function of a Cestui Que Vie Trust were to form a temporary Estate for the benefit of another because some event, state of affairs, or condition prevented them from claiming their status as living, competent and present before a competent authority. Therefore, any claims, history, statutes, or arguments that deviate in terms of a Cestui Que Vie Trust's origin and function, as pronounced by these canons, is false and automatically null and void. A Cestui

Que Vie Trust may only exist for seventy (70) years, being the traditional accepted "life" expectancy of the estate.

In 1534, before the 1st Cestui Que Vie Act (1540), Henry VII declared the first Cestui Que Vie type estate with an Act of Supremacy, which formed the Crown Estate. Seventy (70) years later, in 1604, James I of England modified the estate as the Union of Crowns. The Crown was viewed as a company by the 18th Century. However, at the beginning of the 19th Century, the company filed bankruptcy in 1814; it became a private Crown Corporation controlled by wealthy European banker families who obtained their wealth through intermarrying with high-status Moors. Since 1581, there has been a second series of Cestui Que Vie Estates concerning the property of "persons" and rights which migrated to the United States for administration, including:

i.    In 1651, the Act for the Settlement of Ireland 1651-52 introduced the concept of "settlements," enemies of the State and restrictions of movement in states of "emergency,"

ii.   In 1861, the Emergency Powers Act 1861, and

iii.  In 1931, the Emergency Relief and Construction Act 1931-32, and

iv.   In 2001, the Patriot Act 2001

Since 1591, there has been a third series of Cestui Que Vie Estates concerning the property of "soul" and ecclesiastical rights which migrated to the United States for administration, including:

    i.    In 1661, the Act of Settlement 1661–62, and

    ii.    In 1871, the District of Columbia Act 1871, and

    iii.    In 1941, the Lend–Lease Act 1941

All Berth Certificates, Birth Certificates, and Stock Certificates are indeed Certificates of Title. All include Stock on banknote numbers referring to a bond pending a matured date. Black's Law Dictionary, Second Edition, defines Certificate of Title as,

> This document certifies ownership of real property or a vehicle. An authorized agency will capture a description of the property and the liens on it on the issued certificate.

A Certificate of title is vastly different from the word entitled, meaning,

> To give a right or title to one who has a right to property in ordination as a minister in ecclesiastical law.
>
> (*Black's Law Dictionary – Second Edition*)

A lien is always displayed on a certificate of title and never to one who possesses entitlement to a title. This is why U.S. citizens continue to pay property taxes on houses and vehicles regardless of a settled mortgage or vehicle sales contract. Until the property (effects) is registered in trust with the local ruling government, taxes are due annually. As long as a Certificate of Title for an automobile exists in the ALL CAPITAL LETTER fictitious name, then the DMV remains the true lienholder. The same applies to a real property having a Satisfaction of Mortgage, with a Grant Deed not recorded in a trust, which has a Settlor, Trustee, and Beneficiaries. Until the house is registered in an Express Trust, property taxes are due annually. The beginning process of reaching the Zero Percent tax bracket comes only by claiming one's title to remove them from being lost at sea in the law of admiralty. One must proceed with the authenticating process of the "berth certificate" backed by the Cestui Que Vie Trust's estate assets. The following steps will include a guide to claiming the estate successfully. It begins by realizing that the birth certificate is on par with a certificate of title to an automobile or grant deed or deed of trust to real property. The purpose of authentication is given in Title 28, Judiciary and Judicial Procedure, Chapter 115 – Evidence; Documentary,

> (b) Properly authenticated copies or transcripts of any books, records, papers, or documents of any department or agency of the United States shall be admitted in evidence equally with the originals thereof.

(Title *28 US Code §1733(b)*)

Authentication of the birth certificate first begins with obtaining a certified copy of the document from the county. If issued by the Public Health Department and not the province of birth, one must first authenticate the record obtaining a Certificate of Exemplification. Once received, the birth certificate with the exemplification must be mailed to the birth state's Secretary of State office, requesting that the record becomes authenticated for international travel to a non-Haque Convention country, such as Thailand or Taiwan. A list of non-Haque countries is available through an Internet search, and each Secretary of State office provides this service with a fee, ranging from $10 to $25. The Secretary of State may take up to 30 days to process. Depending on the state, an apostille or certificate of authentication will come back attached to the birth certificate. The next step is to finalize the authentication by sending the returned birth certificate to the Department of State with their DS-4194, Request For Authentications Service form. The applicant should provide their name and mailing address in section one. Leave section two blank and select a Self-Addressed Stamped Envelope for the delivery method in section three. Provide the non-Hague Country in section four; the number of documents, which is one, and the document type, which is the birth certificate. And finally, section five must include the estimated cost, which is $8.00. Below is the Office of Authentications mailing address,

U.S. Department of State

Office of Authentications

CA/PPT/S/TO/AUT

44132 Mercure Cir.

PO. Box 1206

Sterling, VA 20166-1206

Be sure to include a Self-Addressed Envelope inside the mailing packet so that the Department of State can return the fully authenticated birth certificate. Once authenticated, the document is now on par with the original Certificate of Live Birth, which the county will never give to the rightful owner. It is now security that has been annexed from the United States, pending a claim of ownership. The final step is to attach an Affidavit of Ownership to the authenticated record. According to the Minnesota Court Rules,

> The Registrar of Titles is authorized to receive for registration of memorials upon any outstanding certificate of title an official birth certificate pertaining to a registered owner named in said certificate of title showing the date of birth of said registered owner, providing there is attached to said birth certificate an affidavit or an affiant who states that he/she is familiar with the facts recited, stating that the party named in said birth certificate is the same party as one of the owners named in said certificate of title; and that thereafter the Registrar of Titles shall treat said

registered owner as having attained the age of the majority at a date 18 years after the date of birth shown by said certificate.

*(Minnesota Court Rules, Rule 220. Birth Certificate – Task Force Comment-1991 Adoption, 4th Dist. R. 11.05)*

The county Assessor-Clerk or Registrar-Clerk can receive a fully authenticated certificate of title with an attached affidavit for the sole purpose of establishing that one is no longer a minor. Until this process occurs, the government will always see the U.S. citizen as a minor not over 18, even if the citizen is of age. The lack of proof of authentication with an affidavit proves to the government, along with the U.S. census, driver's license, voter registration, SS-5 forms, and U.S. Passport applications, precisely the number of inhabitants of the age of 21 that can rightfully elect the whole number of representatives for the choice of electors in their respective State. The one named in the certificate is the one stating the claim as the registered owner. The testimony should be titled "Affidavit of Claim of Ownership of Certificate of Title," and the exact wording of Minnesota Rule 220 should be quoted in the affidavit. Here is a guide to follow:

## **AFFIDAVIT OF CLAIM**

## **OF OWNERSHIP OF CERTIFICATE OF TITLE**

I, Last Name, First Name Middle Name doing business as FIRST NAME MIDDLE NAME LAST NAME, said affiant/registered owner, being duly sworn, declare and state that I am of full age and legally competent and to have firsthand knowledge of the facts stated herein and believe these facts to be true and correct to the best of my knowledge and that the said affiant is the same party described in the said Birth Certificate (Real Property);

1.  The attached document is the authenticated true copy of the original document of title of which I am the holder of the Certificated Title whose name also appears on the face of the instrument as FIRST NAME MIDDLE NAME LAST NAME (Trust/Estate) by reference to the Official Certificate of Live Birth (Title/Warehousing Receipt), recorded and filed dated Month Day, Year [birth registration date; NOT D.O.B.], in the Office of Clerk, Registrar, Land of [Birth State], as the same appears to be held for safekeeping by [Birth State] Vital Records; and

2.  Affiant is aware, The Registrar of Titles is authorized to receive for registration of memorials upon any outstanding certificate of title an official birth certificate pertaining to a registered owner named in said certificate of title showing the date of birth of said registered owner, providing there is attached to said birth certificate an affidavit or an affiant who states that he/she is familiar with the facts recited, stating that the party named in said birth certificate is the same party as one of the owners named in said certificate of title; and that thereafter the Registrar of Titles shall treat said registered

owner as having attained the age of the majority at a date 18 years after the date of birth shown by said certificate; and

3.  Should any Constitution Officer, whether Executive, Judicial, Legislative or deputy, dispute the above-foresaid statements of facts, let it be known that Last Name, First Name Middle Name, is aware that his/her breath of life, dated [Birth Month Birth Day, Birth Year], on the nation of [Birth State] State, the territory of [Birth County] and not the United States (District of Columbia) and not The State of [Birth State]. Therefore, Last Name, First Name Middle Name, (the creditor) doing business as FIRST NAME MIDDLE NAME LAST NAME (the debtor) is a fourteenth amendment citizen known as an ENS LEGIS, created by the Certificate of Live Birth Contract & SS-5 form, which by law is unconstitutional per [affiant's birth states, No expost facto law section. i.e., search the Bill of Rights or Declaration of Rights] and affiant hereby grants, conveys and or gift said Certificate of Title to the Registered Owner known as [EXPRESS TRUST] Trust, the Secured Party, further documented via a Nine Billion Dollar Lien substantiated by an Equity Secured Promissory Note and Pledge and Security Agreement, listed in the organic public record on a non-Uniform Commercial Code. Any rebuttal or dispute to the above-foresaid statements of facts shall provide proof that such contracts have NOT placed [Last Name, First Name

Middle Name] under "legal disability" (Lack of legal capacity or qualification, such as that of a minor or mentally impaired person, to enter into a binding contract) per the Baby Act and per the 1877 Georgia Constitution, Article I – Bill of Rights – Section IV – Paragraph 1.

4. Take judicial notice; Affiant/Registered Owner is aware that Full Faith and Credit shall be given in each State to the public Acts, Records, and Judicial Proceedings of every other State. And the Congress may by general Laws prescribe the Manner in which such Acts, Records, and Proceedings shall be proved and the Effect thereof; and

5. Affiant/Registered Owner is aware properly authenticated copies or transcripts of any books, records, papers, or documents of any department or agency of the United States shall be admitted in evidence equally with the originals thereof;

**PROOF OF SERVICE**

I, the undersigned, say: I am over the age of 18 years, and I am a party to the action or proceeding. My business address is in care of 1234 Main Street, City, in the Republic of (State) of the united States of America.

On [today's date], I served the foregoing document(s) described as Affidavit of Claim of Ownership of Certificate of Title on all interested parties, including but not limited to [Registrar-

Recorder/County-Clerk name], in this action by recording this day the proper documents within the following office(s):

[Full Registrar-Recorder/County-Clerk address]

The documents were served by the following means (specify):

[X] BY MAIL – I deposited such envelope in the mail at [City, State], with first-class postage thereon fully prepaid. I am readily familiar with the business practice for the collection and processing of correspondence for mailing. Under that practice, it is deposited with the United States Postal Service on that same day at [City, State] the ordinary course of business. I am aware that on the motion of the party served, service is presumed invalid if postage cancellation date or postage meter date is more than (1) day after the date of deposit for mailing in an affidavit; and or

I declare under penalty of perjury under the laws of the United States of America [28 U.S. Code §1746(1)] that the foregoing is true and correct.

Executed on [today's date] at [City, State]

Last Name, First Name Middle Name

The next page should be a valid state-approved Notary Acknowledgment signed by the notary and affiant. It is essential that the affiant always sign everything under the United States of America and not under the United States alone. Title 28 U.S. Code 1746 (1) states,

1) If executed without the United States: "I declare (or certify, verify, or State) under penalty of perjury under the laws of the United States of America that the foregoing is true and correct.

Executed on (date).

(Signature).

2) If executed within the United States, its territories, possessions, or commonwealths: "I declare (or certify, verify, or State) under penalty of perjury that the foregoing is true and correct.

Executed on (date).

(Signature).

The difference is clear; option one takes the person out of the United States (federal district) jurisdiction. A critical portion of an affidavit is its jurisdiction distinction. Now how exactly does one register an authenticated birth certificate with an attached affidavit? The Uniform Commercial Code gives detailed instructions regarding proper registration of any certificate of title. The process consists of perfecting one's security interest (titles and property) within the county's real estate records section or the probate section of the superior, circuit, or district court. The document used is a Financing Statement, sometimes referred to as a U.C.C.1, but how the material is validated before registration is the secret that leads to the Zero Percent tax bracket. Every State has a U.C.C. department at the Secretary of State level and also within each county municipality. The Uniform Commercial Code is a standard source of laws established by the Mehomitan Nation, operating commerce throughout the old world. The U.C.C. code was created because it became increasingly difficult for companies to transact business across interstates given the various country laws. The Uniform Commercial Code is vital since it helps companies in different states to negotiate with one another by providing a standard legal and contractual foundation. The laws have been fully adopted by most countries in the U.S., although there are some slight variations from country-to-country (states), the U.C.C. code consists of nine separate articles. The U.C.C. articles govern various types of transactions, including banking and loans. All lenders are supposed to perfect their contracts with their alleged borrowers using the financing statement, stating that the lender is the creditor. The borrower is the debtor with a description of the property as collateral exercised by a lien amount. Once the debtor pays off the balance, the creditor would then remove the lien.

Article one pertains to general provisions, definitions, and specific parameters of how the U.C.C. is applied. Article two relates to the sale of goods, excluding real estate and service contracts. Article three pertains to checks, drafts, and other negotiable instruments. Article four pertains to bank deposits and collections, and Article five details the regulations of letters of credit. Article six pertains to bulk sales, auctions, and liquidations of assets. Article seven provides rules on title documents, including warehouse receipts, bulk sales, and bills of lading. Article eight pertains to investment securities, and Article nine states the regulations of secured transactions of personal property, agricultural liens, promissory notes, consignments, and security interests. Regarding perfecting security interests such as certificates of titles (birth certificates, titles to automobiles, real property, or other personal property), article nine states,

(a) [Security interest subject to other law.]

Except as otherwise provided in subsection (d), the filing of a financing statement is not necessary or effective to perfect a security interest in property subject to:

(1) a statute, regulation, or treaty of the United States whose requirements for a security interest's obtaining priority over the rights of a lien creditor with respect to the property pre-empt Section 9-310(a);

(2) [list any statute covering automobiles, trailers, mobile homes, boats, farm tractors, or the like, which provides for a security interest to be indicated on a certificate of title as a condition or result of perfection, and any non-Uniform Commercial Code central filing statute];

*(U.C.C. § 9-311 (a)(1)(2))*

Article nine states that a financing statement is not necessary to perfect a security interest or rightfully claim title unless a non-U.C.C. is registered. The actual financing statement form has a small box selected to lawfully request and adequately register the property in the right jurisdiction. How to complete the financing statement as a non-U.C.C. is quite simple but first requires creating a trust, specifically an Express Trust. As mentioned before, trust is the only real entity any government truly respects as a natural person because it is a trust that further creates private corporations. Every other entity is viewed as a dead fictitious corporation (corpse). To take part in the Zero Percent tax bracket, a foreign trust must be the foundation of any person and or business in the form of a holding trust. If JOHN DOE works for Walmart, Inc., a foreign Express Trust must be the foundation, holding all of JOHN DOE's assets, including its income from Walmart. If JOHN DOE starts a mobile car wash business named MOBILE CLEANING, LLC, a foreign Express Trust must be the foundation and owner, holding all LLC business assets as collateral. A foreign Express Trust must have a foreign trustee and not a domestic trustee. To have a domestic trustee would ultimately give the United States control over the trust at all times, which can then be taxed and controlled. A foreign trustee means anyone who does not have a United States green card, United States of America birth certificate, Certificate of Citizenship or Naturalization, Social Security Number, or ITIN. The trustee must have a foreign country passport, identifying the I.R.S. or any United States court, the trust jurisdiction. Without a foreign trustee, obtaining the goal of operating in the Zero Percent tax bracket is impossible.

To complete the financing statement as a non-U.C.C. is as follows:

(Note: Upper and Lower case spelling is necessary)

Box B: [your name]

U/D [Name of Trust] Express Trust

c/o [mailing address]

Chino Hills, California [00000-9998]

Section 1a: FIRST MIDDLE LAST NAME

Section 1c: ADDRESS OF BIRTH COUNTY COURTHOUSE

Section 2b: Last Name, First Name

Section 2c: Address of birth county courthouse

Section 3a: [foreign trustee name], trustee under Declaration of [Name of Trust] Express Tr Dtd [date of trust created]

Section 3c: Foreign mailing address

Section 4: WITH TRUST – Constructive Notice that all of debtor's [every derivative of the name] Interest(s) in certificated securities (Note: include Department of State authentication number, top of gold document), Authenticated Certificated Security No. (note: birth certificate number) uncertificated securities (xxx-xx-1234, last four of SSN) including licenses, permits, insurance contracts, commodities, accounts public and private, all assets, all personal property(ies) whether tangible and or intangible and real property(ies), forever in fee simple is now owned and held in covenant by the trustee for the Beneficial Owner herein known as [Name of Trust] Express Trust d/b/a [Name of Trust].

Exhibit 1.23:

EQUITY SECURED PROMISSORY NOTE: For Valued Received, Debtor (the "Borrower") promises to pay to the order of "Name of Trust" Express Trust, herein known as, Lender (the "Secured Party") in lawful money of the United States, the principal sum of Nine Billion Dollars, secured by Last, First Middle Name for a loan received by the Express Trust.

Exhibit 1.23.4:

PLEDGE AND SECURITY AGREEMENT: Entered into as of Month Day, Year by and among FIRST MIDDLE LAST (the "Borrower") and "Name of Trust" Express Trust (the "Creditor") for itself as the Secured Party.

Section 5: Check box (Held in a Trust)

Section 6a: Check box (Public-Finance Transaction)

Section 6b: Check box (non-U.C.C. Filing)

Section 7: Leave blank

The final step in completing a financing statement is to draft the actual financing detail. For the Express Trust to place a legitimate lien on the ens legis (birth name), it must have a note followed by a security agreement, to which the ens legis has received a loan from the trust as its creditor and promises to re-pay the loan listed as a borrower. In this case, the trust loaned Nine Billion Dollars to the ens legis (FIRST MIDDLE LAST) secured by the labor and energy of the real man (LAST, FIRST MIDDLE). Ever since birth, the County, State, Courts, Banks, and the District of Columbia have created notes against the ens legis without the real man's consent, estimating how much money could be generated and circulated in the economy backed by the real man's labor. The trust, as a creditor, must do the same securing a Nine Billion Dollar note, allowing the trust to have the first lien position of all property in the name FIRST MIDDLE LAST. This is the same procedure when it comes to financing a house with federal government-backed security. The deed of trust or warranty deed (security agreement) is secured by the borrower's promissory note or 1003 Mortgage Application form. If a borrower undergoes a foreclosure, the bank must legally record the amount loaned via a non-U.C.C. to substantiate their right to a first position lien on the property seeking satisfaction of debt before any other potential creditor in pursuit of equity. The non-U.C.C. with the promissory note and security agreement, including the Authenticated Birth Certificate with the attached Affidavit of Claim of Ownership, must be sent to the applicant's birth county recorder's office and the county recorder's office where the applicant is doing business. Some states and counties are more complicated than others because officials know the applicant's intentions and the process's power. No owner wants to free their voluntary slaves from the matrix. It should take anywhere from a month or two for the financing statement to return. Section four pertains to all collateral in the debtor's name, owned by the Express Trust. In trust law, the goal is to control everything but own nothing! The language in section four covers all accounts listed in the name of the social security number, such as bank accounts, business accounts, DMV applications, and the like. After the county records the non-U.C.C., it must be recorded with the Secretary of State as a notice of lien. To do this, the very same Financing Statement form is used. Almost all of the information will remain the same except box 4 and box 6b. Box 4, the collateral, will only state the county's clerk of court recording information such as file number, book number, deed number, dates, and page count. Box 6b, non-U.C.C. filing will be left "unchecked." This will ensure that the financing statement will file as a U.C.C. 1 notice of lien for all corporations to take equitable notice. In addition to receiving a certified copy of the U.C.C. 1 and both non-U.C.C.'s from the birth county and applicant's business county; filing a U.C.C. 11 Debtor Search with the Secretary of State will provide proof that the Express Trust is the "only" creditor of the ens legis and its Nine Billion Dollar lien hold's first position. All creditors thereafter must obtain permission from the Express Trust. The debtor search certificate can now supply the natural person (trust) the admissible evidence to challenge alleged creditors such as lenders holding mortgages or electronic liens held at the Department of Motor Vehicles. Lenders of today, operating in public such as banks after the United States bankruptcy of 1933, are indeed alleged creditors because no corporation or its agents can lend money, credit, or in other words, valuable consideration when it is currently bankrupt. Banks can only act as a pass-through agent to deliver funds. When an applicant provides its name and social security number or ITIN, the alleged lender routes the application to one of the twelve Federal Reserve Banks to wire the funds back to the pass-through agent in exchange for bank credits. Each SSN/ITIN acts as a "checking account number" while the number on the back of the social security card acts as a "Federal Reserve bank routing number." A letter is referenced on the back of each SSN/ITIN card describing the bank origination, such as,

- 1st Bank of Boston, with the letter A;

- 2nd Bank of New York, with the letter B;

- 3rd Bank of Philadelphia, with the letter C;

- 4th Bank of Cleveland, with the letter D;

- 5th Bank of Richmond, with the letter E;

- 6th Bank of Atlanta, with the letter F;

- 7th Bank of Chicago, with the letter G;

- 8th Bank of St. Louis, with the letter H;

- 9th Bank of Minneapolis, with the letter I;

- 10th Bank of Kansas City, with the letter J;

- 11th Bank of Dallas, with the letter K;

- 12th Bank of San Francisco, with the letter L;

One enormous benefit of operating in a trust is that it allows the creditor to collapse the fourteenth amendment trust. The fourteenth amendment certificated and uncertificated securities tied with the Securities and Exchange Commission can then be released to the creditor. This process has been done repeatedly with the wealthiest families worldwide, and the Uniform Commercial Code gives its instruction.

(d) The interest of a debtor in a certificated security for which the certificate is in the possession of a secured party, or an uncertificated security registered in the name of a secured party, or a security entitlement maintained in the name of a secured party, may be reached

by a creditor by legal process upon the secured party.

(*Uniform Commercial Code § 8-112(d). Creditor's Legal Process*)

The Express Trust is the creditor over the debtor (ALL CAPITAL LETTER NAME) and takes ownership of everything the debtor could never own and thus becomes the secured party. The birth certificate is the certificated security, which is in the trust's possession after its authentication process. The certificated security, backed by the estate, is the foundation for the United States, creating the social security benefits, which is the uncertificated security, now registered in the secured party's name via the non-U.C.C. The applicant would then petition the court to affix a new name onto the birth certificate, particularly a name recognized with a high-status Title of Nobility that the U.S. government is fully aware of. For example, the U.S. citizen known as JOHN DOE SMITH of the JOHN EL EXPRESS TRUST would seek a name change to JOHN DOE EL. John Doe El is the name that does not have a social security number or was never registered as a debtor in the United States private corporation trust, which substantiates its commercial status as a creditor and not a debtor slave. The title of El belongs to the lineage of the Moors (i.e., Black or African American), and its inheritance is held in trust just waiting to be claimed. The same applies to English Noble Titles such as Baron, Duke, Marquess, Viscount, or Senor (Lord). The Express Trust could then enter a court of equity and file a suit against the county where the former JOHN DOE SMITH fictitious ens legis was created to collapse the fourteenth amendment trust, terminating all intermediaries fiduciaries managing the trust fund. The Express Trust's trustee would then receive all of the monetary securities in the debtor's name on behalf of the beneficiaries. In addition to the name change, the true nationality/race of the Moor or foreign nation would be affixed to the birth certificate via Vital Statistics, allowing the trustee to petition the court to release all descendible funds in the name of the debtor's forefathers and foremothers. A certified genealogical blood record would be necessary as admissible evidence to the court. Wealthy families utilize the Express Trust and the tools provided in probate court, referred to as the king's court, to fund their trust and enter generational wealth.

# CHAPTER FOUR

# Persons Not Required To File

By now, it may be clear who is required to file a 1040, 1041, or 1065 Tax Return Statement and who is not required to file. If not, then the best source is the Internal Revenue Manual (I.R.M.), which is also codified in Title 26 - Internal Revenue Code. Let their words reveal how wealthy families have obtained prosperity for over a century. An interesting fact about taxes is the actual definition of the word in Title 31, "Money and Finance."

(d)(1) The Secretary of the Treasury may accept, hold, administer, and use gifts and bequests of property, both real and personal, for the purpose of aiding or facilitating the work of the Departments of the Treasury. Gifts and bequests of money and the proceeds from sales of other property received as gifts or bequests shall be deposited in the Treasury in a separate fund and shall be disbursed on order of the Secretary of the Treasury. Property accepted under this paragraph, and the proceeds thereof shall be used as nearly as possible in accordance with the terms of the gift or bequest.

(2) For purposes of the Federal income, estate, and gift taxes, property accepted under paragraph (1) shall be considered as a gift or bequest to or for the use of the United States.

*(Title 31 U.S. Code § 321. General authority of the Secretary(d)(1)(2))*

Taxes are indeed voluntary! They are not needed to run the government, and the services Americans use on a day-to-day basis. All taxes acquired from real property meaning real estate, and all taxes acquired from personal property, whether tangible or intangible, meaning social security numbers, stocks, shares, etc., are considered "gifts" to Washington D.C. There is no need to transfer all hard-earned wealth to the United States corporation when its only motive is inflating the dollar and controlling as many alleged citizens as possible through deceptive voluntary contracts.

Before diving into the I.R.M., understanding how the fraud of being classified as a domestic U.S. citizen and not being recognized as a countryside national is paramount. Each state is its own country; therefore, being born in Oregon State makes the newborn an Oregonian National per the 2016 GPO Style Manual, page 95. Parents have unknowingly provided evidence that their offspring is a federal district franchise such as Black/African American, White, Asian, Hispanic, American Indian, Latino, Alaskan, or Pacific Islander, including evidence stating that their offspring were born in a ZIP Code; the District of Columbia deems the child lost at sea, abandoned and state-less.

This unconstitutional act by the District of Columbia is an act of paper genocide, which is described as,

> The deliberate and systematic destruction of Native American Indian culture, language, and identity as a unique racial group by way of the illegal and oppressive race reclassification imposed on Native American Indians or "Blood Indians" to the Non-Indian races of Black/African American, White, or Latino/Hispanic. With the stroke of a pen or the click of a mouse, Native American Indian ancestry can be suppressed on government records. ★The United States Supreme Court struck down Walter Plecker's Racial Integrity Act in 1967 within Loving v. Virginia.

> (*Urban Dictionary*)

The "Affidavit of Claim of Ownership of Certificate of Title" template mentions in section four, the Full Faith and Credit Clause from the United States Constitution, Article IV, Section I. It means that any law or record in one state shall be applied in any other country/state. Observe the 1877 Georgia Constitution, Article I, Bill of Rights, Section IV, Paragraph I, which is law in every other state,

> Laws of a general nature shall have a uniform operation throughout the State, and no special law shall be enacted in any case for which provision has been made by an existing general law. No general law affecting private rights shall be varied in any particular case, by special legislation, except with the free consent, in writing of all persons to be affected thereby; and no person under legal disability to contract is capable of such consent.

The latter of this law explains that each person must consent to any contract they have willfully agreed to, and no person under legal disability can consent to such an agreement. The definition of legal disability is defined,

> Lack of legal capacity or qualification, such as that of a minor or a mentally impaired person, to enter into a binding contract

> (*Business Dictionary*)

In this case, all Americans are not and have never been U.S. citizens. The District of Columbia is committing fraud by contracting with infants who are incompetent of entering into a legally binding contract. Which contract? The Certificate of Live Birth, to be exact. By issuing a birth certificate, an American can voluntarily apply for a social security number, register to vote, apply for a driver's license, apply for a U.S.A. passport, or life insurance. However, the mother and father or legal guardian submitted the information on behalf of the infant to the county or province registrar to create a contract. It is against the 1877 Georgia Constitution and every other constitution. Its law holds uniformity in all other states as well. Everyone is a national because the United States is located in that ten square mile radius known as Washington D.C., permitted by the Organic Act of 1871. Therefore all nationals are foreign to the United States. All Americans are lawfully placed in the category of a plea of infancy, known as the Baby Act.

> Plea of infancy, interposed for the purpose of defeating an action upon a contract made while the person was a minor, is vulgarly called "pleading the baby act." By extension, the term is applied to a plea of the statute of limitations.

> (*Baby Act, Blacks Law Dictionary - Second Edition*)

The Baby Act and Legal Disability are major lawful components to being recognized as nationals by birthright. Wouldn't it mean that all contracts in the ALL CAPITAL LETTER, FIRST MIDDLE

LAST NAME or LAST, FIRST MIDDLE NAME fictitious name considered invalid contracts? Contracts require one to be a U.S. citizen to be approved for financings, such as mortgages, auto loans, student loans, and more. What would happen to these obligations if a national claimed their estate, removing the estate from the fourteenth amendment trust into an Express Trust, and the Express Trust sued the alleged lien holder based upon an invalid agreement? Would all false financial obligations be discharged?

The true location and meaning of the United States are the ten square miles of Washington D.C. Most American nationals, born outside of that radius, are foreign to the domestic United States concerning their country. Discovering how the Internal Revenue Manual determines who is required to file income tax returns is not simple. Regardless of the entity type as an individual or a business, first, analyze how an employee or a business owner can set up a foundation to enter the Zero Percent tax bracket. Section 21.7.13.3.2.7, subsection 2, states,

Telephone calls from foreign entities requesting an EIN (Employer Identification Number) are assigned EIN Prefix 98 and are only worked by Cincinnati and Ogden International Units. If a call is received in any other location, provide the caller with the:

- EIN International phone number (267) 941-1099 (not a toll-free number) Hours of operation 6:00am to 11:00pm. Eastern time Monday through Friday

- EIN International fax number (855) 215-1627 if faxing from within the U.S. and

- EIN International fax number (304) 707-9471 if faxing from outside the U.S.

Anyone may use any of these options to set up their foundation; however, calling to speak to an agent is the fastest method. So, what exactly is the foundation that needs to be acquired to achieve a tax-free lifestyle? Well, according to the Internal Revenue Code § 7701 Definitions,

> The term "domestic," when applied to a Business Entity, means created or organized in the United States or under the law of the United States or of any State unless, in the case of a partnership, the Secretary provides otherwise by regulations. A Business Entity created or organized both in the United States and in a foreign jurisdiction is a domestic entity.

> The term "foreign," when applied to a corporation or partnership, means a corporation or partnership which is not domestic.

> The term "domestic trust" means a trust in which a court within the United States is able to exercise primary supervision over the administration of the trust, and one or more U.S. persons have the authority to control all substantial decisions of the trust.

The term "foreign trust" means any trust other than a domestic trust described above.

*(I.R.S. Manual 21.7.13)*

The term "domestic estate" means any estate other than a "foreign" estate.

*(I.R.S. Manual 21.7.13)*

The term "foreign estate" means an estate the income of which, from sources outside the United States which is not effectively connected with the conduct of a trade or business within the U.S., is not included in gross income under subtitle A of Title 26 of the U.S. Code.

Notice the I.R.S. is very descriptive with terms describing domestic, but not so much with foreign terms other than it is the opposite of domestic. As nationals, the people of the united States of America are foreign to the domestic U.S.; therefore, it is imperative to set up a foreign trust as the foundation to hold all assets. The golden rule of trust is to own nothing but control everything cannot be stressed enough. This means that the foreign trust will own all of the earnings from employment or the earnings generated from business practices. Regarding the earnings from an employer, a social security number, or ITIN (uncertificated security), was given to the employer via I.R.S. Form W-4 to begin working as an employee. To remove the obligation of federal and state taxes from each employee's paycheck, first, convert the uncertificated security (SSN/ITIN) from a domestic estate to a foreign estate, as mentioned above. The foreign estate will be housed under the foreign trust for total tax exemption through the trustee alerting the employer to no longer provide payments in the domestic estate name but now in the foreign trust. All foreign trusts seeking lawful tax exemption use the I.R.S. Form SS-4 to receive an EIN assignment 98 Prefix number from the I.R.S., and it must be done over the telephone. If the foreign trust receives any number other than a 98 Prefix, the process must be completed repeatedly until it is received. Here are all of the reasons the I.R.S. will assign an EIN 98 Prefix number by the Cincinnati or Ogden Campus:

A corporation or limited liability company indicates on Line 9b that it was incorporated in a foreign country.

There is language anywhere on Form SS-4 suggesting foreign status, such as:

Tax treaty

Foreign entity

Treas. Reg. §1.1441-1(e)(4)(viii)

897(I) Election

Form 1120-F

Form 5471

Form W-8IMY

Form W-8EXP

Form W-8BEN

An entity checks the box on Line 10 for "Compliance with I.R.S. withholding regulations."

*(I.R.S. Manual 21.7.13)*

The I.R.S. Form SS-4 must have the above information detailed on the form given to the I.R.S. agent over the telephone to receive their EIN 98 Prefix foreign number to own everything in a trust held by the trustee successfully. An employee trading hours for dollars becomes liable to pay all forms of taxes, of course, from using the uncertificated security as a domestic estate and failing to provide the employer with consent that the employee agrees for taxes to be withheld from their earnings. The I.R.S. Form W-4 is simply not a complete, valid consent. The law requires that all employees furnish a separate "statement" in writing to be attached to the W-4. How many employers follow this imperative rule? Most would agree not many, and therefore, many employers face a legitimate lawsuit for not providing the information upfront with the new hire employee. This is another deceptive tactic that the United States uses to entrap "nationals" into voluntary servitude. Many employers would rather not hire the new employee when presented with such a statement out of fear of dealing with the I.R.S. If the statement is addressed to the employer from the trustee's attention of a foreign trust, then the responsibility of reporting tax exemption would be in the hands of the I.R.S. and not the employer. The foreign trust is the only entity the I.R.S. respects because it is viewed as a natural person and outside of their jurisdiction. Title 26 CFR § 31.3402(p)-1 - Voluntary withholding agreements, states,

> (a) Employer-employee agreement. An employee and his employer may enter into an agreement under section 3402(p)(3)(A) to provide for the withholding of income tax upon payments of amounts described in paragraph (b)(1) of § 31.3401(a)-3, made after December 31, 1970. An agreement may be entered into under this section only with respect to amounts which are includible in the gross income of the employee under section 61, and must be applicable to all such amounts paid by the employer to the employee. The amount to be withheld pursuant to an agreement under section 3402(p)(3)(A) shall be determined under the rules contained in section 3402 and the regulations thereunder. See § 31.3405(c)-1, Q&A-3 concerning agreements to have more than 20-percent Federal income tax withheld from eligible rollover distributions within the meaning of section 402.

> (b) Form and duration of the employer-employee agreement. (1)(i) Except as provided in subdivision (ii) of this subparagraph, an employee who desires to enter into an agreement under section 3402(p)(3)(A) shall furnish his employer with Form W-4

(withholding exemption certificate) executed in accordance with the provisions of section 3402(f) and the regulations thereunder. The furnishing of such Form W–4 shall constitute a request for withholding. (ii) In the case of an employee who desires to enter into an agreement under section 3402(p)(3)(A) with his employer, if the employee performs services (in addition to those to be the subject of the agreement), the remuneration for which is subject to mandatory income tax withholding by such employer, or if the employee wishes to specify that the agreement terminate on a specific date, the employee shall furnish the employer with a request for withholding which shall be signed by the employee, and shall contain –

(a) The name, address, and social security number of the employee making the request,

(b) The name and address of the employer,

(c) A statement that the employee desires withholding of Federal income tax, and applicable of qualified State individual income tax (see paragraph (d)(3)(i) of § 301.6361-1 of this chapter (Regulations on Procedures and Administration)), and

(d) If the employee desires that the agreement terminate on a specific date, the date of termination of the agreement.

If accepted by the employer as provided in subdivision (iii) of this subparagraph, the request shall be attached to, and constitute part of, the employee's Form W-4. An employee who furnishes his employer a request for withholding under this subdivision shall also furnish such employer with Form W-4 if such employee does not already have a Form W-4 in effect with such employer. Instead of providing an employer a statement attached to Form W-4 as a domestic estate; a foreign estate should be provided on behalf of the foreign trust via an Assignment Notice to the employer human resources department. All employees who do not provide a statement as required in section c, as a foreign estate, qualifies their wages as "effectively connected with the conduct of a trade or business with the United States" and are therefore taxed at the highest tax bracket. To convert a domestic estate (SSN or ITIN) into a foreign estate, a 98 Prefix foreign tax identification number must first be acquired using the IRS Form SS-4 and calling the (267) 941-1099 number.

Before completing Form SS-4, understanding the rules to obtain the 98 number is very important. Section 21.7.13.3.2.7.1 (5-16-2018), titled Foreign Entities/ Persons Not Required to File a U.S. Tax Return, states,

> (1) Foreign corporations and individual not engaged in a trade or business in the United States (and foreign partnerships, foreign trusts, and foreign estates that do not have gross income that is (or is treated as) effectively connected with the conduct of a trade or business) are not required to obtain an EIN unless they otherwise have United States source income on which the tax liability was not fully satisfied by the withholding of tax at the

source. However, a foreign entity may need an EIN to comply with I.R.S. withholding regulations or to claim tax treaty benefits. In this case, the taxpayer should complete Form SS-4 as shown below:

a. Line 7b-provide an ITIN or SSN if appropriate, otherwise write "N/A."

b. Line 10-check the Compliance with I.R.S. withholding regulations box, or in the case of claiming treaty benefits, check the Other box and specify on the line For Tax Treaty Purposes Only, Treasury. Reg. 1.1441-1 (e) (4) (vii).

c. Lines 11-17 enter "N/A."

(2) Establish these entities on the "0" file.

(3) If the foreign entities/individuals above receive a letter from the I.R.S. soliciting the filing of a U.S. tax return, the foreign entity/individual should respond to the letter immediately by stating that it has no requirement to file any U.S. tax returns. Failure to respond to the I.R.S. letter may result in a procedural assessment of tax by the I.R.S. against the foreign entity.

(4) If the application is received over the phone, ask the caller's name, SSN/ITIN, address, date of birth, and position with the entity If the caller does not have an SSN/ITIN (and therefore cannot be authenticated using CC INOLE), the new EIN will still be disclosed to the caller, as long as their position with the

entity authorizes them to receive it. See I.R.M. 11.3.2.4, Persons Who May Have Access to Returns and Return Information Pursuant to IRC 6103(e).

The Internal Revenue Manual simply explained that those considered foreign to the United States could obtain their foreign tax identification number to remove all tax liability. Once the 98 number is obtained, the I.R.S. will enter the foreign trust EIN on the "0" file list as an entity that never has to file, not one tax return. Usually, the I.R.S. sends a letter, known as the CP-575, detailing all information given about the entity, such as its name, address, EIN, date of establishment, responsible party, and request tax return by a specific date. The trustee of the trust must respond, stating that the entity has no requirement to do so under Title 26 U.S. Code § 7701(30) and Title 26 U.S. Code § 7701 (31)(B). Before filling out Form SS-4, the foreign national must determine three important key factors.

First, the trust's name should be entirely different from the name on the birth certificate or social security card. Depending on the nationality, research titles of nobility are given to families of notoriety within the applicant's nation.

Second, a domestic address as the trust mailing address and a foreign address from a foreign country as the principal place of business where the trust was established. Although the republic of the united States of America is foreign to the United States, a.k.a the District of Columbia; a foreign address from a foreign country is required because the I.R.S. agent on the telephone are not trained to understand the difference between a republic address and a domestic federal address by way of the ZIP code. This is not an illegal action; a trust can decide when and where it began and what nation it is established under. It is a standard practice among corporations to have a principal address offshore, yet doing business within North America. For example, Experian plc, corporate headquarters is addressed Newenham House, Northern Cross, Malahide Road, Dublin 17 Ireland, but Experian is doing business in Canada and Costa Mesa, California.

The third key factor, and most important, is a foreign trustee. The trust will need a person who has never had a U.S.A. birth certificate, derived from one of the Internal Revenue District States, a social security card, a green card (legal permanent resident card), or any citizenship document issued by the U.S. Citizenship and Immigration Services. The identity and nationality of a trustee determine the overall jurisdiction the United States has over a trust. (Note: If the applicant's primary language is American English, it is wise to select a foreign address in Amsterdam, Netherlands, such as a hotel or available office space or any country where inhabitants have a native tongue similar to American English. If the applicant is indeed from another country, then, by all means, use the familiar accent of the native foreign country to validate the foreign address further.)

For this example, in completing Form SS-4, Christopher Alexander Wellington is an American National born in the land of

California, the territory of Los Angeles. He is employed with Target, Inc., with plans of starting a small business in California. By birth, Mr. Wellington is foreign to the United States' jurisdiction as a Native Californian National seeking to enter the Zero Percent tax bracket. The name of the foreign trust is Heinz Wolfgang Express Trust, whose trustee is Ahmed-El Ben (a New South Wales Australian) with an established foreign address as Dam 9, 1012 JS Amsterdam, Netherlands, and domestic address as 9999 Peppertree Blvd, Ste Q03, Los Angeles, CA 11119. Mr. Wellington will use a private mailbox from iPostal1 and not his residence. iPostal1.com is an excellent option to receive mail and no longer receiving personal mail where he lays his head. Remember U.C.C. 9-307; a debtor is located at their primary place of residence belonging to the District of Columbia.

The below SS-4 (Revised December 2019) instructions are as follows:

Section 1. Legal name of entity (or individual) for whom the EIN is being requested: HEINZ WOLFGANG EXPRESS TRUST

Section 2. Trade name of business (if different from name on line 1): N/A

Section 3. Executor, administrator, trustee, "care of" name: care of Ahmed-El Ben, trustee

Section 4a. Mailing address: 9999 Peppertree Blvd. Suite Q03

Section 4b. City, state, and ZIP code: Los Angeles, CA 11119

Section 5a. Street address: Dam 9

Section 5b. City, state, and ZIP code: 1012, JS Amsterdam, Netherlands

Section 6. County and state where the principal business is located: Los Angeles County, California

Section 7a. Name of responsible party: Ahmed-El Ben

Section 7b. SSN, ITIN, or EIN: "N/A" (Note: The foreign trustee was never issued a social security number. Suppose the applicant is still working on finding a foreign trustee and want to obtain their 98 number. In that case, the applicant can use themselves as the initial trustee in section 3 and the responsible party in section 7a. The applicant (CHRISTOPHER WELLINGTON) should use a new First and Last Name such as Kristopher Oliver or Kristopher El, and state they were never given a social security number. – This was a reference to the two-fold message by Yahusha when he stated in John 3:3, "Yahusha answered and said to him, Most assuredly, I say to you unless one is born again, he cannot see the kingdom of God."– To be born again is to take on a new name that does not belong to the State and also to be made new, walking in newness of life because of what Yahusha was going to do and as of today, has already done. Isn't it fascinating that absolutely no one in the Bible has a last name? What new bibles have done was merge titles of nobility such as Dani'

El, Gabri' El, Micha' El, Isra'El, Melchi'zedek, or Mary of Magdalene.)

Section 8a. Is this application for a limited liability company (LLC) (or a foreign equivalent)?: No

Section 8b. Skip

Section 8c. Skip

Section 9a. Type of entity: Trust (TIN of grantor) - Express Trust

Section 9b. Skip

Section 10. Reason for applying: Other (specify) W-8BEN PURPOSES ONLY

Section 11. Date business started or acquired (month, day, year): Select a date three months before the current day

Section 12. Closing month of accounting year: December 2021 (Note: Always the last month of the year and the current year-end of the application)

Section 13. Skip

Section 14. Skip

Section 15. Skip

Section 16. Check one box that best describes the principal activity of your business: Other (specify) - Unincorporated Church

Association. (Note: Why an unincorporated church association? Trust law is derived from biblical treaties, and the government follows the rules and regulations of the Bible. A trust requires a minimum of two persons, a Settlor, and a Trustee, to fulfill three positions: a settlor, a trustee, and a beneficiary. Just as the Bible states, God is a triune God, the father, the Son, and the Holy Spirit; man comprises three parts. Flesh, mind, or soul, and spirit. In like manner, the government has a minimum of two persons, the President and the Vice President, with three branches as legislative, executive, and judicial. The Bible states that man is the church, and wherever a man goes or whatever activity a man is engaged in, God will be in the midst. Every man is a church, and therefore every man is an unincorporated church association, who occasionally enters into partnerships. The unincorporated church association is automatically tax-exempt as described under Title 26 U.S. Code § 508(c)(1)(A) and completely distinguishable from a religious organization Title 26 U.S. Code § 501(c)(3), which can be taxed if the religious organization "does not" adhere to the rules of subsection 501(c)(3). The Bible is surprisingly one big trust book. The church is tax-exempt, avoiding usury, also known as interest, stated throughout the Old Testament, which the government has codified as law under Public Law 97-280 - OCT. 4, 1982, 96 STAT. 1211).

Continuing with the foreign 98 application,

Section 17. Skip

Section 18. Has the applicant entity shown on line 1 ever applied for an received an EIN?: No

That's it! Congratulations! If the applicant provided the above information to the I.R.S. agent over the telephone, the applicant should have a 98 Prefix tax identification number. As previously mentioned, the I.R.S. may send the applicant its CP-575 letter confirming all of the provided information and may state the following,

"Based on the information received from you or your representative, you must file the following form(s) 1041, 1040, 1065 by the date(s) shown."

Regardless of receiving this letter, the trustee should send some type of statement to the I.R.S. to altogether confirm its lack of tax return liability. The statement provided below using the example used in the SS-4 instructions will guarantee a confirmed statement from the I.R.S. that the trust is on the "0" file list. (Note: The following abbreviations are defined, U/D as under-declaration, ttee as trustee, and TR as trust.)

Month/Day/Year

Ahmed-El Ben, ttee or Kristopher Olive or El, ttee

U/D HEINZ WOLFGANG EXPRESS TR

care of: 9999 Peppertree Blvd, Suite Q03

Los Angeles, California Republic united States of America.

ATTN: DEPARTMENT OF THE TREASURY

INTERNAL REVENUE SERVICE

CINCINNATI, OH 45999-0023

RE: I.R.S. Form SS-4 Application, CP-575; EIN 98-########

I, Ahmed-El Ben, trustee of the HEINZ WOLFGANG EXPRESS TRUST on behalf of the trust beneficiaries, wish to provide the Internal Revenue Service with additional information regarding the trust. The trust is aware that the Internal Revenue Service may request an entity's I.R.S. Form(s) 1040, 1041, or 1065 by a determined date.

T A K E J U D I C I A L N O T I C E, that the HEINZ WOLFGANG EXPRESS TRUST is a "Foreign Trust" established in Amsterdam and was assigned EIN 98-######## for tax classification purposes. The foreign entity and its representatives have no requirement to file any U.S. Tax Return, according to I.R.M. 27.7.13.3.2.7.1 (05-16-2018). The foreign trust and its representatives are not United States Persons per Title 26 U.S. Code § 7701 (30) and not a domestic trust under the supervision and jurisdiction of any court within the United States (District of Columbia) per Title 26 U.S. Code § 7701 (31)(B).

Please be advised that submitting an EIN application is for W-8BEN purposes only, as stated on the attached I.R.S. Form SS-4. Should you have any questions or concerns, you may write to our attention via the address listed above.

Attached: Internal Revenue Service Form SS-4

Thank you for your prompt attention to this matter!

Signed:

Ahmed-El Ben, ttee or Kristopher Olive or El, ttee

Office: (999) 123-4567

It is best to include a copy of the exact information on the I.R.S. Form SS-4, given to the I.R.S. agent over the telephone. The I.R.S. may take up to 6 months to process your statement, but once the I.R.S. has accepted your letter, a correspondence from them should state,

Dear Taxpayer:

Thank you for the inquiry dated Month Day, Year.

Our records show you are no longer required to file such forms.

The next step is to proceed with a two-step process in converting the employees' public insurance bond (i.e., SSN/ITIN) into a foreign estate. It will first be classified as a domestic estate, which will further be converted into a foreign estate. To accomplish this, the same SS-

4 is needed except this time; it will be done online by searching "apply for EIN online" and select www.irs.gov, "Apply for an Employer Identification Number (EIN) Online." The application can only be completed Monday to Friday during the operating hours of 7 a.m. to 10 p.m. Eastern Standard Time. The only thing required to complete this process is the applicants/employee public insurance bond (SSN/ITIN), uncertificated security. The process is as follows,

After selecting "Begin Application Now," the first set of options given is the entity selection. The correct entity to choose is the "estate." People are led to believe the estate is only chosen upon a loved one's death in an attempt to settle their financial affairs. According to the I.R.S., there are two kinds of taxes owed by an estate, first, on the transfer of assets from the decedent to their beneficiaries and heirs (the estate tax), and second, on income generated by assets of the decedent's estate (the income tax). When someone passes away, their assets become the property of their estate. All income generated by the assets is part of the estate and may cause the filing of an estate tax return. The decedent's estate may generate assets including but not limited to savings accounts, CDs, stocks, bonds, mutual funds, and rental property. I.R.S. Form 1041, U.S. Income Tax Return for Estates and Trusts, is required if the estate generates more than $600 in annual gross income.

Interestingly, the estate number can be used for much more than a death benefit. It is a 9-digit number like any SSN, ITIN, or business EIN, also known as a credit profile number. It can be used to access high-limits of corporate credit. This is a necessary skill to learn as the social security number and ITIN are surrendered and abandoned going forward, except if the applicant wishes to finance real estate and obtain a mortgage to convey the property to a trust. It should be noted that an inactive SSN becomes on par with a dissolved corporation after three years. To continue to use the public insurance bond (SSN/ITIN) in the form of credit cards, cell phone contracts, auto loans, all insurance accounts, or bank accounts, knowing that nationals are not U.S. citizens would be counter-productive, accepting the United States benefits and privileges. Therefore, it is recommended to use the foreign estate credit profile as a replacement to the SSN/ITIN, in the same name and only maintain installment credit accounts in the SSN/ITIN credit profile rather than revolving accounts, for the sole purpose of obtaining a mortgage, which is optional. The trust will protect the asset and the applicant's commercial status to remain a national but not a U.S. citizen.

In continuing with the online estate application, after selecting an estate, the next page requires the applicant to confirm this selection, and the I.R.S. provides a little more information as to what an estate is. One key component that the I.R.S. points out is that the estate consists of the deceased person's real and personal property. Remember, the United States and the I.R.S. are referring to the fourteenth amendment fictitious entity, previously mentioned during the explanation of the Cestui Que Vie Act of 1666. This entity is a corpse, a corporation on paper only. The personal property that the applicant is taking control of is the corporate public insurance bond, backed by the certificate of birth (berth). To verify one of the estate's security accounts, perform a google search: treasury direct calculator and select treasurydirect.gov/BC/SBCPrice. Inside of the savings bond calculator, under Series, select EE Bonds; under Denomination, select $10,000; under Bond Serial Number, enter the "berth" certificate number or driver's license, passport number or SSN/ITIN; and lastly under Issue Date, enter the correct issued date and year of the security chosen. The results will populate the bond's interest and value, and there are many bonds in the name on the "berth" certificate.

The application's next page requires the applicant to provide information about the deceased corporation, the applicant's FIRST MIDDLE AND LAST NAME, including ANY SUFFIX that matches the social security card and birth certificate. It may be shocking to know that the estate contains trust fund money logged into accounts where the Registrar first created the fourteenth amendment person. The funds are held within the County CAFR (Comprehensive Annual Financial Report) and the Depository Trust and Clearing Corporation. Many corporations worldwide use the labor of U.S. citizens as collateral for the corporation's taxes, dues, and liabilities. For example, many Americans are familiar with the 13.4 billion dollars "2008 General Motors Bailouts," causing all taxpayers to pay General Motors' debt. This is why all U.S. citizens (ens legis corporations) are listed as human capital on the NASDAQ.

Only corporations can settle another corporation's debt, and the fourteenth amendment fictitious corporation is doing just that. To see evidence of the many corporations doing business in an alleged U.S. citizen's name, simply go to www.gmeiutility.org, click on the search icon, and enter the social security number with dashes. All of the companies and trust companies revealed are doing business in the name of the U.S. citizen's fictitious corporate name and holding them accountable for all debts, liabilities, and losses. To remove oneself from this immense level of fraud, claiming the estate is paramount and must be completed with the 98 foreign tax identification number, owning the estate's assets. A foreign trust is similar to a Holding Co. or Lis Pendens, otherwise known as a Notice of Pendency, alerting the world that the trust has a lien via the non-U.C.C. filing on the estate.

The applicant should enter their name in the EIN application in the ALL CAPITAL LETTER format, CHRISTOPHER (in the First Name box), ALEXANDER FAMILY OF (in the Middle Name box), and WELLINGTON (in the Last Name box). Select Jr, Sr, etc., if applicable. And lastly, enter the applicants' SSN/ITIN.

The following page requires information about the Executor, Administrator/Personal Representative. If the principal person is processing this application, then the Executor is the proper selection. In the upper and lower case format, enter Christopher (in the First Name box), Alexander (in the Middle Name box), and Wellington (in the Last Name box). Enter the SSN/ITIN again and select

Executor as the Fiduciary Title. The last question on this page must confirm the identity of the one completing this application. Again, if the principal person is completing this application, then there is no third party or power of attorney to be listed; therefore, the first selection applies: "I am the executor, administrator, or the personal representative of this estate." On the contrary, if another person, such as a third party or delegated Executor, their information, including SSN/ITIN, will be required.

The next page asks for the applicant to provide a valid mailing address. According to the U.C.C. 9-307(b) Debtor's Location (2), A debtor is an organization and has only one place of business located at its place of business. Therefore, it is necessary to use a private mailing address that is separate from where the principal applicant rests regularly and cannot be a United States Postal Mail Box. The correct address would be the origin of the fourteenth amendment fictitious entity, created by the Registrar at the county office or the county courthouse headquarters. Mr. Wellington was born in Los Angeles, California. Per the Los Angeles County government, the Registrar-Recorder/County-Clerk office is located at 12400 Imperial Highway, Norwalk, CA 90650, and the Los Angeles County Superior Court is 111 N. Hill Street, Rm 204, Los Angeles, CA 90012. Since Mr. Wellington provided the county courthouse address as the debtor residence on the non-U.C.C. filing, the Registrar address would suffice on the estate application. The birth certificate was the first security created to bring about the ens legis.

On the next page, the applicant must provide information regarding the origins of where the estate is probated. Probate court always deals with equity matters, sometimes referred to as chancery court or the kings' court. It allows the government to determine what is their property and what is not. The applicant's trust fund and or inheritance, held within probate and the county courts, have the records of what assets are descendible. This is why upon death and in the absence of a will or trust, the local county assumes all of the decedent's property, further administering the estate assets in their fourteenth amendment trust. Simply provide the county of the applicants' birthplace in the first box, in the ALL CAPITAL LETTER format. Mr. Wellington would provide LOS ANGELES (the county where the estate is probated), CALIFORNIA (State/Territory where Estate is probated, AUGUST 1999 (Date Estate created/funded/probated). (Note: the year cannot be more than 25 years from the current year. Why? As previously stated, the fourteenth amendment fictitious entity was created within the fourteenth amendment trust itself, such as a corporate trust, which is perpetual and is governed under statutes and codes. Any trust that provides a specific amount of years, up to 20-25 years, is automatically considered an Express Trust and is governed under equity law. The I.R.S. is seeking to find out if the estate is under equity law or statutory law. Mr. Wellington is 22 years old, born in 1999, and the current year is 2021. If the applicant is older than 25 years of age, take the difference of 24 years from the current year, which will be the maximum date allowed. And DECEMBER as the closing month of the accounting year).

The application's following page asks if the applicant will have or expect any employees in the next 12 months. At this time, the correct answer is No. However, the estate could hire employees in the future. As the application comes to an end, the applicant can receive their EIN Confirmation Letter online or via the mail. Selecting online is the fastest and most efficient option. The final page allows the applicant to verify and confirm everything is correct. The applicant should see the Legal name as CHRISTOPHER ALEXANDER FAMILY OF WELLINGTON ESTATE. This is the correct format. Upon accepting the estate's confirmation, the applicant should receive the first stage of a domestic estate number. It is wise to save the pdf, I.R.S. Form CP-575, and make copies for safekeeping.

Now that the SSN/ITIN has its estate, the applicant should have a 9-digit number encoded as its domestic estate. The second part of the two-step process is converting the domestic estate into a foreign estate by way of I.R.S. Form 8832, "Entity Classification Election." Filing the two-page form is as follows,

Name of eligible entity making election: CHRISTOPHER ALEXANDER FAMILY OF WELLINGTON ESTATE

Employer Identification Number: 85-####### (domestic estate)

Number, street, and room or suite no. If a PO box, see instructions: 12400 Imperial Highway, (Registrar Address)

City or town, state, and ZIP Code: Norwalk, CA 90650

Part I -

Section 1. Type of election: (a) Initial classification by a newly-formed entity. Skip lines 2a and 2b and go to line 3.

Section 3. Does the eligible entity have more than one owner? (No) You can elect to be classified as an association taxable as a corporation or disregarded as a separate entity. Go to line 4.

Section 4. If the eligible entity has only one owner, provide the following information: (a) Name of Owner -> HEINZ WOLFGANG EXPRESS TRUST

(b) Identifying number of owner -> 98-#######

Section 5. If the eligible entity is owned by one or more affiliated corporations that file a consolidated return, provide the name and employer identification number of the parent corporation: (a) N/A & (b) N/A

Section 6. Type of entity: (f) A foreign eligible entity with a single owner electing to be disregarded as a separate entity

Section 7. If the eligible entity is created or organized in a foreign jurisdiction, provide the foreign country of organization: AMSTERDAM

Section 8. Election is to be effective beginning (month, day, year): Today's Date

Section 9. Name and title of contact person whom the I.R.S. may call for more information: Ahmed-El Ben, ttee

Section 10. Contact person's telephone number: Office Number

Consent Statement and Signature(s): Provide two signatures, two dates, and the titles of each signature. The first should be the Executor's print name, today's date, their title as Executor, and signature. The second should be the trustee of the foreign trust; Ahmed-El Ben or Kristopher Oliver or El print name, today's date, their title as Beneficial Owner, and signature.

The completion of I.R.S. Form 8832 finalizes the conversion of the SSN/ITIN from a domestic to a foreign estate. The estate is now under the jurisdiction of the 98 Foreign Express Trust. Depending on the state the applicant is filing from, will determine whether I.R.S. Form 8832 should be sent to Kansas City, Missouri, or Ogden, Utah. See the instructions page provided with the 8832 Form. The I.R.S. may reply with a correspondence stating that the applicants' arguments were found frivolous. If such a letter is received, don't panic; the applicant did nothing wrong. It is merely because the I.R.S. has a specific quota of how many 98 foreign tax identification numbers can be issued in 3 months and how many estate reclassifications can be allowed under a foreign jurisdiction. A frivolous correspondence is just the Internal Revenue Service's funny way of saying they can't complete the applicant's request at the moment. Simply resubmit I.R.S. Form 8832 precisely as before, and the second attempt is certainly a guarantee. The approval letter will state,

Important information about your Form 8832

WE APPROVED YOUR FORM 8832, ENTITY CLASSIFICATION ELECTION

We have approved your election as a foreign eligible entity with a single owner to be disregarded as a separate entity. The effective date of this election is Month Day, Year.

The foreign trust will own all wages earned by the employee's estate and all earnings produced by any businesses in the jurisdiction of the foreign trust. Since the trust is on the "0" file list, every other entity under its classification is also on the "0" file list. This is how wealthy families preserve their wealth for generations. The United States Debt is up 300% from $20.4 trillion in the year 2000 to $62.3 trillion in the year 2009, according to David Walker, the former U.S. Comptroller General who served under three U.S. Presidents. The national debt is the United States' obligation, not the people, and it can be avoided; however, the people do play a part in the debt's existence. The process of tax avoidance is lawful, but tax evasion is illegal. Some tax code practitioners use other corporations, partnerships, or LLCs as holding companies for other businesses to preserve wealth or save on the amount of taxes due. However, this method will promote slight savings, but taxes are still due, anywhere from 15% to 20% per Internal Revenue Codes 541 to 547.

In the recent example, the employee Christopher Alexander Wellington is employed with Target, Inc. in California. He has completed the estate conversion under his trust name, the HEINZ WOLFGANG EXPRESS TRUST. Which both entities are now in the Zero Percent tax bracket. Mr. Wellington can now update his tax reporting information in one of two ways.

The first option is by remaining an employee with Target, Inc. and filing the 2020 I.R.S. Form W-4 with his SSN or ITIN; manually write "EXEMPT" in Step 4, section (c) to claim federal tax exemption from withholding, and also manually write "EXEMPT" in section 3 of California's 2020 Employee Withholding Allowance Certificate, regarding state tax exemption. Social security and Medicare taxes will continue to be withdrawn from Mr. Wellington's paycheck until the human resources department at Target, Inc. receives a statement from the trustee of the 98 foreign trusts. This statement is the I.R.S. Form 4029, "Application for Exemption From Social Security and Medicare Taxes and Waiver of Benefits." This exemption is only granted if the I.R.S. finalizes and returns a copy to Mr. Wellington approved to forward to his employer. Part I of the application requires the applicants, Name, Social Security Number, Address, and Date of Birth. Box 5: Check, do not send me my Social Security Statement. This form works in correlation to the 98 Foreign Trust being described as a Religious Group. The applicant would complete the following sentence in Part I as, "I certify that I am and continuously have been a member of the HEINZ WOLFGANG EXPRESS TRUST (name of religious group) Treaty of Marrakesh, 1012, JS Amsterdam, Netherlands (foreign district or congregation address) since Month, Day, Year, and as a follower of the established teachings of the group, I am conscientiously opposed to accepting benefits of any private or public insurance that makes payments in the event of death, disability, old age, or retirement; or makes payments for the cost of medical care, or provides services for medical care. Public insurance includes any insurance system established by the Social Security Act. Part II of the application must be completed by the Trustee or Authorized Representative, hired by the trustee to certify the above statements. Mr. Wellington must make two copies of the original I.R.S. Form 4029 and mail all three copies, including a W-9 with the 98 foreign tax identification number, the recorded Declaration of Express Trust, which provides information about the foreign sole trustee as the holder of all estate assets to Social Security Administration, Security Records Branch, ATTN: Religious Exemption Unit, P.O. Box 7, Boyers, PA 16020. Information regarding the Express Trust will be provided in the upcoming chapters. Once the SSA department approves their portion of the application, they will forward the necessary copies to the I.R.S. for final approval, to which Mr. Wellington will receive proper notice to deliver to his employer. All Medicare and Social Security taxes will cease from this point on. Treaty law is the supreme law of the land.

The Express Trust operates fully in conjunction with the several treaties connected with the United States, dating back to the corporation's beginning. The updated W-4, DE 4, and I.R.S. Form 4029 are only necessary if the employer refuses to accept to pay Mr. Wellington earnings as an independent contractor, using I.R.S. Form W-9 with the Foreign Estate EIN. Most employers will not accept the W-9 due to the ongoing court battles of determining an employee's finalized definition and a contractor. W-4 forms have been the only "non-belligerent" method of the hiring process in the United States. Furthermore, there will be no need for Mr. Wellington to file a tax return at the end of the year since he has kept all of his earnings throughout the year. His employer will provide him with I.R.S. Form W-2 to file his taxes. Instead, Mr. Wellington would discharge any tax bill consisting of federal and state obligations using the Express Trust unless Mr. Wellington wishes to utilize the Foreign Express Trust and claim the entire annual debit, credit, and cash transactions as business deductions to receive every dollar back, as a tax refund. The foreign trust can claim all of its expenses as deductions and losses, in a sense, receive its income in the form of a tax refund.

The second option Mr. Wellington could do is update his work status from employee to a contractor with Target, Inc. Filing the W-4 is optional, and as mentioned before, providing the W-9, as an independent contractor with the foreign estate EIN would remove all Federal, State, Social Security, Medicare and other withholdings from each paycheck, if the employer is willing. Mr. Wellington would need to complete the W-9 precisely, which is explained in the upcoming chapters. However, this is the only form Mr. Wellington would need to work as a contractor completely, and he would have the chance to have the foreign Express Trust file taxes at year-end to receive his annual income as a second occurrence.

In the meantime, Mr. Wellington would like to start a pet grooming business in California. Most advisors would advise him to move to a more tax-friendly state like Nevada due to the high annual state tax of $800 in California. The $800 tax is mandatory, no matter if the business has earned one cent; it is a privilege tax to do business in California. However, most advisors do not know Mr. Wellington is on the "0" file list, and all he has to do is exercise his valid Determination Letters with the State. It is necessary to determine what type of entity would best serve its nature to begin a California business. Any business entity selected such as a Corporation, Limited Liability Company, Limited Partnership, General Partnership, Limited Liability Partnership, or Sole Proprietorship will need a business employer identification number. The objective is to generate as much money as possible with any business plan and reduce the amount of taxes owed to Zero Percent from its inception by reclassifying the entity to a foreign entity under the jurisdiction of the 98 foreign trusts. For this example, Mr. Wellington will use a General Partnership for the dog grooming business, which will consist of two partners; his fiancé as the Co-Partner and himself as the General

Partner. According to California Corporations Code, Title 3, Chapter 1, Section 18035,

> (a) Unincorporated association means an unincorporated group of two more persons joined by mutual consent for a Common Lawful purpose, whether organized for profit or not.

The definition of an unincorporated association has similarity to a trust. Requiring a minimum of two persons and under Common Law, which is reminiscent of an Express Trust. Common-Law finds its jurisdiction heard only in a court of equity. Mr. Wellington and his fiancé have decided to call the name of their business SoCal Pet Spa and have confirmed the availability of the business name via the Secretary of State website and the county Recorders-Clerk office by filing a fictitious business name statement, providing its principal place of business address. A General Partnership EIN was obtained from the I.R.S. EIN Online process, which was then converted to a foreign entity using I.R.S. Form 8832. The approval of Form 8832 allowed Mr. Wellington to further submit a correspondence letter to the I.R.S. stating that the General Partnership is not obligated to file any tax return. In response, the I.R.S. provided an I.R.S. Determination Letter, stating that their entity is not required to file 1040, 1041, or 1065 tax returns. The partners will open a general partnership bank account by providing a copy of a bilateral partnership agreement, fictitious business name statement, and their I.R.S. CP-575 EIN Confirmation. The bank will also require the partners to file their short-form general partnership agreement with the California Secretary of State office by filing Form GP-1 (Statement of Partnership Authority). The information to the GP-1 can be derived from the bilateral partnership agreement within Common Law jurisdiction provided on the next page.

## GENERAL PARTNERSHIP AGREEMENT

This Partnership Agreement ("Agreement") is made on Monday Day, Year by and between the following, who shall be referred to in this Agreement as "Partners":

Wellington, Christopher Alexander 1234 Main St, Ste 102, 90210

name address

Johnson, Tiffany Burton 2211 Broadway Blvd, Ste 54, 91201

name address

### Article I: Overview

### Type of Business

1.1 The Partners shall associate to form a General Partnership for the purpose of Investments, Securities, and render services to the several communities and shall have the power to do all lawful acts to further the Partnership business as an Unincorporated Church Organization.

## Partnership Name

**1.2** The Partnership name shall be SOCAL PET SPA GENERAL PARTNERSHIP Dtd MM-DD-YYYY under the laws of California State.

## Partnership Term

**1.3** The Partnership shall commence on the day that this Agreement is executed and shall continue until dissolved by agreement of the Partners or terminated under provisions of the Agreement.

## Place of Business

**1.4** The Partnership's principal place of business shall be at [9876] Central Avenue, Suite 537, [Santa Monica] California Republic, [Near] 90404. The Partnership shall operate in other places of business agreed upon by the Partners.

## Purpose

**1.5** The nature of the General Partnership is hereby declared to exercise its Religious Instructions and Beliefs [Title 42 U.S. Code § 2000bb(a) & (c)], holding consultations, offering goods, publishing, promoting, filing statements, procuring applications, recording invoices in the furtherance of education, science, transportation and giving to the public within various incorporated counties and territories of California State honoring the covenant of God with all of mankind (Acts 20:35, Hebrews 13:16, etc.). Each Partner shall be known as a Church and exercise their inalienable God-given right protected by the 1849 California State Constitution - Article I - Declaration of Rights - Section IV and per the United States of America Constitution "Full Faith and Credit" clause, the 1877 Georgia Constitution - Article VII - Section II - Paragraph II, shall apply in uniform to the nature of the General Partnership in California State.

## Article II: Capital and Accounting

### Initial Capital

**2.1** The Partnership's initial capital shall be One Hundred Dollars and Zero Cents (USD 100.00). Each Partner shall contribute the initial capital by depositing the following amounts in the Partnership business account at any National Association, Credit Union on or after this Day of Month, Year, or any Federal Reserve Bank.

Wellington, Christopher Alexander Fifty Dollars and Zero Cents

name contribution

Johnson, Tiffany Burton Fifty Dollars and Zero Cents

name contribution

### Capital Withdrawals

**2.2** No Partner (known as Co-Partner) shall withdraw any portion of the Partnership capital without the other Partner (General Partner) express written consent.

## Profits and Losses

**2.3** The Partners shall share equally in Partnership net profits and shall bear Partner losses equally.

## Books of Account

**2.4** Partnership books of account shall be accurately kept and shall include records of all Partnership income, expenses, assets, and liabilities. Each Partner shall have the right to inspect the Partnership books at any time.

## Fiscal Year

**2.5** The Partnership's fiscal year shall end on December 31 each year.

## Accounting

**2.6** Complete accounting of the Partnership affairs shall be provided at end of quarter and provided to each Partner within 15 after quarter-end. At the time of each accounting the net profits of the Partnership shall be distributed to the Partners. Net profits shall be profit as designed by generally accepted accounting standards, less required working capital as determined by the Partners.

## Article III: Management

### Time Devoted to Partnership

**3.1** Each Partner shall devote undivided time to and use the utmost skill in the Partnership business.

### Management and Authority

**3.2** Each Partner shall have an equal right in the management of the Partnership. Each Partner shall have the authority to bind the Partnership in making contracts and incurring obligations in the Partnership name or on its credit. No Partner, however, shall incur obligations in the Partnership name or on its credit exceeding One Hundred Thousand Dollars (USD 100,000.00) without the other Partner's express written consent. Any obligation incurred in violation of the provision shall be charged to and collected from the Partner who incurred the obligation.

## Article IV: Statement of Partnership

**4.1** Concurrent with the execution of this Agreement, the Partners, are fully aware and acknowledge the rules and laws that this General Partnership does not require any filings or recordings of a Statement of Certificate of Partnership Authority with the California

Secretary of State office pursuant to California Code - Corporations Code - Title II. Partnerships - Article I. General Provisions - Section 16105(a) with respect to partnership property located in or transactions that occur in this state.

## Article V: Withdrawal and Purchase of Partnership Interest

### Withdrawal of Partner

**5.1** Upon 45 days written notice of intent to the other Partner (s), a partner may dissociate from the partnership by withdrawing as a partner. Notice shall be United States mail, certified, first-class postage prepaid via Certificate of Service, addressed to a Partner at the Partner's address set forth in the Agreement or to such other place as may be specified in a notice given pursuant to this Paragraph as the address for service of notice on that Partner.

### Option to Purchase Dissociated Interest

**5.2** On dissociation by a Partner due to the death, withdrawal, or other act, the remaining partners may continue the Partnership business by purchasing the outgoing Partner's interest in the Partnership assets and goodwill. The remaining Partners shall have the option to purchase the dissociated Partner's interest by paying to the outgoing Partner or the appropriate personal representative the value of the dissociated Partner's interest as determined by an outside appraiser. If the remaining Partners do not exercise this opinion, the Partnership shall be dissolved.

## Article VI: Miscellaneous Provisions

### Consents and Agreements

**6.1** All consents and agreements provided for or permitted by this Agreement shall be in writing. Signed copies of all consents and agreements pertaining to the Partnership shall be kept with the Partnership books.

### Notices

**6.2** Any notice to be given or served upon the Partnership or any party hereto in connection with this Agreement must be in writing at the address shown in Article I, Section 1.4. Any party may designate any other address in substitution of the foregoing address by giving five days written notice to all Members.

### Governing Law

**6.3** This Agreement shall be governed by the California Uniform Partnership Act of 1994 as amended, and shall in all respects be a contract under the 1849 California Constitution and other constitutions of the several states in the union pursuant to the 1789 Constitution of The United States of America - Article IV - Section

I – "Full Faith and Credit" clause, Article I – Section X – Clause I – "Contract" clause and [Title 26 U.S. Code § 508(c)(1)(A)].

**Attorney Fees**

**6.4** As between the parties to this Agreement, the prevailing party in any dispute arising from or relating to this Agreement shall be awarded costs and attorney fees whether or not the matter is resolved by trial or appeal.

**Sole Agreement**

**6.5** This instrument contains the Partner's sole agreement relating to their partnership. It correctly sets out the Partner's rights and obligations. Any prior agreements, promises, negotiations, or representations not expressly set forth in this instrument have no force or effect.

**CERTIFICATE OF ACKNOWLEDGEMENT**

WE THE UNDERSIGNED, declare (or certify, verify, or state) under penalty of perjury under the laws of the United States of America that the foregoing is true and correct [28 U.S. Code § 1746(1)], and was signed as a free and voluntary act and deed for the uses and purposes stated therein executed in the County of Los Angeles, California, this day.

Wellington, Christopher Alexander MM/DD/YYYY

signature (Gen. Partner) date

Johnson, Tiffany Burton MM/DD/YYYY

signature (Co-Partner) date

The above is a complete general partnership agreement that covers every aspect of any business plan. Any business requiring more than one employee and multiple managers, then an LLC or Corporation should be established. There are several examples available on the internet as a rule of thumb to draft Articles of Incorporations or Articles of Organization, to be filed with the Secretary of State in the proper commerce state. The most important language to include in any business structure is found in section 6.3 regarding the governing law. By successfully reclassifying the entity via I.R.S. Form 8832, the operating agreement must state its jurisdiction being a separate contract from the United States and does not seek any tax-exempt benefit or protection of the United States, such as Title 26 § 501(c)(3). Instead, it operates as a church under Title 26 § 508(c)(1)(A). According to the California Secretary of State website,

> a California GP must have two or more persons engaged in a business for profit. Except as otherwise provided by law, all partners are liable jointly and severally for all obligations of the partnership unless agreed by the claimant. Profits are taxed as

personal income for the partners. To register a GP at the State level, a Statement of Partnership Authority (Form GP-1) must be filed with the California Secretary of State's office.

(Note: Registering a GP at the state level is optional.)

Form GP-1 is optional because a general partnership has the same characteristics of a trust, which is a private contract that no "State of" jurisdiction can control and therefore does not need the permission of any entity to exist. However, it should be filed for two reasons. First, opening a bank account for deposits and withdrawals for the nature of the business and, secondly, obtaining a California state entity number to file a specific form with the California Secretary of State office regarding state taxes. This form is known as California Form 3500A, Submission of Exemption Request. The objective is to inform the Secretary of State that the business is not required to file any state tax return to the Franchise Tax Board per the Internal Revenue Service. Remember, due to California ceding its jurisdiction over to the District of Columbia, and the State will heed the I.R.S direction. If the I.R.S. Determination Letter states that the entity is not obligated to file a federal tax return, then the State will determine there is no obligation to pay state taxes. A California business can obtain exemption based on Internal Revenue Code sections 501(c)(3), 501(c)(4), 501(c)(5), 501(c)(6), 501(c)(7), 501(c)(19) or a Federal Determination Letter. The federal letter is precisely what Mr. Wellington has obtained from his efforts of adequately setting up his pet grooming business as one that is foreign to the United States. Below is a guide to complete Form 3500A,

Enclose a copy of the Federal Determination Letter.

Organization Information:

California Corporate Number/California Secretary of State file number: CA#############

FEIN (Federal Employer Identification Number): 85-#######

Name of organization as shown in the organization's creating document: SOCAL PET SPA GENERAL PARTNERSHIP

Web address: www.website.com, If any

Street address : [9876] Central Avenue, Suite 537,

City: [Santa Monica]

State: CA

Zip code: [90404]

Telephone: Business telephone, if any.

Fax: Business fax, if any

Representative Information:

Name of representative: Christopher Alexander Wellington

Email Address: info@socalpetspa.com, if any.

Representative's mailing address: [1234] Main Street, Suite 102

City: [Beverly Hills]

State: CA

Zip Code: [90210]

Telephone: Business telephone, if any.

Fax: Business fax, if any

Part I - Entity Information

Has the Franchise Tax Board (FTB) previously revoked the entity's tax-exempt status? No

Is the entity a trust? No

When did the organization establish, incorporate, organize, or conduct business in California? MM/DD/YYYY

Provide gross receipts for the current year and the three immediately preceding taxable years in existence. Gross receipts are defined as the organization's total amounts from all sources during its annual account period without subtracting any costs or expenses. If the organization has been in existence for less than one year, provide the projected amount of gross receipts for the entire year. List the accounting period beginning to the accounting period ending.

Example mm/dd/yyyy: From MM/DD/2020 To 12/31/2020; Projected Gross Amount: $0.00 USD

Part II - Group Exemption

Is the parent organization applying for a group exemption? No

Is a subordinate unit applying for tax-exempt status using a parent's I.R.S. group determination letter? Yes, (Note: include a copy of the 98 Determination Letter from I.R.S. stating that it is not required to file federal taxes and provide a copy of the I.R.S. letter corresponding to I.R.S. Form 8832 application, which should state the general partnership has been approved as a foreign entity classification.)

Mail form FTB 3500A and a copy of the federal determination letter to:

EXEMPT ORGANIZATIONS UNIT, MS F120, FRANCHISE TAX BOARD, PO BOX 1286, RANCHO CORDOVA, CA 95741-1286

MM/DD/YYYY

date

Wellington, Christopher Alexander [28 U.S.C. 1746(1)]

signature

General Partner

title

Part III - Purpose and Activity

Exemption based on IRC 501 Section(c)(3) Federal Determination Letter: "Church"

The application is complete. Providing a restricted endorsement [28 U.S.C. 1746(1)] in Part II's signature section reserves the applicant's rights within Common Law. It removes the assumption and jurisdiction of agreeing to penalties of perjury under the State of California's statutory law, which is the District of Columbia. That's it! No more $800 minimum state tax obligation in the State of California or any tax due to the business's amount earned. Mr. Wellington and his soon-to-be bride have successfully created a tax-free business from its inception. The Secretary of State will provide an approval letter of the FTB 3500A Form, which is guaranteed. In the meantime, the two partners can open a business bank account with any bank or credit union that offers business accounts. The required documentation needed is two forms of ID, social security card or ITIN letter (from each Partner), General Partnership Agreement (signed by both partners), California Secretary of State Statement of Partnership Authority (Form GP-1) showing the California File Number, the I.R.S. CP-575 showing the Federal Employer Identification Number and $100.00 initial deposit. The bank will make copies of the provided documentation and use the FEIN to open the account. Mr. Wellington is now on his way to generating the wealth that he deserves, transacting commerce as a Native Californian National but not a citizen of the United States. Even if Mr. Wellington decides to put the business on hold and continue working with Target, Inc. or any employer, he is earning money with his social security number as a foreign estate in the I.R.S. system, not subject to 37% withholdings. The foreign estate avoids being in the United States jurisdiction by not having any federal or state taxes withheld from his earnings, which is not effectively connected with the conduct of a trade or business within the U.S. His general partnership business is also not effectively connected with the conduct of a trade or business within the U.S. because it is operating in a foreign country to the U.S. known as the republic of California. Every state has a similar process with similar forms to accept the Internal Revenue Service's Determination Letters. The only procedure left to accomplish is to draft the irrevocable foreign instrument, known as the HEINZ WOLFGANG EXPRESS TRUST, and register the trust in probate court or the county recorder's office, which will be explained thoroughly in the upcoming chapters.

# CHAPTER FIVE

# Eradicating Public Debt

Most would argue whether or not there is Lawful Money circulating in today's economic system. In 1933, the United States corporation asked the people to turn in all of their gold and silver and give it to the U.S. Treasury. The U.S. Constitution, Article I, Section 8, Clause 5, states,

> To coin Money, regulate the Value thereof, and of foreign Coin, and fix the Standard of Weights and Measures;

And Section 10, Clause 1 reads,

> No State shall enter into any Treaty, Alliance, or Confederation; grant Letters of Marque and Reprisal; coin Money; emit Bills of Credit; make any Thing but gold and silver Coin a Tender in Payment of Debts;

The Treasury, permitted by the Constitution, is only allowed to issue precious metals in gold and silver coins as tender of payment. In the year 2021, gold and silver coins are not issued by banks or traded in any market as a form of payment for services; but instead, the United States circulates Federal Reserve notes, better known as cash or fiat paper. All fiat paper printed from 1933 and beyond has the specific language stating, "THIS NOTE IS LEGAL TENDER FOR ALL DEBTS, PUBLIC AND PRIVATE." It would make sense that due to the confiscation of all gold and silver and circulating fiat currency, the Treasury has all lawful money. For the people to have this lawful money, the people must use the Treasury to get it. Lawful money cancels out public debt created by interest applied to negotiable instruments. Gold and silver is a fixed weight of value and, therefore, not negotiable such as Federal Reserve notes. There are two sides to the dollar bill: a public and private side to the Federal Reserve note. Before 1933, all paper bills displayed a different language than all 1933 and beyond paper bills. Within any search engine, there are images of "lawful money of the United States." There are bills in the images, such as a five-dollar bill issued in 1928, which says REDEEMABLE IN GOLD DEMAND AT THE UNITED STATES TREASURY, OR IN GOLD OR LAWFUL MONEY AT ANY FEDERAL RESERVE BANK. This wording comes from Title 12, Banks and Banking, Chapter 3, Federal Reserve System, Subchapter XII. Federal Reserve notes, section 411. In July of 1933, the Columbus Dental Manufacturing Company submitted an application to the Federal Reserve Bank of Cleveland in the amount of $10 grand worth of precious metals.

The bank approved the application in just one day of submitting the application, acquiring 476.92 ounces of gold and valued at $9,867.14. In the depths of the Great Depression, anyone would question why was the Cleveland Fed supplying gold to an unsuccessful firm rather than supplying gold coins and gold-backed currency to banks? Does the Federal Reserve supply gold to any business today? The answer to these questions revolves around President Roosevelt's gold program, which began in 1933. It first restricted the private use of gold, requiring businesses like Columbus to apply to the Fed for precious metals. The Gold Reserve Act of 1934 was signed by President Roosevelt in January of 1934, which transferred ownership of all precious metals in the U.S. to the Treasury, according to Section 2 of the Act. Monetary gold included all coins and bullion held by individuals and institutions, including the Federal Reserve. In return, the individuals and institutions received currency at a rate of $35 per ounce of gold. This rate reduced the gold value of the dollar to 59 percent of the value set by the Gold

Act of 1900, which equaled $20.67 per ounce. That rate had prevailed until the spring of 1933, when the Roosevelt administration began its campaign to devalue the dollar. The Glass-Steagall Act effectively separated commercial banks from the process of investment banking and created the Federal Deposit Insurance Corporation (FDIC), among other public programs. It was one of the most debated legislative initiatives that President Franklin D. Roosevelt signed into law in June 1933. According to the Federal Reserve History,

In the wake of the 1929 stock market crash and the Great Depression, Congress was concerned that commercial banking operations and the payments system were incurring losses from highly volatile equity markets. An important motivation for the Act was the desire to restrict the use of bank credit for speculation and direct bank credit into what Glass and others thought to be more productive uses, such as industry, commerce, and agriculture. In response to these concerns, the main provisions of the Banking Act of 1933 effectively separated commercial banking from investment banking. Senator Glass was the driving force behind this provision. Commercial banks, which took in deposits and made loans, were no longer allowed to underwrite or deal in securities, while investment banks, which underwrote and managed securities, were no longer allowed to have close connections to commercial banks, such as overlapping directorships or common ownership.

Another relevant provision of the Act created the Federal Deposit Insurance Corporation (FDIC, which insures bank deposits with a pool of money collected from banks. This provision was the most controversial at the time and drew veto threats from President Roosevelt. It was included at Steagall's insistence, who had the interest of small rural banks in mind. Small rural banks and their representatives were the leading proponents of deposit insurance. Opposition came from large banks that believed they would end up subsidizing small banks. Past attempts by states to install deposit insurance had been unsuccessful because of moral hazard and because local banks were not diversified. After the bank holiday, the public showed vast support for insurance, partly hoping to recover some of the losses and partly because many blamed Wall Street and big bankers for the Depression. Although Glass had opposed deposit insurance for years, he changed his mind and urged Roosevelt to accept it. A temporary fund became effective in January 1934, insuring deposits up to $2,500. The fund became permanent in July 1934, and the limit was raised to $5,000. This limit was raised numerous times over the years until reaching the current $250,000. All Federal Reserve member banks on or before July 1, 1934, were required to become stockholders of the FDIC. No state bank was eligible for membership in the Federal Reserve System until it became a stockholder of the FDIC and became an insured institution, with required membership by national banks and voluntary membership by state banks. Deposit insurance is still viewed as a great success, although the problem of moral hazard and adverse selection came up again during the banking failures of the 1980s. In response, Congress passed legislation that strengthened capital requirements and required banks with less capital to close.

Today's fiat paper currency says, "This note is legal tender for all debts public and private." How exactly does an American obtain a public debt or a private debt? To understand these questions, a couple of definitions that govern the United States dollar are essential and can provide America's remedy for eradicating the national public debt. Title 12 US Code § 411 states,

> Federal reserve notes, to be issued at the discretion of the Board of Governors of the Federal Reserve System for the purposes of making advances to Federal reserve banks through the Federal reserve agents as hereinafter set forth and for no other purpose, are authorized. The said notes shall be obligations of the United States and shall be receivable by all national and member banks and Federal reserve banks and for all taxes, customs, and other public dues. They shall be redeemed in lawful money on demand at the Treasury Department of the United States or at any Federal Reserve Bank.

Title 12 informs everyone who uses Federal Reserve notes that they are obligations of the United States. If Federal Reserve notes are obligations of the United States, shouldn't the Federal Reserve or the U.S. Treasury and its representatives be responsible for the taxes, customs, and public dues? Public debt originates from negotiable instruments, and private debts are associated with non-negotiable instruments or contracts involving entities not associated with the Federal Reserve, such as private investors. The Uniform Commercial Code defines a negotiable instrument as,

> 2(a) Except as provided in subsections (c) and (d), "negotiable instrument" means an unconditional promise or order to pay a fixed amount of money, with or without interest or other charges described in the promise or order,

When observing any denomination of a Federal Reserve note, it displays a fixed amount of money, and interest can be applied to the fixed amount or not.

(1) is payable to bearer or to order at the time it is issued or first comes into possession of a holder;

Anyone who possesses any denomination of a Federal Reserve note can exchange the note as soon as it is in the holder's hands.

(2) is payable on demand or at a definite time; and

Anyone who possesses any denomination of a Federal Reserve note can exchange the note as soon as it is in the holder's hands or anytime in the future.

(3) does not state any other undertaking or instruction by the person promising or ordering payment to do any act in addition

to the payment of money, but the promise or order may contain (i) an undertaking or power to give, maintain, or protect collateral to secure payment, (ii) an authorization or power to the holder to confess judgment or realize on or dispose of collateral, or (iii) a waiver of the benefit of any law intended for the advantage or protection of an obligor.

The latter explained that any negotiable instrument (fiat paper bill, aka Federal Reserve notes) has no restrictions. Still, it obligates the exchanger, and the exchanger has no other protections of the law. If a negotiable instrument refers to the public side of the dollar bill, it would mean that a non-negotiable instrument is in reference to the dollar bill's private side.

(b) "Instrument" means a negotiable instrument.

(c) An order that meets all of the requirements of subsection (a), except paragraph (1), and otherwise falls within the definition of "check" in subsection (f) is a negotiable instrument and a check.

(d) A promise or order other than a check is not an instrument if, at the time it is issued or first comes into possession of a holder, it contains a conspicuous statement, however, expressed, to the effect that the promise or order is not negotiable or is not an instrument governed by this Article.

All bills before 1933 contained a conspicuous statement, stating redeemed in lawful money on demand at the U.S. Treasury or any Federal Reserve Bank. Therefore, they are not negotiable. This is the key to reducing the national public debt. Non-negotiable instruments (demand notes) must be exchanged in every commercial transaction to discharge public debt created by negotiable instruments.

(e) An instrument is a "note" if it is a promise and is a "draft" if it is an order. If an instrument falls within the definition of both "note" and "draft," a person entitled to enforce the instrument may treat it as either.

(f) "Check" means (i) a draft, other than a documentary draft, payable on demand and drawn on a bank or (ii) a chaser's check or teller's check. An instrument may be a check even though it is described on its face by another term, such as "money order."

(g) "Cashier's check" means a draft with respect to which the drawer and drawee are the same bank or branches of the same bank

Take, for example, an American writing a check to the Internal Revenue Service for a payment towards a tax bill. The check would be considered a cashier's check because the I.R.S. is the public side to the U.S. Treasury private sector. They are both the same bank on which the same account is drawn or deposited.

(h) "Teller's check" means a draft drawn by a bank (i) on another bank or (ii) payable at or through a bank.

(I) "Traveler's check" means an instrument that (i) is payable on demand, (ii) is drawn on or payable at or through a bank, (iii) is designated by the term "traveler's check" or by a substantially similar term, and (iv) requires, as a condition to payment, a countersignature by a person whose specimen signature appears on the instrument.

(j) "Certificate of deposit" means an instrument containing an acknowledgment by a bank that a sum of money has been received by the bank and a promise by the bank to repay the sum of money. A certificate of deposit is a note of the bank.

*(U.C.C. § 3-104. Negotiable Instrument)*

Take a look at any birth certificate issued from Vital Statics or any Public Health Department that warehouses birth certificate receipts. It will state a banknote at the bottom of the certificate with a series of numbers. The birth certificate is a certificate of deposit within the U.S. stock market on behalf of international bankers and creditors for the United States. Again this pertains to U.S. citizens being listed as human capital on the NASDAQ. According to Senator James Traficant, Jr. of Ohio, on March 17, 1993, addressing the House,

Mr. Speaker, we are here now in chapter 11. Members of Congress are official trustees presiding over the greatest reorganization of any Bankrupt entity in world history, the U.S. Government. We are setting forth, hopefully, a blueprint for our future. There are some who say it is a coroner's report that will lead to our demise.

(United States Congressional Record March 17, 1993, Vol. #33, page H-1303)

It is an established fact that the United States Federal Government has been dissolved by the Emergency Banking Act, March 9, 1933, 48 Stat. I, Public Law 89-719; declared by President Roosevelt, being bankrupt and insolvent. The receivers of the United States Bankruptcy are the International Bankers, the United Nations, the World Bank, and the International Monetary Fund. All United States Offices, Officials, and Departments are now operating within a de facto status in name only under Emergency War Powers. This democratic form of Government is an established Socialist/Communist order under a new governor for America. This Act was instituted by transferring and or placing the Office of the Secretary of Treasury to that of the Governor of the International Monetary Fund. Public Law 94-564, page 8, Section HR 13955 reads in part,

The U.S. Secretary of Treasury receives no compensation for representing the United States.

The Federal Reserve describes what lawful money is and how it is applied to specific case law on its website. It reads,

"Lawful money" is a term used in the Federal Reserve Act, the Act that authorizes the Board of Governors of the Federal Reserve System to issue Federal Reserve notes. The Act states that Federal Reserve notes "shall be obligations of the United States and shall be receivable by all national and member banks and Federal reserve banks and for all taxes, customs, and other public dues. They shall be redeemed in lawful money on demand at the Treasury Department of the United States, in the city of Washington, District of Columbia, or at any Federal Reserve bank. "The Act did not, however, define the term "lawful money," but up until 1913, the only currency issued by the United States that was legally recognized as "lawful money" was various issues of "demand notes" (subsequently known as "old demand notes") and "United States notes" authorized by Congress during the Civil War.

At the time, some currency was not considered legal tender, although it could be used by national banking associations as "lawful money reserves." Thus, the term "lawful money" had a broader meaning than the term "legal tender."

In 1933, Congress changed the law so that all U.S. coins and currency (including Federal Reserve notes), regardless of when issued, constitutes "legal tender" for all purposes. Federal and

State courts since then have repeatedly held that Federal Reserve notes are also "lawful money." MILAM V. U.S., 524 F.2D 629 (9TH CIR. 1974), is typical of the federal and State court cases holding that Federal Reserve notes are "lawful money." In Milam, the United States Court of Appeals for the Ninth Circuit reviewed a judgment denying relief to an individual who sought to redeem a $50 Federal Reserve Banknote in "lawful money." The United States tendered Milam $50 in Federal Reserve notes, but Milam refused the notes, asserting that "lawful money" must be gold or silver. The Ninth Circuit, noting that this matter had been put to rest by the U.S. Supreme Court nearly a century before in the Legal Tender Cases.

(JULLIARD V. GREENMAN), 110 U.S. 421 (1884) rejected this assertion as frivolous and affirmed the judgment.

*(What is lawful money? How is it different from legal tender? - "http://federalreserve.gov" \t "_blank" federalreserve.gov)*

Taking a closer look at the Milam case, the Federal Reserve Bank is using to determine what is lawful money and what is not. The Mobley M. Milan, Appellant, v. United States of America et al., Appellees, 524 F.2d 629 (9th Cir. 1974) is a memorandum before Kilkenny and Trask, Circuit Judges and Craig,★ District Judge:

Appellant has filed a substantial brief and an adequate reply brief and has argued his full share of allowed time insupportable for a demand that his $50.00 Federal Reserve Banknote be redeemed in "lawful money" of the United States, which he says, in effect, must be gold or silver. Appellant refused appellees' tender of an equivalent value in Federal Reserve notes.

Appellant's contentions, in our view, were put to rest close to a century ago in Julliard v. Greenman, 110 U.S. 421, 448, 4 S. Cti. 122, 130, 28 L. Ed. 204 (1884), in which it was said:

"… Under the power to borrow money on the credit of the United States, and to issue circulating notes for the money borrowed, its power to define the quality and force of those notes as currency is as broad as the like power over a metallic currency under the power to coin money and to regulate the value thereof. Under the two powers, taken together, Congress is authorized to establish a national currency, either in coin or in paper, and to make that currency lawful money for all purposes, as regards the national Government or private individuals…"

While we agree that golden eagles, double eagles, and silver dollars were lovely to look at and delightful to hold, we must at the same time recognize that time marches on and that even the time-honored silver dollar is no longer available in its last bastion of defense the brilliant casinos of the houses of chance in the State of Nevada. Appellant is entitled to redeem his note, but not in precious metal. Simply stated, we find his contentions frivolous.

Judgment affirmed.

The appellant did not realize that the Federal Reserve note has two sides. The Supreme Court informed the appellant that the Constitution is the contract that allows them to determine what is lawful money and what is not. According to contract law and the terms of the law, both cases mentioned, the Federal Reserve has determined that Federal Reserve notes are lawful money and equal to that of gold and silver, as long as they are used as treasury notes on the private side. Depending on the user's knowledge and understanding of the Federal Reserve note, it will determine its tender of payment. Whether it is a negotiable instrument on the public side with interest or a non-negotiable demand note on the private side without interest. The dollar bill has two sides; the public side is a Federal Reserve note, and the private side is a U.S. Treasury demand note. Upon looking at a dollar bill, it may not be noticeable how contract law applies in this manner. The words Federal Reserve note is located at the top of the bill in a black box, referring to the four corner rules. In contract law, the four-corner rule simply stipulates that if two parties enter into a written agreement, they cannot use oral or implied agreements in court to contradict the terms of the written agreement. It is the Federal Reserve and the United States Treasury, who are the two parties entering into an agreement, which removes their responsibilities or liabilities for the instrument, transferring its liability to whoever uses the instrument as a negotiable instrument. There are two signatures on every denomination of a Federal Reserve note, one for the Treasurer of the United States and the other for the Secretary of Treasury. Keep in mind; the Secretary of Treasury is now the Governor for the International Monetary Fund, which is the public side to the actual U.S. Treasury. Therefore the Treasurer of the United States is the actual Treasurer of the private side.

Reducing the public debt is obtainable by steering away from Federal Reserve notes as the beginning and end to Americans' daily commerce. The issuer must reserve their rights upon their signature when using lawful money. Although a Federal Reserve note is already signed by the Treasurer of the U.S. and the Secretary of Treasury (Governor of IMF), American's are not supposed to reserve their rights on the actual Federal Reserve note but instead, on their own demand notes, checks, or whenever using credit cards. Simply, exchange Federal Reserve notes for United States Postal Money Orders or money orders or checks issued by any Federal Reserve bank such as Chase, Wells Fargo, Bank of America, etc. and add the conspicuous statement of Title 12 U.S.C. § 411, that was once provided on all United States denominational bills before 1933 in the memo section. The imperative language is "Redeemed in Lawful Money or on-demand at the U.S. Treasury or at any Federal Reserve bank," and provides a signature followed by the words All Rights Reserved. This is called a restricted endorsement, which removes the obligation from the public and puts the obligation back onto the United States Corporation to reduce the national public debt lawfully. The U.C.C. informs everyone that unless the conspicuous statement and or rights are reserved, the person using the instrument is held responsible.

(a) If a person acting, or purporting to act, as a representative signs an instrument by signing either the name of the represented person or the name of the signer, the represented person is bound by the signature to the same extent the represented person would be bound if the signature were on a simple contract. If the represented person is bound, the signature of the representative is the "authorized signature of the represented person," and the represented person is liable on the instrument, whether or not identified in the instrument.

(b) If a representative signs the name of the representative to an instrument and the signature is an authorized signature of the represented person, the following rules apply:

1.  If the form of the signature shows unambiguously that the signature is made on behalf of the represented person who is identified in the instrument, the representative is not liable on the instrument.

(U.C.C. § 3-402 Signature By Representative)

When the Treasurer of the United States and the Secretary of Treasury sign a negotiable instrument (i.e., dollar bill), which is a contract, without restricting their rights, they become responsible for the debt attached to the dollar bill. This is why Title 12 U.S.C. § 411 states that all forms of money are the United States' obligations. Since many Americans are using negotiable instruments (dollar bills) without restricting their rights (restricted endorsement) on their demand notes such as money orders or checks, Americans become responsible for the national public debt, through the fourteenth amendment fictitious ens legis as one of the entities called the States United. This is how the Government is off the hook from all liability and can tax the U.S. citizen and their children to pay down extreme amounts of debt. All checks linked to any checking account at any bank will have a section for the issuer to sign their name on the provided line. What's interesting is that line is not a line at all. If zoomed in closely, the words "authorized representative" can be seen, followed by the letters MP, meaning Micro Print. Anyone who signs their name without restricting their rights becomes responsible for the negotiable instrument they are creating.

The national public debt is not entirely the federal Government's fault. Unfortunately, it is the fault of the American people. Americans have been given a choice from the Federal Government to use any Federal Reserve note as a negotiable instrument or a non-negotiable demand note. There is no budget plan discussed in political campaigns that will magically reduce the national debt. The national debt in North America has increased more than 21% since President Trump took office in January of 2017, with the debt-to-gross domestic product (GDP) ratio approaching 110% in 2019. Under President Obama's administration, the national debt increased 100%, from $10 trillion to $20 trillion. As of April 13, 2020, the U.S. government debt is up to $24.22 trillion. It is codified within Title 31, Money and Finance subsection 3101, that the public debt is limited. The face amount of obligation issued and the face amount of obligations whose principals and interest are guaranteed by the United States Government may not be more than $14,294,000,000,000. That is $9,926,000,000,000 over the legal public debt limitations. It is easy to understand why so many Americans (beyond politicians and economists) are starting to pay close attention to this issue. Unfortunately, how the debt level is explained to the public is usually glossed over. Pair this problem with the fact that many individuals do not understand how the national debt level affects them on a daily basis, including their future generations.

Regarding banking, most Americans are misinformed of the workings of the Federal Reserve System or how money is circulated in the United States economy. It all starts with politicians requesting to be put into office, promising to provide more free benefits to the public than the opposition. The main issue the politician faces is the need for more money to provide the promised free stuff. However, the State spends more than its income, which is called Deficit Spending. To pay for that deficit spending, the Treasury borrows currency by issuing a bond. A bond is a fixed income instrument that represents a loan made by an investor to a borrower. It could be thought of as an IOU. Between the lender and the borrower, that includes the details of the loan and its payments. Treasury bonds are indeed the national public debt, stealing prosperity from the future for spending today, to be paid in the form of taxes. The American people could put an end to it by merely using non-negotiable instruments. Once the bond is created, the Treasury then holds a bond auction, and the world's largest banks compete to buy a large part of the national debt and make a profit by earning interest. After the auction, the banks enter an open market operation to sell the bonds to the Federal Reserve for their profit. To pay for the bonds, the Federal Reserve begins to write a check on an account with nothing in it. According to the Boston Federal Reserve Bank,

> "When people write a check, there must be sufficient funds in our account to cover the check, but when the Federal Reserve writes a check, there is no bank deposit on which that check is drawn. When the Federal Reserve writes a check, it is creating money."

The Federal Reserve then delivers the bad checks to the banks, and at this point, currency comes into existence. The big banks then use that currency to buy more bonds at the next Treasury auction. What is a check? A check is surprisingly an IOU for cash, requiring the receiver to go to the bank and pick it up. In all actuality, the U.S. Treasury and the Federal Reserve exchange IOUs, enriching the banks as middlemen and indebting the people. This is the origination of all of the paper fiat currency! The Treasury then deposits the newly created currency to several government branches, and the Government then proceeds to deficit spending, which is directed to public works, social services, and wars. The employees of Government, hospitals, local school districts, and others then deposit their paychecks into local commercial banks or institutions. This is where things get interesting. When an employee deposits their earnings from labor, they are not depositing into an account to be safely held in trust. Instead, the employee is loaning the bank their earnings, and within certain legal limits, the banks can do anything with it to their benefit. This includes purchasing shares in the stock market or the foreign exchange market and loaning them to the public without giving the employee their fair share of profit. Instead, should the employee choose to keep their earnings in a savings account, the bank sees fit only to give 0.01% to 1% interest back to the employee while the bank made a fortune. At this point, the Federal Reserve System's primary operation comes into play once the employee deposits their earnings. A process called Fractional Reserve banking is the primary function of all banks in America. It is a system in which only a fraction of bank deposits are backed by actual cash on hand and available for withdrawal. This happens to expand the economy by freeing capital for lending theoretically. Loan ratios vary from institution to institution. Using the Target, Inc. employee, Christopher Alexander Wellington, from the previous chapter, as an example to show how earnings affect the economy from a 10% reserve ratio. Suppose Mr. Wellington received a separate bonus check from Target, Inc. for $100 to be deposited into Citibank, N.A. The bank can legally take $90 and loan it out to the public without informing Mr. Wellington. Citibank must hold $10 of his deposit in a reserve account in case Mr. Wellington wants to come back to make a withdrawal. Of course, his withdrawal of the entire $100 comes from a pool of other 10% reserves from other people; these reserves are called vault cash. How exactly does Mr. Wellington's bank account statement remain a total of $100 as an available balance? Because the bank created a $100 I.O.U. as bank credit in its place. According to the Federal Reserve Bank of New York,

> Commercial banks create checkbook money whenever they grant a loan, only by adding new deposit dollars in accounts on their books in exchange for a borrower's IOU.

(*Federal Reserve Bank of New York, "I Bet You Thought," p. 19*)

Under this example, Mr. Wellington's deposit of $100 allowed Citibank to create an additional 10% bank credit of $90, and therefore there is $190 in existence. People take out loans from the bank to buy a house, a car, have operating money for a business plan, or consolidate debt. A borrower who wishes to buy a car then takes out a loan of $90 from the same bank that was created as bank credit from Mr. Wellington's account and pays the seller for the car. Then the seller deposits the $90 into their Wells Fargo account, and their bank then loans out 90% of that deposit, creating another set of bank credits, which would be $81 for a total of $271 in existence. This process repeats and repeats up to $1,000 bank credit, all backed by just $100 of vault cash. As mentioned before, some reserve ratios are 10%, 3%, and some are 0%. This is where the vast majority of the currency supply in America comes from. In fact, 92%-96% of all currency in existence is created not by the Government but within banks. The result of this currency expansion by the banks is far higher than this example. This tremendous expansion of currency causes the everyday prices of goods and services to act as a sponge on this never-ending expanding supply. The more currency circulating in existence, the more prices rise to use all of the currency equally. This is where inflation is derived; rising prices are nearly a symptom! Sadly this is the entire makeup of America's currency supply. The U.S. Treasury and the Federal Reserve exchange IOUs printing 4%-8% of the money into existence, and the other 92%-96% is nothing but numbers typed into a computer by the banks as bank credits. Unfortunately, the American people work for that currency supply, trading moments of their lives, hour by hour, day by day, year by year in exchange for numbers someone printed on pieces of paper or typed into a computer.

In the United States, neither paper currency nor deposits have value as commodities. Intrinsically, a dollar bill is just a piece of paper; deposits merely book entries. Coins do have some intrinsic value as metal but generally far less than their face value. What, then, makes these instruments - checks, paper money, and coins - acceptable at face value in payment of all debts and for other monetary uses? Mainly, it is the confidence people have that they will be able to exchange such money for other financial assets and for real goods and services whenever they choose to do so.

(*Modern Money Mechanics - A Workbook on Bank Reserves and Deposit Expansion, Federal Reserve Bank of Chicago*)

The numbers printed or typed now represent Americans' blood, sweat, tears, labor, ideas, and talents so that they can save some of those numbers and pay the tax collector, known as the Internal Revenue Service. The I.R.S. then delivers the taxes over to the U.S. Treasury so that the Treasury can pay the principal and interest on the bonds that the Federal Reserve bought with a check, drawn on an account with NOTHING in it! Much of the taxes collected are not used for schools, public roads, and services but to pay interest on bonds that the Federal Reserve bought with a check drawn on an account with nothing in it. Is the Federal Reserve committing fraud on the American people, or are the American people unknowingly allowing the Federal Reserve to play their game? Before the establishment of the Federal Reserve, there was no need for personal income tax. The Federal Reserve was created in 1913, and in that very same year, the Constitution was amended to allow income tax, stemming from section 5 of the fourteenth amendment. How many hours and dollars were siphoned away from Americans and into the hands of the owners of the Federal Reserve? The Federal Reserve bank is not a federal entity at all; it has stockholders. A stockholder is a share of stock representing a percentage of ownership in a corporation; therefore, the stockholders are the owners of that corporation. The Federal Reserve is a private corporation with owners, according to their website, which says,

Appendix B. Dividends

B.1 Payment of Dividends from Surplus

After all necessary expenses of a Federal Reserve bank have been paid or provided for, the stockholders shall be entitled to receive an annual dividend of six per centum on the paid-in capital stock, which dividend shall be cumulative.

(*Federal Reserve Act, Section 7. Division of Earnings*)

The American people know all too well that whenever the issue of reducing the national debt or talk of the debt ceiling, the federal Government always prints more money or raises taxes to settle the enormous debt. Here's why talk of the debt ceiling is delusional. If the federal government prints the very first dollar into existence and that is the only dollar that exists, but the Government promises to pay it back plus another dollar's worth of interest, where does the Government get the second dollar to pay interest? The answer is that the Government will have to borrow the second dollar into existence and promise to pay it back with interest. Now there are two dollars that exist, but four dollars is owed, and so on—leading to never enough currency to pay the debt, atlas, not with this method. The only way to stop increasing the national public debt, created by negotiable instruments, is by issuing lawful private money, also known as non-negotiable instruments. But to reduce the current national debt is entirely different.

Title 31, Money and Finance, the U.S. Treasury informs the American people,

(a) To provide the people of the United States with an opportunity to make gifts to the United States Government to be used to reduce the public debt -

(1) the Secretary of the Treasury may accept for the Government a gift of

(A) money made only on the condition that it be used to reduce the public debt;

(B) an obligation of the Government included in the public debt made only on the condition that the obligation be canceled and retired and not reissued;

(*Title 31, U.S.C. § 3113. Accepting gifts*)

To discharge the public debt, such as student loans, bank loans, mortgages, etc., the Secretary of Treasury has informed the public of how to successfully aid the Government in debt reduction. Non-negotiable demand notes cancel out negotiable instruments by providing the words of Title 12 U.S.C. § 411. There must also include the words of section (A) of Title 31 U.S.C. § 3113 on the American people's demand notes. For example, suppose the Target, Inc. employee, Christopher Alexander Wellington, has an auto loan for $16,500 and a monthly payment of $378.47 with Ford Motor Credit. Mr. Wellington has had this loan for three years now and has decided to cancel the obligation of interest affecting the overall national economic health. The first thing Mr. Wellington must do is understand the laws of making conspicuous statements on negotiable instruments. This rule comes from the Uniform Commercial Code, known as Accord and Satisfaction By Use of Instrument.

(b) Unless subsection (c) applies, the claim is discharged if the person against whom the claim is asserted proves that the instrument or an accompanying written communication contained a conspicuous statement to the effect that the instrument was tendered as full satisfaction of the claim.

*(U.C.C. § 3-311(b))*

Every State has encoded this U.C.C. rule into its state code. Being that Mr. Wellington is a Californian National, the state code for accord and satisfaction is CA CIV Code, Chapter 4, Section 1526,

(a) Where a claim is disputed or unliquidated, and a check or draft is tendered by the debtor in settlement thereof in full discharge of the claim, and the words "payment in full" or other words of similar meaning are notated on the check or draft, the acceptance of the check or draft does not constitute an accord and satisfaction if the creditor protests against accepting the tender in full payment by striking out or otherwise deleting that notation or if the acceptance of the check or draft was inadvertent or without knowledge of the notation.

(b) Notwithstanding subdivision (a), the acceptance of a check or draft constitutes an accord and satisfaction if a check or draft is tendered pursuant to a composition or extension agreement between a debtor and its creditors and pursuant to that composition of the extension agreement, all creditors of the same class are accorded similar treatment, and the creditor receives the check or draft with knowledge of the restriction.

A creditor shall be conclusively presumed to have knowledge of the restriction if a creditor either:

(1) Has, previous to the receipt of the check or draft, executed a written consent to the composition or extension agreement.

(2) Has been given, not less than 15 days nor more than 90 days prior to receipt of the check or draft, notice, in writing, that a check or draft will be tendered with a restrictive endorsement and that acceptance and cashing of the check or draft will constitute an accord and satisfaction.

(c) Notwithstanding subdivision (a), the acceptance of a check or draft by a creditor constitutes an accord and satisfaction when the check or draft is issued pursuant to or in conjunction with a release of a claim.

(d) For the purposes of paragraph (2) of subdivision (b), mailing the notice by first-class mail, postage prepaid, addressed to the address shown for the creditor on the debtor's books or such other address as the creditor may designate in writing constitutes notice.

According to the law mentioned above, Mr. Wellington first needs to provide the Ford Motor Credit Company a certified mail notice with an attached proof of service, made attention to the Chief Executive Officer. The notice should inform their office will receive a check or draft with a "restrictive endorsement" not less than 15 days or not more than 90 days from the date of receipt of the notice. Once 15 days have passed, and Mr. Wellington has received a returned certified mail receipt with either no response from Ford Motor Credit Company or a positive confirmation, he may begin to provide his non-negotiable demand note with a restrictive endorsement. Mr. Wellington should use a United States Postal Money Order because of the Post Office's contractual relationship with the United States Treasury via the Post Master General. The Post Office is the closest form of lawful money from the U.S. Treasury that Americans have available. Per Title 39 of the United States codebook, all officers and employees are constitutional officers,

Before entering upon their duties and before receiving any salary, all officers and employees of the Postal Service shall take and subscribe the following oath or affirmation:

"I, ___, do solemnly swear (or affirm) that I will support and defend the Constitution of the United States against all enemies, foreign and domestic; that I will bear true faith and allegiance to the same; that I take this obligation freely, without any mental reservation or purpose of evasion; and that I will well and faithfully discharge the duties of the office on which I am about to enter."

*(Title 39, U.S.C. § 1011. Oath of office; Pub. L. 91-375, August 12, 1970, 84 Stat. 733)*

Title 39, U.S.C. § 2006. The relationship between the Treasury and the Postal Service reads,

(c) Notwithstanding section 2005(d)(5) or 2011(e)(4)(E) of this title, obligations issued by the Postal Service shall be obligations of the Government of the United States, and payment of principal and interest thereon shall be fully guaranteed by the Government of the United States, such guaranty being expressed on the face thereof, if and to the extent that –

(1) the Postal Service requests the Secretary of Treasury to pledge the full faith and credit of the Government of the United States for the payment of principal and interest thereon; and

(2) the Secretary, in his discretion, determines that it would be in the public interest to do so.

Mr. Wellington has purchased a United States Postal Money Order in the amount equal to his monthly car payment of $378.47. The "pay to the order" would state Ford Motor Credit Company, with its address right below the company name. The memo section is the most crucial, converting the pre-made negotiable instrument to a non-negotiable demand note. The memo should have the following exact language, "Payment in Full For The Reduction of Public Debt Account No. 1234567890 (i.e., car loan account number); Redeemed in Lawful Money on Demand at the U.S. Treasury or at any Federal Reserve bank." Mr. Wellington would then provide his name, followed by the words "All Rights Reserved," and provides his address right below. The next step is to properly register the demand note as an extension to Mr. Wellington's U.C.C. 1 Financing Statement, as explained in Chapter Three: Existence of Life. The extension of the uniform commercial code is the form U.C.C. 3 Financing Statement Amendment. Mr. Wellington would provide the initial U.C.C. 1 Financing Statement File No. from the Secretary of State's office in box 1a. Box 3, the option for continuation would be checked, any secured party of record would be checked in box 5, as this continuing statement affects the Express Trust. In box 8, the third option would be checked as giving an entire restated collateral description. Mr. Wellington would provide the full automobile details, the full Ford Motor Credit Company account details (including contract sales date), and a full description of the demand note. The HEINZ WOLFGANG EXPRESS TRUST would be provided in box 9a for the secured party organization name. The U.C.C. 3 must be directed to the Secretary of State for recording. A certified copy of both the U.C.C. 1 and 3 should be obtained from the Secretary of State, and Mr. Wellington is now prepared to delegate discharge instructions to the United States Post Master General. Both U.C.C. forms, with the actual U.S.P.S. Money Order, and a certified copy of the Declaration of Express Trust (further explained in the upcoming chapters), and lastly, an introductory trustee letter made attention to the Post Master General, with the I.R.S. Form W-8BEN would complete Mr. Wellington's accord and satisfaction discharge packet. The W-8BEN will further be explained as well. The introductory letter should provide brief detail introducing the foreign express trust as well as advising the postmaster general to register the demand note as a treasury note with the Secretary of the U.S. Treasury Department and forward the demand note to Ford Motor Credit Company in respect to Title 31 U.S.C. 3113, Accepting Gifts. The Chief Executive Officer of the Board of Governors of the United States Postal Service can receive the packet at 475 L'Enfant Plaza SW, Washington, D.C. That's it! Once Mr.

Wellington sends the payment to Ford Motor Credit Company, and they have cashed the money order, his $16,500 obligation of the United States has just been canceled, reducing the national debt minus $16,500 and would then receive a 1099-C from the lender. The HEINZ WOLFGANG EXPRESS TRUST must settle the amount reported in the 1099-C by using the same method or by sending an Explanatory Statement to the I.R.S. stating that the entity is not required to file nor pay taxes. The I.R.S. will definitely need the trust to cancel the amount provided in the informational 1099-C to clear their books, or else it will be considered as an income to Mr. Wellington's social security account.

A mortgage or credit card payment would operate just the same. In the event that one is in the middle of purchasing an automobile using an installment sales contract or at the closing table regarding real estate, a restrictive endorsement is still required to help reduce the national public debt. All installment sales contracts and mortgage promissory notes are obligations of the United States, just waiting to be circulated from one party to another as a negotiable instrument. Adding the language "Redeemed in Lawful Money on Demand at the U.S. Treasury or at any Federal Reserve bank" with a signature, followed by the words "All Rights Reserved," will most assuredly prevent a negotiable instrument.

If all Americans proceeded to issue demand notes in all areas of commercial transactions, with the intent to discharge the public debt to stop assuming liability for the use of Federal Reserve notes, the national debt could be eradicated in no time at all. The Federal Reserve note is legal tender for all debts, public and private. All paper fiat currency bills have two sides. A public side from the use of negotiable instruments requires interest, and a private side from the use of non-negotiable instruments that have no interest but act as lawful money and or treasury notes. Besides the United States Postal Service offering Americans the best access to the United States Treasury, there is also the United States Coin. The majority are led to believe that the Federal Reserve has all the power to create money when indeed, all the power they have is to print Federal Reserve notes but never to coin money. Minting coin has always been the responsibility of the United States Treasury per the constitution. Despite the smallest amounts of silver, gold, and copper in the current U.S. coin, it will always hold more value than a Federal Reserve note. An article entitled "Contracts Payable in Gold," by George Cyrus Thorpe, Showing the Legal Effect of Agreements to Pay in Gold – Senate Resolution No. 62, April 17, 1933, quotes,

> The laws of the United States recognize two kinds of money, namely coin, and paper. The term "dollars in species" means gold or silver coined dollars. "Dollars in currency" means dollars in notes or any paper money current in the community.
>
> *(Trebilcock v. Wilson (1872) 12 Wall. 687, 20 L. Ed. 460)*

As of today, the current median income is $34,466 in North America, which is $2,872.17 per month that the average household is bringing in to support their families. Back in 1913, the dollar to gold ratio was just $29.01, and today, one gold dollar is still measured by the same gold dollar value, which was used in 1849 to 1889, weighing in at 1.672 grams or 0.04837 troy ounces. One gold dollar is equal to $91.91. So, if gold and silver are the standards for real tangible money that will never lose its value in contrast to paper fiat money, and if the average family brings in $2,872.17 fiat per month; then in actuality, an average family truly brings in just $31.25 of gold per month. As stated before, if all Americans proceeded to issue demand notes in all areas of commercial transactions, with the intent to discharge the debt to stop assuming liability for the use of Federal Reserve notes, the national debt could be eradicated in no time at all.

One final thought in relation to the National Public Debt, which is highly talked about every year, especially in the year 2020 with the wide-spread of the Global Economic Pandemic, known as COVID-19; is that the name of a U.S. citizen, U.S. resident, or Legal Permanent Resident and its Social Security Number or ITIN, creates the securities needed for the federal government to then package those securities into bonds to be sold around the world to investors. All U.S. citizens have been naturalized via the birth certificate. All birth certificates have a listed Registrar or Assessor Clerk, and according to Title 8 U.S.C. § 1101(a)(7), the term "clerk of court" means a clerk of a naturalization court. As the bonds are sold, the federal government cannot get away with 100% of fraud, earning a profit from the U.S. citizens labor; therefore, the government gives a portion of the securities to its citizens on the private side called the

CAFR funds and given to the citizens on the public side via old-age insurance, workers compensation, social security insurance, 401k, Medi-Cal, Medicare and other means of public insurance. Every created security goes into the CAFR accounts in the county and continues to grow. Whenever there's talk about the debt ceiling or debt clock in New York City, it is money ($27 Trillion) that is owed to nationals on the private side of the ledger and ($27 Trillion) of dischargeable debt on the public side. The private side is also inheritance funds that are uncollectable unless the national operates completely in trust in the name of their forefathers and foremothers of the Mehomitan Nation, which means the national is descendible who is able to collect what is rightfully theirs. Only nationals of an Express Trust, a.k.a Natural Persons, can own property fully protected by the United States Constitution "contract clause.".

> Section 1. The rights protected by the Constitution of the United States are the rights of natural persons only. Artificial entities, such as corporations, limited liability companies, and other entities, established by the laws of any State, the United States, or any foreign state shall have no rights under this Constitution and are subject to regulation by the People, through Federal State, or local law. The privileges of artificial entities shall be determined by the People through Federal, State, or local law and shall not be construed to be inherent or inalienable.

> *(116th Congress 1st Session, H.J. Resolution 48, February 22, 2019)*

# CHAPTER SIX

# Credit Secrets, Investing & Banking

T he economy is changing, and it is changing rapidly in the eyes of Money. There are precious metals, notes, bonds, certificates, commodities, and most recently, bitcoin (digital dollar and digital wallets) per the 116th Congress, 2D Session, "Financial Protections and Assistance for America's Consumers, States, Businesses, and Vulnerable Populations Act." Even states in America, such as Nevada, Utah and Texas, now mint, and print gold-backed currency exchangeable in their states for goods and services.

Everyone has heard that cash is king; however, this new system is not the case. Credit is king, and the world is preparing for two monetary systems for two types of people. The first system is a credit digital dollar system for all U.S. citizens operating outside of a natural person. The second, precious metals for all nationals operating within a natural person, known as an Express Trust.

Credit is king; therefore, it is wise to review a couple of useful credit tips that any FICO professional would advise.

Credit Tip #1; how many credit cards should one have? Well, the answer is as many as possible. The more, the better, but the real question is, what is the minimum amount of credit cards one should have? The answer is three credit cards. FICO (the Fair Isaac Company) has implemented a scoring model based on revolving credit as 40% of the entire FICO score, ranking higher than late payments, mortgages, or student loans. The key is to have three credit cards open at all times, with balances maintained at 7% or less. FICO has figured out that if a borrower can maintain three credit cards under 7%, the likelihood of having a derogatory item over the next 24 months is extremely low, so the score increases. If borrowers go over 7% up to 17%, then the score drops 10 points. It is about 10 points for every 10% of the credit limit. If the limit is 100% maxed, it will lose approximately 100 points.

Credit Tip #2; does canceling credit cards boost the credit score? The answer is an absolute no! Jumping back to the first credit tip, FICO always wants to see at least three credit cards because it shows responsibility. If borrowers closed all accounts and canceled all credit cards, thinking that no credit is good credit, FICO will then view the debtor as an alcoholic that avoids the local bars. In this case, the proper term to use is a "crediholic" (one who abuses credit). FICO will not trust the borrower with credit if they don't trust themselves. It is also good to practice using specific types of credit cards to avoid cancelation. Using VISA or Mastercard pay networks is highly preferred over department store credit cards. Department cards can only be used at the participating stores and not anywhere VISA or Mastercard is accepted. Therefore, it forces the card user to shop more than they need to, and if the card user doesn't make purchases, then the credit card company will decrease the card limit or cancel the account, which will decrease the FICO score drastically. It is best to have three major credit cards that can be used anywhere. One for living expenses, the second for monthly bills, and the third for miscellaneous spendings, such as batteries for the smoke detector or auto repair maintenances. It is imperative to use credit cards every month sparingly. If the credit user chooses to max the cards to receive the cashback or rewards, pay off or pay down to the credit limit's 7% mark. And last but not least, pay off 100% of the balance two months before applying for new credit or new loans.

Credit Tip #3; does paying off installment loans early increase the FICO score? No! Before diving into this question, determining the difference between installment credit and revolving credit is critical. Revolving and installment credit come in the form of secured and unsecured credit. Installment credit is an extension by fixed and scheduled payments made until the loan is paid in full. If the scheduled payment is $10 per month at 50 months and the borrower paid 49 payments of $10 each month, the remaining payoff balance would be $10, and the $4,900 paid to the bank would not be available to the borrower. Revolving credit is renewed as the debt is paid, allowing the borrower access to a credit line whenever needed. FICO's scoring model for early installment loan payoff is likened to the medical field when a pregnant woman is in the care of a physician. Here's a fair question. Would the physician prefer the pregnant woman to go into delivery in the ninth month or early in the sixth month? Of course, the physician and the mother would prefer to go to the full term for a healthy delivery. It is the same concept for installment loans. Banks set out an agreement for principal and interest and prefer the debtor to go the full term in paying off their loans. So how exactly can the debtor maintain good credit, save money and not procure an early installment loan penalty? Applying the Target, Inc. employee, Mr. Wellington, once more, Mr. Wellington has a $10,000 personal loan, with a scheduled payment term of 57 months at $184.46 per month. To avoid a prepayment penalty, Mr. Wellington will pay down the loan to the number of scheduled payments. In this case, the remaining balance goal would be $57; therefore, Mr. Wellington would work to submit a principal payment of $9,943 and, for the next 57 months, he would pay $1 plus interest (in change) per month. With this method, Mr. Wellington has avoided prepayment penalty, reduced the monthly debt obligation, and maintained excellent payment history for the installment loan, fulfilling the 57-month term. If Mr. Wellington did not have the $9,943 in cash, he could select to use a revolving credit card and utilize the credit card payment system provided in Credit Tip #5.

Credit Tip #4; is it best to use debit cards or credit cards? Never use debit cards but always use credit cards! When it comes to practicing good credit management, using credit cards in the same manner as a debit card is more rewarding. Most credit cards offer 2% cashback on groceries, gas purchases, or all purchases as a whole. Debit cards are a one-time payment transaction without interest, which does not provide purchasing power or FICO points. There are more debit card transactions than there are credit transactions in North America. Switching all debit cards to credit card use would maximize the 40% FICO scoring model and have the banks begging consumers to take new credit card offers. The average American household family income is an annual $35,977, according to the 2019 U.S. Census Bureau, at $2,998 per month. This family would comfortably spend approximately $3,000 per month using this budget, precisely 30% of a $10,000 credit limit. With $3,000 in monthly transactions to pay for all bills and living expenses, the family would pay off the $3,000 on payday, ready for next month's transactions, taking advantage of all of the available cashback rewards. The use of a credit card offers additional protection at local gas stations because the user's funds are not immediately withdrawn from the user's bank account. In contrast, debit cards are riskier, as credit thieves favor gas stations and might be able to access user's accounts with their PIN.

Credit Tip #5; what is the fastest way to increase the credit score? The fastest and most efficient strategy to increase the credit score is by forcing the credit bureaus to report payments twice per month, legally. The key is to pay attention to the statement closing date because most creditors report payment activity 3-4 days after the statement closing date. For instance, a credit card payment due on the 13th of every month and a statement closing date on the 21st of every month with a $150 monthly payment; the borrower should pay $75 (first half) on the 1st and $75 (second half) on the 13th. Paying on the 1st allows enough time for the payment to post before the second payment is applied on the actual due date. The borrower can use the card at any time in the month, except during the closing cycle, which is 3-4 days from the statement closing date (21st-25th). The borrower can also spend any amount within their means, ensuring that the balance is within 7%-30% before the statement closing date. The first half of the payment is usually right on schedule with the creditor's statement date. This method will decrease the interest due and cause a double payment reported to the credit bureaus.

These helpful credit tips have maintained healthy personal and business credit reports. When it comes to living in trust, deciding to operate in the public or private can be jarring. But with full knowledge and understanding, choosing one or the other is easy. Utilizing both sides of the ledger is necessary. For credit purposes, using the foreign estate EIN to build corporate business credit, obtaining a Paydex Score and personal credit, obtaining a FICO Score is possible. The truth about the estate is that it is the highest form of credit anyone could ever access. And, the best way to access its treasures is through bankruptcy court, paired with the foreign Express Trust.

Companies build their corporate credit profiles for a certain pre-determined number of years with a plan to bankrupt the entity while storing all of its assets (property) inside of the trust. Consequently, all corporate debts, such as loans and credit lines, are forgiven without selling the assets to cover the debt. It's no wonder prominent investors such as Donald Trump and Mitt Romney utilize the bankruptcy strategy. Whenever bankruptcy occurs, the social security number or the company's employer identification number is used to obtain a bankruptcy estate number, which has an abundance of securities to pay off the existing debt. This strategy has worked well for those who know how to plan with real estate. Suppose a potential borrower's application is approved for financing a $580,000 house in their name using the social security number and then proceeds to transfer the title into the name of the foreign Express Trust, removing all county tax liability. The applicant files for bankruptcy to avoid foreclosure. The court utilizes the estate to pay off the mortgage obligation without selling the property or processing a short sale. The applicant is not the owner but only the Express Trust with the trustee as the title's legal owner. Therefore, the trustee remains the holder and legal owner of the title, and the mortgage obligation is discharged from the borrower's credit report; since the Express Trust is the secured party holding a "nine billion dollar lien" against the First Middle Last Name, debtor, as the holder-in-due-course. During this 7-8 year period, the debt-free individual can apply for all the credit they want. Credit card companies often flood the mailboxes of recent bankruptcy filers because creditors know the applicant's name, social security number, and a signature will allow the creditor to have instant access to the estate as a claim to the abandoned securities. Within the 7-8 year window, the bankruptcy estate continuously pays off debt! Financiers would have the general public believe there is no credit available during a bankruptcy. It would much serve the courts, the county, and the State to not inform the people of the bankruptcy court's truth. During this 7-8 year period, the municipalities are taking advantage of the estates' abandonment. The municipalities use I.R.S. Form 1099-A (Acquisition or Abandonment of Secured Property) and 1096 (Annual Summary and Transmittal of U.S. Information Returns) procuring all of the abandoned securities with the State and County Comptroller/Controller office.

Chapter 7 bankruptcies are occasionally referred to as "liquidation" bankruptcies. Firms and associations experiencing this form of bankruptcy are past the reorganization stage and must sell off any "non-exempt" assets to pay creditors. To qualify for a chapter 7 relief, the debtor can be a corporation, an individual, or a small business. However, one is forbidden from filing for bankruptcy if another bankruptcy petition was dismissed within the previous 180 days due to the debtor's failure to show up in court. A debtor likewise forgoes the right to file for bankruptcy if the debtor agrees to dismiss a former case after creditors asked the bankruptcy court to grant them the right to seize properties on which they hold the liens. The critical takeaway is having all property and assets held in the Express Trust, resulting in an exempted status. The Express Trust holds the real lien, exempting the assets from being sold to pay off the creditors. The law of the land obtains this Chapter 7 rule from the bible, specifically from the book of Deuteronomy chapter 15:1-2, which reads,

At the end of every "seven" years, you shall grant a release of debts. And this is the form of the release: Every creditor who has lent anything to his neighbor shall release it; he shall not require it of his neighbor or his brother because it is called the Lord's release.

*(New King James Version)*

When it comes to building private personal credit, using the foreign estate EIN to avoid using the social security number is easy and perfectly legal under the Section 7 of the Privacy Act of 1974 (Title 5 U.S. Code § 552a) provides,

> "It shall be unlawful for any Federal, State or local government agency to deny to any individual any right, benefit, or privilege provided by law because of such individual's refusal to disclose his social security account number."

*(Sec. 7(a)(1))*

The first step is to file a Fictitious Business Name or DBA with the county of business operations. The name should be in the format First Name Middle Name Family of Last Name Estate d/b/a First Name Middle Name Last Name, using the Registrar address as the principal place of residence, a different mailing address, a different email address, and a new phone number not connected with any past SSN/ITIN credit profile. The second step is to create an Internet presence with the name, new address, new phone, and new email address (Hotmail, Yahoo, Gmail) using listyourself.net, followed by signing up with different department stores, airlines, and fuel rewards cards or programs. The third step is to wait 30 days before applying for the Capital One Auto Finance program, Apple-Card, Amazon, and American Express to deny credit. The denial will create a credit profile with the major credit bureaus using the information provided with different department stores, airlines, and fuel rewards cards or programs. The fourth step is to wait another 30 days to finalize the credit profile before re-applying to Capital One for their Capital One Secured Mastercard, providing a refundable deposit anywhere from $49-$200. This same process should take place with Discover I.T. and Merrick Bank or the like. The goal is to have three major credit cards reporting for a high credit score and to have the credit limit of all three credit cards eventually equate to 3.5 times the amount of the credit user's monthly bills. For example, if Mr. Wellington consistently pays out $4,500 per month in living expenses, then each of the three credit cards should have a minimum limit of $5,250, totaling $15,750. With a combination of all three cards and spending only 30% of $15,750, Mr. Wellington would have paid all of his monthly living expenses and maintained a 30% credit card utilization, which secures the credit profile to sustain a 760 to 800 FICO score. The estate must only be used for credit cards and rental/lease agreements in place of using the SSN/ITIN but never for mortgages or auto loans as an SSN/ITIN. Federal mortgages must always utilize government-backed uncertificated securities such as the SSN/ITIN. (Note: The estate EIN can utilize its credit to obtain auto loans or leases but only in the form of a business application, using the EIN format 12-3456789, not the SSN/ITIN format 123-45-6789.)

To build corporate business credit using the same foreign estate EIN, some additional steps are necessary. Upon completing the fictitious business name statement or DBA, the first step is to draft the Estate's articles of Unincorporated Business Association in the fictitious business name such as FIRST NAME MIDDLE FAMILY OF LAST NAME ESTATE and file it with the Secretary of State. Being that Mr. Wellington is from California, he would use the California Secretary of State's UA-100 Form to properly file his estate's association using the Registrar's address as the business address, in the same manner, provided on the I.R.S. EIN Online estate application. This will prepare the business to file for a DUNS (Dun & Bradstreet) number, an essential step to ensure the corporate business profile is viewed as a legitimate company, leading to the opening of an Unincorporated Business Association bank account. Chase Bank, among others, is a great bank that offers this type of business bank account with easy requirement instructions on their website. When applying for a DUNS number, the business address, mailing address, business phone number, and business email address must be separate from the personal estate credit profile. (Note: The business email address must not be generic such as Hotmail or Gmail. Mail.com is an available option to satisfy this requirement. For example, cwestate@accountant.com.) The information previously used to obtain the estate number online with the I.R.S. should be consistent with the DUNS application. It is essential to select the correct SIC (Standard Industrial Classification) or NAICS (North American Industrial Classification System). As a final step, the corporate business estate should obtain a corporate seal expressing its full corporate name and establishment date. The seal is placed alongside any signatures approved by its President or board members. To get a jump on building the credit immediately, switch all personal utility accounts such as cell phone providers, home internet, gas company, electric company, and water company, from the personal SSN/ITIN name at home or rental unit to the estate business, First Name Middle Name Family of Last Name Estate.

Furthermore, signup with eCredable Business Solutions and link all of the newly transferred utility accounts into the eCredable Business Solutions profile. They will report the past 24 months of payment history to the business credit bureaus, whereas the individual companies would not. These accounts can be reported in as little as 14 days up to 45 days, providing an instant business credit score.

After successfully obtaining a DUNS number, it's time to obtain vendor credit from commercial vendors that provide Net-30 payment terms to report to the major credit bureaus, such as Dun & Bradstreet, Equifax, Experian Business, Transunion, Credit Safe, SBFE, Ansonia, and NACM. These accounts must be paid within 30 to 60 days. The following vendors will provide instant corporate Net-30 or Net-60 payment terms for new businesses, and it is advised to regularly purchase items for the business.

- Shirtsy

- Crown Office Supplies

- Creative Analytics

- Uline

- Grainger

- Quill

- Summa Office Supplies

- Office Depot/OfficeMax

- H.D. Supply

- Strategic Network Solutions

- NAV Business Boost – NAV is a credit monitoring system that can provide all credit report information for the corporate estate (Paydex Score) and the personal estate (FICO Score) for $39.99/month as of 1st quarter 2021. The payments are reported to all major business credit bureaus as a tradeline.

The process of opening an Unincorporated Business Association bank account in the name of the estate, as previously mentioned, will require obtaining an additional EIN due to National Associations (banks) can only do business with EIN's that have a responsible party's social security number attached to the creation of the EIN for insurance guarantee purposes. Another important reason to obtain an additional EIN in the estate's name is bank rules and regulations. If a potential account holder, such as Mr. Wellington, were to walk into a bank to open an estate account using the foreign estate EIN that he has established credit with, the bank manager wouldn't know what to think of the situation. In the bank's eyes, an estate account only applies to a descendant, and a third party or an executor would open the account on behalf of the deceased. Even if Mr. Wellington used a proxy or third party to open this type of account, the bank would require a death certificate as proof of death, which is a dead-end. Therefore, obtaining another EIN that does not have any language within the I.R.S. CP-575 form such as, "the EIN will identity your estate or trust," will be required to open a business account in the name FIRST NAME MIDDLE NAME FAMILY OF LAST NAME ESTATE without raising any concern. This new EIN would serve for bank purposes only. Mr. Wellington would apply the following steps via the I.R.S. EIN Online:

- 1. Identity: Select "View Additional Types, Including Tax-Exempt and Government Organization"

- 1. Identity: Select "Other Non-Profit/Tax-Exempt Organizations"

- 1. Identity: Select "Banking Purposes"

- 2. Authenticate: Enter "Full Birth Name as the responsible party with a social security number"

- 3. Address: Enter "a private mailing address"

- 4. Details: Enter "CHRISTOPHER ALEXANDER WELLINGTON ESTATE" followed by the county and of the place of business and month and year the original estate number was obtained

- 4. Details: Enter "No for the five required questions"

- 4. Details: Select "Other"

- 4. Details: Again Select "Other and type Unincorporated Business Association"

- 5. EIN Confirmation: Select "Receive Letter Online"

Once the I.R.S. has provided the EIN via the CP-575, Mr. Wellington can then provide it with the Secretary of State stated articles of association (Form UA-100), the county fictitious name statement or DBA, and two forms of I.D. from the association's Secretary to open the account at Chase bank or any other bank. The fictitious name statement reveals to the bank that the account can receive any payment in the name FIRST NAME MIDDLE NAME FAMILY OF LAST NAME ESTATE or FIRST NAME MIDDLE NAME LAST NAME. The bank will provide a debit card to the Secretary with Mr. Wellington's full name to administrate everyday transactions as he would a regular checking account. The sole purpose is to avoid creating securities under the SSN/ITIN with the banks. Whether debit or credit under an Unincorporated Business Association EIN, all transactions can now account for business expenses during the annual tax filing period using the foreign Express Trust. The trust office will never owe a tax but instead receive tribute under treaty law because the trust was forced to pay sales tax and interest attached to the standard pricing of everyday business expenses, which the trust is exempt from. Therefore, a refundable payment on every accountable dollar is due to the Express Trust. This is the ultimate tax-saving strategy that can take place now rather than in retirement. After the bank account is securely opened, Mr. Wellington or his Secretary can begin the reclassification process, converting the newly obtained domestic Unincorporated Association EIN to a foreign association under the Express Trust 98 number using I.R.S. Form 8832, as previously instructed. This business bank account should be the primary account used by Mr. Wellington to embrace the new private banking lifestyle that the Zero Percent tax bracket requires. All other accounts in the birth name using the SSN/ITIN should be closed in good standing.

Anyone in business who relies on business credit will advise that it is crucial to never become late on any payment due with vendors or credit card companies. Once the estate business credit profile has six months of established Net-30 payments, a commercial fleet and secured credit cards can be obtained. This will lead to high-limit credit unsecured cards from American Express, Brex Credit Card, Amazon, eBay, Ollo, Capital One, Paypal, Lowes, just to name a few. The foreign estate EIN should be the lifeline to the user's estate for all commercial purposes. The goal is to avoid creating SSN/ITIN "public insurance" uncertificated securities through contracts. Being a part of the Zero Percent tax bracket is a lifestyle change.

Again, the estate is to be used for business accounts to achieve a Paydex Score and a personal "private" account achieving a FICO score. If anyone ever needed to press the reset button in the world of credit, this is the way to do it. Obtaining a mortgage should be the only reason to maintain good credit on the SSN/ITIN credit profile, which means only keeping "specific" installment accounts open and avoiding credit cards, insurance accounts, bank accounts, auto loans, and personal loans that induces interstate transactions. The following installment accounts are a suggested source to keep open on the SSN/ITIN credit profile for obtaining mortgage financing:

- Credit Strong Savings/CD Account

- Self Lender CD account

- MyJewelers Account

- Newcoast Direct

As of February 2021, two of the above-suggested accounts, MyJewelers and Newcoast Direct, will report up to a $5,000 tradeline limit. Self Lender will provide a maximum of $1,663 Certificate of Deposit at $150 per month as a savings account. At the end of the term, the user will receive their savings in the form of a check. It is advised to reuse that money on auto-pay from the Unincorporated Business Association account for the next new CD term. Credit

Strong will apply a maximum of $10,000 installment account reported to the credit bureaus for $110 per month. Combine these accounts to the SSN/ITIN credit profile for a total of $21,663 as installment credit to maintain good credit when the time comes to obtain financing for a mortgage, which will be gifted from CHRISTOPHER ALEXANDER WELLINGTON (grantor) to HEINZ WOLFGANG EXPRESS TRUST (grantee).

To ensure instant approval when filing a credit application, the SSN/ITIN credit profile information must not cross-reference or mix with the personal estate credit profile. Utilize the United States Postal Office change of address and mail forwarding service, which cost only one dollar. This will ensure that the SSN/ITIN profile records the County Courthouse as the residence address, including a separate mailing address. The personal estate profile has a record of the County Registrar as the residence address with its own separate mailing address. Lastly, the corporate business estate profile records the selected iPostal1 address as its place of business and mailing address. The SSN/ITIN credit profile place of residence would include the birth county courthouse address; after all, this is the origin of the ens legis creation, and the CAFR accounts were held. No mail will come to this address because the new private mailbox will be on file as the current mailing address (i.e., new iPostal1 account). Ensure the SSN/ITIN credit profile has consistent credit application information such as its phone number, email address (Hotmail, Yahoo, or Gmail), place of employment, annual salary amount, U.S. citizen, date of birth, and rent/mortgage amounts. Once all of the information is obtained, list it within the listyourself.net database, register the information with the three credit bureaus, and apply with three auto dealers on three separate credit applications with the exact information. Approval or denial does not matter in this case. If approved, do not accept it, walk away informing that the credit union may provide a better interest rate.

After 30 days have passed, the applicant should attempt to remove all of the credit inquiries created by the auto dealerships by contacting SageStream, LLC, and LexisNexis via mail or online to place a security freeze on the SSN/ITIN credit report. This will prevent any further consumer credit pulls without the consumer's consent and easily allow invalid information to be removed, including the previous three auto credit inquiries. Suppose the credit bureaus are unable to validate the inquiries due to a credit freeze. In that case, the requested items are then removed atop utilizing section 604 of the Fair Credit Reporting Act (15 U.S. Code 1681b) as a dispute to the credit bureaus.

The auto dealerships are the best choice for this method because dealerships are notorious for running more than one permitted credit pull to get the application approved that day. Some dealerships will continue to pull credit with other lenders up to a week later. The law that the dealerships break regularly is known as impermissible credit pulls, to which they must have a permissible purpose. A permissible purpose is established "following the written instructions of the consumer to whom it relates." The institution must obtain permission from the consumer, in writing, to obtain their consumer report. In this case, the consumer's verbal consent is not good enough even if documentation of such consent is maintained. For instance, if a potential borrower applies for a auto loan on December 21st, is it permitted that a financial institution utilize said consumer's December 21st credit report for a HELOC application on January 5th? The answer is no. Once an institution establishes a permissible purpose to obtain a consumer's credit report, it is suitable only for one application and no more, regardless of the amount of time between subsequent applications for credit. Once the credit report is frozen, submit a 604 letter to the credit bureaus without a signature to prevent cross-matching credit application signatures and watch the inquiries fall off the credit report with an increased credit score. At this point, removing the credit freeze is necessary to add the suggested installment accounts.

Keeping these three credit profiles separate will allow for easy credit approvals while maintaining a private commercial lifestyle without jeopardizing the national status. To recap, the requirements to establish a "public insurance" SSN/ITIN credit profile for mortgage approval (optional) only includes:

- FIRST NAME MIDDLE NAME LAST NAME

- DOB

- U.S. CITIZEN

- SOCIAL SECURITY NUMBER OR ITIN

- BIRTH COUNTY COURTHOUSE ADDRESS

- iPOSTAL ONE MAILING ADDRESS

- NEW HOTMAIL, AOL, GMAIL OR YAHOO EMAIL ADDRESS

- EMPLOYMENT INFO

- ANNUAL SALARY

- NEW PHONE NUMBER (GOOGLE NUMBER)

- RENT/MORTGAGE AMOUNT

- REGISTER WITH LISTYOURSELF.NET

- UDPATE CHANGE OF ADDRESS WITH U.S.P.S

- ESTABLISH INSTALLMENT CREDIT ACCOUNTS

To establish a corporate business credit profile includes:

- FIRST NAME MIDDLE NAME FAMILY OF LAST NAME ESTATE d/b/a FIRST NAME MIDDLE NAME LAST NAME ESTATE

- ESTATE EIN

- UNINCORPORATED ASSOCIATION EIN – BANKING PURPOSES

- DUNS NUMBER

- UNINCORPORATED BUSINESS ASSOCIATION ARTICLES OF ORGANIZATION
- MAIL.COM PROFESSIONAL EMAILING ADDRESS
- CORPORATE BUSINESS PHONE NUMBER
- CORPORATE BUSINESS ADDRESS
- iPOSTAL ONE BUSINESS MAILING ADDRESS
- BUSINESS SERVICES OR REAL ESTATE/PROPERTY MANAGEMENT
- REGISTER WITH LISTYOURSELF.NET
- CORPORATE ESTATE SEAL
- ESTABLISH VENDOR CREDIT, CREDIT CARDS, BUSINESS AUTO LOANS AND LEASES

And lastly, to establish a "private" personal credit profile includes:

- FIRST NAME MIDDLE NAME LAST NAME
- DOB
- U.S. CITIZEN
- ESTATE EIN IN LIEU OF SSN/ITIN
- BIRTH COUNTY REGISTRAR ADDRESS
- iPOSTAL ONE MAILING ADDRESS

- NEW HOTMAIL, AOL, GMAIL OR YAHOO EMAIL ADDRESS

- SELF-EMPLOYED INFO

- ANNUAL SALARY

- NEW PHONE NUMBER

- RENT/MORTGAGE AMOUNT

- REGISTER WITH LISTYOURSELF.NET

- ESTABLISH SECURED CREDIT CARDS, RENTAL/LEASE PROPERTY

Of course, maintaining a healthy SSN/ITIN credit profile to obtain a mortgage is a choice and not the only way to obtain property. One could take over a borrower's property who may be in distress and cannot afford to continue their mortgage payments by way of "subject to," which uses a quitclaim deed, avoiding any mortgage credit application. There is also obtaining property through private lenders, also known as hard money lenders. The interest rates are slightly higher than public FHA (3.5%) or USDA (0%), and the deposits are usually not less than 20%. However, the obligation is never reported to the credit profile. It is a private transaction, and the credit report is only pulled to determine payment credibility.

As mentioned before, a large portion of millionaires in the world have earned their profits from real estate, and it's time to reveal its trade secrets that will provide a massive return on investment. This trade secret is known as Seller Financing, and it is a tool that has been used for centuries around the world. Seller financing is a sale made where any part of the sales price becomes a note back to the seller. In real estate, owners have a note, a mortgage, or deed of trust instrument depending on the property's whereabouts. Some states are mortgage states, and others are trust states. The note is the debt instrument containing the amount, interest, payment, and term. The document requires a guarantee by most lenders, and it is the document responsible for litigating in pursuit of collections. The mortgage or deed of trust documents is used to attach the note to the house as collateral. There are many advantages to utilizing seller finance strategies. Lowering closing costs on both sides of the transaction, lower interest rates, lower payments, no credit reports, no banks, reliable flexibility, no negative cash flow, no personal liability when using trusts, eliminates the due-on-sale clause or balloon notes when buying, provides quick closings, eliminates seller's and seller's attorney's anxiety regarding selling subject to, allows the investor to create almost instant profits and huge monthly cash flows very quickly. It also provides the seller a provable income stream to wash out their debt payment to qualify for another loan and, most of all, no maintenance, taxes, insurance, or vacancies when sold.

A big question in real estate when using Seller Financing is how to avoid the "due-on-sale clause" when transferring title from one owner to another. A bank cannot stop a seller from selling with owner financing. However, they can call the loan due because it will trigger the due-on-sale clause, and this vital fact should always be disclosed with the seller. However, transferring a title into an entity such as an Irrevocable Express Trust with a foreign owner (a foreign national trustee) would not trigger the due-on-sale clause. Using an Irrevocable Foreign Express Trust would exempt the trust from property taxes indefinitely. This strategy would be best only when deciding to keep the property from generation to generation. Should the investor plan to take over the property intending to sell the property for a profit, then a Revocable Land Trust would be necessary, significantly reducing or exempting the property from county taxes. The Garn-St. Germain Depository Institutions Act of 1982 (Public Law 97-320, H.R. 6267) allowed a significant consumer change regarding the title. The act granted anyone to place real estate in their trust without alerting the due-on-sale clause, allowing lenders to foreclose on a current loan upon transfer to another. This greatly facilitates the use of a trust to pass property to heirs and minors and protects wealthy owners' property against a possible future lawsuit from creditors because the trust owns the property, not the individual beneficiaries at risk. Investors use Revocable Land Trust to quickly obtain property from distressed sellers or sellers looking for another way to sell, taking on the existing payments. It is unlikely that the banks will call the loan due if payments continue to be received, and there is a way to cash out or pay off the loan if necessary, even if the investor sells on installments.

One of the best and secure seller finance strategies widely used amongst investors is a Wrap or Wrap-Around Mortgage. It is merely one loan that encompasses another loan or loans of smaller value. Here is a typical example:

The investor buys a house and takes over a $140,000 first mortgage and a $20,000-second mortgage for $160,000. In the world of seller financing, the value of the house is determined by what the buyer is willing to pay. Now the investor sells the house for $180,000 with a $20,000 (non-refundable) down payment and takes a mortgage, land contract, or AITD (All-Inclusive Trust Deed) for $160,000. See Table 1.

**Table 1.**

| Note to Inv. | $160,000 10% - 30 | yrs $1,447.27 monthly income |
|---|---|---|
| Existing 1st | $140,000 7% - 30 yrs - | $987.78 monthly outgo |
| Existing 2nd | $20,000 9% - 15 yrs | - $221.44 monthly outgo |
| | | $238.05 Net |

The $160,000 note wraps around the $140,000 and the $20,000. The total debt is $160,000. In this case, the investor has no equity in the note. The principal would collect $1,447.27 and payout the first note payment of $987.78 and the second note payment of $221.44 and keep the difference. When paid off, the investor must pay off the $160,000 to clear the title. So, why sell on a wrap with no equity? Well, first, to make sure the underlying note gets paid. Second, to receive $238.05 per month cash flow and three possible defaults of buyer and forfeiture of $20,000 down payment.

There are multiple ways to sell using Seller Financing. One way is via Long Term on a free and clear house, meaning no encumbrances or mortgages on the title. Suppose the seller calls the investor with a house worth $140,000 in good condition. The seller is asking $140,000, with no loan, and after prescreening, the investor finds that the seller would be willing to seller finance with a 10% down payment ($14,000). That would leave a balance of $126,000 Mortgage, Land Contract, or Deed of Trust to the seller at the requested rate of 6% for 30 years with a 10-year balloon. In real estate, it is always wise to counter offer for a potential discount so that the investor may look forward to a fair return (profit) on investment. Offering a purchase price of $126,000 with $4,000 as the down payment, leaving a balance of $122,000 at 5%, 30 years, and 10-year balloon, with a payment of $721 principal and interest with the first payment due in 3 months, no due-on-sale clause. Once the deal is accepted, the principal, the investor, take advantage of their equitable interest and sells the property for $149,900 with no less than a $20,000 down payment from their end-buyer. This would leave a remaining balance of $129,900 Deed of Trust, Wraparound Mortgage, or Land

Contract to the investor at 9.9% for 30 years with a 5-year balloon. A principal and interest monthly payment of $1,197 would be rewarded. Structuring the deal in this matter would provide the following:

- $16,000 profit on down payment ($20,000 from the end-buyer less $4,000 to the initial seller), plus two months income of $1,197 with no payment,

- $476 per month on payment spread ($1,197 incoming less $721 outgoing),

- $7,900 minimum on the back end of the sale ($129,900 owed to the investor less $122,000 the investor owes the initial seller). Profit increases each month because the incoming debt pays off slower than the outgoing due to the difference in interest rates,

- ? Discount when the principal is ready to pay off the initial seller due to their end-buyer refinancing or selling,

- When possible, closing the sale the same day of purchase

Another possible deal structure would be a strategy known as Subject To Plus, a Second To the Seller. A seller calls the investor with a house in good condition worth for $130,000. There is a due-on-sale loan for $61,000 with a payment of $699.40 per month, including taxes and insurance. The seller is asking $130,000 cash for the house. Upon prescreening, the investor learns he would consider carrying a second for his equity if he gets a $13,000 down payment. It would provide the seller with a $56,000 equity payout as a second mortgage. Instead, the investor offers a $110,000 purchase price with an $8,000 down payment, and they take over the existing due-on-sale loan of $61,000 via subject to and the payment of $699.40 P.I.T.I. ($500 principal and interest + $199.40 taxes and insurance). The remaining balance of $41,000 would be a second mortgage to the seller at 5% for 30 years with a 10-year balloon. Payment of $227.67 beginning in 3 months and a total outgoing payment of $927.07 P.I.T.I. ($699.40 + $227.67 = $927.07). Now, here is the interesting part. The investor sells the house at $139,900 with a minimum down payment of $15,000, which leaves a remaining balance of $124,900 Land Contract, Trust Deed of Wraparound Mortgage 9.9% with a 5-year balloon. The object payment would come to $1,177.07 P.I.T.I. ($977.67 P&I + 199.40 taxes and insurance). Structuring a deal in this matter would provide the following:

- $7,000 instant profit from the down payment spread plus a two-month income of $1,177.07 with no payment due.

- Monthly payment spread

- $22,900 when the investor's end-buyer pays off the loan ($124,900 - $41,000 - $61,000).

- ? Large discount possibility.

- When possible, close the sale on the same day.

The main objective is to target specific properties. Beautiful houses in significant areas at the median price or above would be ideal. Low-priced properties attract buyers with no money and incur large default rates. Any property where the seller will agree to wait for their money or equity until the investor is cashed out from their end-buyer or accept payments is a high prospect property. Targeting ugly properties with a lot of equity, the investor can raise cash on their house is ideal as well. Conducting business with little to no risk with the best houses in the best areas would promote:

- Better quality tenants and end-buyers.

- Great houses in significant areas, meaning no junk.

- The investor as the principal would make much more profit on all income streams:

- More significant down payments due to higher valued houses

- Bigger monthly spreads

- Larger back end payouts. High value makes it easier to negotiate bigger spreads.

If the investors sell with owner financing, there's less chance an end-buyer will default because they're in a higher income bracket and have more money or equity at risk. Buying with seller financing, the principal can create larger payouts by discounting the note later.

The tools utilized to engage in selling with owner financing are a Wraparound Mortgage, Land Contract, Land Installment Contract, Agreement for Deed, Contract for Deed, Bond for Deed, Deed of Trust, or All Inclusive Trust Deed (AITD). The Wrap is an all-inclusive loan encompassing underlying financing, collecting a larger payment from the end-buyer than what is paid out to the lender. Seller deeds to the buyer and takes back a note and mortgage. It must be prepared by a professional and will vary from state to state. The Contracts and Agreements are all terms that mean the same thing, but the name will vary from state to state. As mentioned before, the word State is synonymous with the country. Every country has its own rules. The contracts and agreements serve the same purpose as a wraparound, but the deed remains with the seller until paid. The buyer acquires equitable interest in the property, which is a straightforward process. It's no more complicated than completing a Purchase and Sales Agreement. A Deed of Trust is a contract by which the property title is conveyed to a trustee for a loan's repayment, usually a non-related entity. This contract involves two remaining parties. The trustor is the owner who borrows from the lender and the beneficiary as the lender. This document should always be prepared by a professional and varies from country to country in America's united States. Having a knowledgeable CPA and real estate attorney to draft all documentation to be recorded inside the county recorders office where the property is located is always recommended. No deal should go without legal counsel.

Seller Financing is but just one method savvy real estate investors use. There are seven more ways to profit quickly in real estate. In addition to seller financing, the second method would be wholesaling. It is a business of locating houses, usually needing repairs, at bargain prices and quickly passing them to bargain hunters well below retail for an all-cash deal transaction. The third method is retailing. This form of business of locating houses at bargain prices, usually rehabbing them and selling to the end buyer for all cash at the top of the market with new financing terms. The fourth method is getting ownership. The business of owning pretty houses in beautiful neighborhoods by taking over existing debt "subject to" or creating seller carry back financing or combining the two. The fifth method is what is known as lease options. It takes control of a property by leasing it from the seller and retaining the option to purchase at an agreed-upon price and terms. It also provides the rights to sub-lease the property to a potential tenant/buyer, giving them the right to purchase from the investor. A sixth method is an option, which is an agreement the investor may buy without the right to sublease. And the final method is known as ACTS. It is an acronym for Assigning Contracts with Terms System to a new buyer or tenant-buyer. The great Ron LeGrand invented the ACTS system and is mostly applied to overleveraged houses, allowing investors to do transactions on properties where most would turn down the deal. For example, a house in good condition is valued at $200,000 with a loan of $220,000 and a monthly payment of $1,650 with 27 years left. The investor agrees to lease purchase for the entire loan balance of $220,000 with a lease payment equal to the seller's mortgage payment of $1,650, which begins when a tenant/buyer is located to assign the investor's contract. Once the tenant/buyer is located, the investor assigns their contract with the initial seller's approval and collects a $10,000 assignment fee. This deal structure lets the investor never buy the house, no closing cost, no money needed, no risk, no costly attachments, and the investor can do two to four or more per month.

In another type of transaction, such as a Sand-which Lease Purchase or Subject To, the investor would buy a house from the seller with the same value of $200,000 with a $0 down payment and loan in the amount of $180,000 with a monthly payment of $1,382. The investor sells to the end-buyer at $219,000 and collects a $20,000 non-refundable down payment, leaving the buyer with a balance of $199,000, contributing a $1,800 first month payment to the investor. $20,000 was collected in just a few days plus the investor will make $418 per month ($1,800 - $1,382 = $418) for years to come. Once tenant/buyer cashes out, they keep all the cash above the loan payoff. Here is a ten year Profit Recap:

- $20,000 Original Down Payment

- $1,800 First Month Payment Received

- $50,160 Monthly Cash Flow (10 years)

- $35,000 Estimated back end cash above loan payoff

That's approximately $106,960 net profit on a property that the investor got for free using no money, no credit, no risk, no repairs, no banks, no realtors, and no short sales. Even better, 100% of the responsibility, including repairs, is passed on to the buyer, including taxes and insurance, finalized in escrow. The privilege of homeownership is automatically given to the tenant/buyer. Therefore, no maintenance cost would come from the investor.

Many wealthy families or several nationalities utilize these real estate techniques to always stay above the water during any depression or financial-economic crisis. Becoming a landlord will always provide a stream of revenue as people will always need a roof over their heads. One important thing that families care about in banking is always having on hand strong financial statements if they may need to apply for credit to access capital, with the attempt to use good debt to make a profit. These families bond together and share their income, rotating each monthly income into each member's bank account as a legitimate deposit. At the end of the month, each member's income would be routed back to them. For instance, looking at a family of four:

- Father earns $15,000 per month

- Mother earns $15,000 per month

- First Son earns $5,000 per month

- Second Son earns $7,000 per month

Each family member would have their monthly earnings deposited into each other's Unincorporated Business Association bank account at least once per month consistently, giving each member approximately $42,000 of monthly income.

This same family would also take advantage of another strategy that banks and top-tier corporations have used for over a century. This method is known as a High Cash Value Whole Life Insurance Policy, which builds generational wealth safely and allows the family to have their economy. Another term for this type of wealth-building strategy is Infinite Banking, which has five fundamental principles.

The first principle is safety. Markets are extremely volatile in the world of the Fractional Reserve banking system. A volatile market only promotes unpredictability. Everyone thinks that the markets will go up forever, and then out of nowhere, all savings, all equity, all foreseeable profits are lost in the blink of an eye. In 2008, 2.1 Trillion Dollars vanished in about the same time it takes for one to brush their teeth in the morning. Many stock traders have a saying such as, "The market has a way of proving the most number of people wrong!" It's all terrifying not knowing what will happen to all of the money backed by hard-earned labor. Many people had to put their retirement on hold due to the events of 2008, and it seems like it will happen again due to this Global Economic Pandemic. Well, with a High Cash Value Policy, it doesn't have to be that way. Strong insurance companies have been through every economic cycle without experiencing a loss and have protected many of their policyholders through good and bad times, such as the Great Depression. Almost all National Associations and Credit Unions have poured their capital into High Cash Value Policies. They call it BOLI, Bank Owned Life Insurance, and for the banks, those policies are put on the books as tier one assets, being the safest assets, the board members and its owners have fewer concerns. As mentioned before, banks take the deposits of account holders and invest in the U.S. Stock Market and the Foreign Exchange Market. Still, most of it goes into their High Cash Value Policies to protect the money from a volatile, unpredictable market. If it's suitable for the banks, then it's good for anyone to take advantage of.

The second principle is that a High Cash Value Policy offers a tax-free growth opportunity. Pair this strategy with an Irrevocable Foreign Express Trust – identified by the EIN 98 Prefix Number, as the policy's beneficial owner and the assets are 100% tax-free on every dollar. The money would be tax-free on income while living and even after death in the hands of the beneficiary(s).

The third principle is there is an unlimited opportunity to access capital. People will always need to access capital, and with this type of High Cash Value Policy, there is always access to cash without the need to apply for a loan.

The fourth principle is the most often overlooked aspect. The most fantastic benefit of a High Cash Value Policy is income at retirement, should the policyholder choose to stop commerce engagement. At some point, retirement will be the subject matter as people move into another phase of their lives. Going from an accumulation plan to an income plan is very viable. It used to be a fact where career employees received a pension when they retired and would have income for life, and now pension plans have been replaced by the 401k, which means the risk is all on the employee due to 401k's are at the risk of the market. After all, the fees are deducted, and taxes are paid, a retiree can't help but wonder if it was worth it at all. The best retirement is safe money, tax-free and predictable.

Last but not least, the fifth principle is all about leaving a legacy. Nationals who are a part of the Zero Percent tax bracket care about leaving an inheritance for the next generation. The inheritance must be protected in trust irrevocably with instructions and plans that will last for centuries. One of the biggest advantages of having a death benefit inside the High Cash Value Policy is that the policyholder can spend down other buckets of assets while living, knowing that the buckets will be replenished at death.

Policy loans can also be taken against the policy's death benefit from its cash value account. Taking a look at a case study to use a High Cash Value Policy to eliminate credit card debt of $30,000 with an interest rate of 11%-28% and $300 per month. For this strategy to work, the policy cash value must be established first, meaning the policyholder must have some time invested to pay into their premium threshold. As mentioned in the third principle, the cash value may be accessed anytime, and loaning from the cash value to pay off the credit card debt, is similar to using a Line of Credit against the homeowner's property. Even though a homeowner takes out an equity line of credit, the home's value continues to rise annually, anywhere from 5%-7%; the actual policy operates in the same manner. It is important to remember that borrowed money from the cash value account will remain at work for the policyholder as if it never left the policy. This is because of the dividends paid to the policyholder annually from the insurance company, and for this reason alone, infinite banking is the best banking tool known to man. A loan of $30,000 against the policy is used to pay off the credit card debt, and the regular $300 per month credit card payment would be used to pay back the policy loan balance, rather than spending the $300 monthly cash flow. Some key advantages to this strategy are:

- Consolidate High-Interest Debt
- Policy Loan Interest Rate is more favorable than Credit Cards (5%-6% Simple Interest)
- The repayment schedule is in the policyholder's control
- Repayments are optional; recommended but optional

One disadvantage to this strategy is that if the policy loan never receives a single payment, the balance will compound the life insurance policy. The results are not necessarily a "problem" in all cases but a fact to be made known, as it will negatively impact the policyholder's Cash Value & Death Benefit Growth. See Table 1.

**Table 1.**

| Year | Age | Annual Outlay | Cash Value | Death Benefit |
|------|-----|---------------|------------|---------------|
| 1 | 31 | $10,000 | $8,568 | $464,104 |
| 2 | 32 | $10,000 | $17,570 | $502,587 |
| 3 | 33 | $10,000 | $27,908 | $540,454 |
| 4 | 34 | $10,000 | **$38,939** | $577,707 |
| 5 | 35 | $10,000 | $50,544 | $614,363 |
| 6 | 36 | $10,000 | $62,748 | $650,472 |
| 7 | 37 | $10,000 | $75,575 | $685,045 |
| 8 | 38 | $10,000 | $89,058 | $721,141 |
| 9 | 39 | $10,000 | $103,222 | $755,760 |
| 10 | 40 | $10,000 | $118,101 | $789,966 |
| 11 | 41 | $10,000 | $133,734 | $823,772 |
| 12 | 42 | $10,000 | $150,158 | $857,260 |
| 13 | 43 | $10,000 | $167,420 | $890,479 |
| 14 | 44 | $10,000 | $185,546 | $923,526 |
| 15 | 45 | $10,000 | $204,583 | $956,383 |
| 16 | 46 | $10,000 | $224,554 | $983,209 |
| 17 | 47 | $10,000 | $245,594 | $1,022,021 |

Table 1, displays the policyholder at age 31, paying roughly $834 per month for a total of $10,000 per year into his High Cash Value Policy. In the first year of contribution, there is $8,568 as immediate cash to take out as a line of credit. At the beginning of year 5, the cash value breaks even at $38,939 and the policyholder is now ready to take out a policy loan to pay the credit card debt. See Table 2.

## Table 2.

| Year | Outlay | Loan | Interest | Repay | Bal | Cash Value | Death Benefit |
|------|--------|------|----------|-------|-----|-----------|---------------|
| 1  | $10k | $0   | $0    | $0    | $0    | $8.5k | $464k  |
| 2  | $10k | $0   | $0    | $0    | $0    | $17k  | $502k  |
| 3  | $10k | $0   | $0    | $0    | $0    | $27k  | $543k  |
| 4  | $10k | $0   | $0    | $0    | $0    | **$38k** | $577k |
| 5  | $10k | $30k | $0    | $0    | $30k  | $19k  | $584k  |
| 6  | $10k | $0   | $1.5k | $3.6k | $27k  | $33k  | $622k  |
| 7  | $10k | $0   | $1.3k | $3.6k | $25k  | $48k  | $660k  |
| 8  | $10k | $0   | $1.2k | $3.6k | $23k  | $64k  | $697k  |
| 9  | $10k | $0   | $1.1k | $3.6k | $20k  | $81k  | $734k  |
| 10 | $10k | $0   | $1k   | $3.6k | $18k  | $98k  | $771k  |
| 11 | $10k | $0   | $920  | $3.6k | $15k  | $117k | $808k  |
| 12 | $10k | $0   | $786  | $3.6k | $12k  | $135k | $844k  |
| 13 | $10k | $0   | $645  | $3.6k | $9k   | $156k | $880k  |
| 14 | $10k | $0   | $497  | $3.6k | $6k   | $178k | $916k  |
| 15 | $10k | $0   | $342  | $3.6k | $3.5k | $200k | $952k  |
| 16 | $10k | $0   | $179  | $3.6k | $166  | $224k | $989k  |
| 17 | $10k | $0   | $8    | $174  | $0    | $245k | $1.02M |
| 18 | $10k | $0   | $0    | $0    | $0    | $267k | $1.05M |

The impact of borrowing on the policy by comparing both tables' death benefits at the end of year four provides an astonishing revelation. Table 1 displays a cash value of $38,939 with a death benefit of $577,707. Table 2 displays the same cash value until year five when the $30,000 loan is withdrawn, leaving a cash value of $19,044. The ending result is a dollar-for-dollar reduction in cash value and death benefit, from $614,363 to $584,363. The policy loan is paid back with the same $300 per month credit card payment at $3,600 per year, which takes twelve years to complete. The loan policy's interest does not go toward the cash value or death benefit but the actual insurance company itself. The advantage to the policyholder is that the loan is paid off in year seventeen. The cash value would be at $245,594, precisely the same cash value amount in year seventeen if no policy loan was ever taken against the policy.

In a worst-case scenario, suppose the policyholder takes out a $30,000 loan to pay off the credit card debt. However, for some unforeseen reason, life happens, and the borrower cannot repay the loan but can still contribute to the $10,000 per year premium. With a $30,000 policy loan, taken out in year five and is never paid back, the balance would reach $62,368 due to compound interest in year 20. At year 20, there would be $315,907 in cash value and $1,120,438 in death benefit without a policy loan, compared to a policy loan resulting in $250,421 cash value and $1,058,070 death benefit. A $65,000 difference due to the 5%-6% dividends paid out by the insurance company to the policy allowing the cash value and death benefit to grow exponentially while ignoring the policy loan. A High Cash Value Policy replaces the need for any bank loan or interest-bearing vehicle altogether. The policy provides access to capital for debt consolidation or investing any time, ultimate savings, a life insurance policy with high dividends, which is highly beneficial.

# CHAPTER SEVEN

# Nationality

T he term "national" means a person owing permanent allegiance to a state according to Title 8, Chapter 12 – Immigration and Nationality U.S.C. subsection 1101(a)(21). To reach the Zero Percent tax bracket, a person must realize that they cannot be anything other than a national listed in the government's system. The terms American Indian, Black, Negro or African American, White or Caucasian, Pacific Islander, Hispanic or Latino, etc., cannot be used with a national's listing. Every State has codified in their libraries the slave laws. Taking a look at Georgia's Slave Laws, titled, "A Codification of the Statute Law of Georgia, including the English

Statutes of Force: In Four Parts; compiled, digested and arranged by William A. Hotchkiss, by the authority of the legislature," states,

46. Jurisdiction of inferior court. – The inferior courts of the several counties of this State shall have jurisdiction of the several offences created or mentioned by this act, in all cases in which, by the constitution of the State, jurisdiction may be entertained by them.

47. Exceptions in favour of aborigines, Moors, and Hindoos. – The provisions, prohibitions, and penalties of this act shall not extend to any American Indian, free Moor, or Lascar; but the burden of proof, in all cases of arrest of any person of color, shall be on such person of color, to show him or herself exempt from the operations of this act.

*(CHAP. XXXIII. FREE PERSONS OF COLOR.; Art. II. Disabilities of Free Persons of Color)*

Many people believe American Indian is the right nationality to assume. Still, as Georgia's slave laws just mentioned, anyone using that term does not have any rights in the inferior courts such as county superior courts except Aboriginals, Moors Hindoos. Any other term is just a franchise classification used by the United States to financially and legally control its citizens. Again, the fourteenth amendment to the Constitution allegedly claims to have been ratified on July 9, 1868, granting citizenship to all persons born or naturalized in the

United States, which included former slaves recently freed. How is this possible? If in 1866, everyone, regardless of skin color, was already free and actual citizens of the united States of America in Congress Assembled. The Civil Rights Act of 1866 explains that everyone held citizenship within the republic confederacy and is, in fact, the written legislation that encouraged the fourteenth amendment, in association with the Organic Act of 1871.

> Be it enacted by the Senate and House of Representatives of the United States of America in Congress assembled, That all persons born in the United States and not subject to any foreign power, excluding Indians not taxed, are hereby declared to be citizens of the United States; and such citizens, of every race and color, without regard to any previous condition of slavery or involuntary servitude,
>
> *(Thirty-Ninth Congress, Session I. Ch. 31, April 9, 1866, Chap. XXXI. – An Act to protect all Persons in the United States in their Civil Rights, and furnish the Means of their Vindication.)*

The first document a U.S. citizen, U.S. national, State Citizen, or Legal Permanent Resident could file to correct their commercial status with the federal government is the Unites States Passport Application, known as the DS-11. In Chapter Two, the Acts or Conditions were explained in detail. It requires a supplementary explanatory statement under oath (or affirmation) from the applicant should be attached and made a part of the application. An affidavit stating the affiant's nationality must be attached to the application before it is delivered to a passport agent. In all actuality, the Department of Secretary of State website at travel.state.gov provides concise instructions on how to complete the application as a national correctly. The government cannot force U.S. citizenship on anyone, owing taxes. They will always provide a way for equity if one has eyes to see and ears to hear. According to the Secretary of State of the District of Columbia, the Department of State occasionally receives requests for certificates of non-citizen national status according to Section 341(b) of the Immigration and Nationality Act (I.N.A.), 8 U.S.C. 1452(b). As defined by the I.N.A., all U.S. citizens are U.S. nationals, but only a relatively small number of persons acquire U.S. nationality without becoming U.S. citizens. Section 101(a) (21) of the I.N.A. defines the term "national" as "a person owing permanent allegiance to a state." Section 101(a)(22) of the I.N.A. provides that the term "national of the United States" includes all U.S. citizens as well as persons who, though not citizens of the United States, owe permanent allegiance to the United States (non-citizen nationals). As the Department has received few requests, there is no justification for creating a non-citizen national certificate. Designing a separate document that includes an anti-fraud mechanism was seen as an inefficient expenditure of resources. Therefore, the Department determined that those who would be eligible to apply for such a certificate may instead apply for a United States passport that would delineate and certify their status as a national but not a citizen of the United States.

If a person believes he or she is eligible under the law as a non-citizen national of the United States and the person complies with the provisions of section 341(b) of the I.N.A., Title 8 U.S.C. 1452(b), he/she may apply for a passport at any Passport Agency in the United States…When applying, applicants must execute a Form DS-11 and show documentary proof of their non-citizen national status as well as their identity.

(b) A person who claims to be a national but not a citizen of the United States may apply to the Secretary of State for a certificate of non-citizen national status. Upon – (1) proof to the satisfaction of the Secretary of State that the applicant is a national, but not a citizen, of the United States; and, (2) in the case of a non-citizen national born outside of the United States of its outlying possessions, taking and subscribing, before an immigration officer within the United States or its outlying possessions, to the oath of allegiance required of an applicant for naturalization.

*(Section 341(b) of the Immigration and Nationality Act)*

The Department of State is very precise with the procedure of being classified as a national. Applicants are applying for a certificate of non-citizen national status via form DS-11 and in return will receive a United States of America Passport, listed as a "National but Not a Citizen of the United States." A national of the United States and a citizen of the United States are the same per Title 8 U.S.C. § 1101, Section (a)22. It is not to be mistaken with a national but not a citizen of the United States. The wordplay can be very deceiving if not careful. Section 341(b) requires that the applicant, mostly foreign nationals from other countries who may be visiting on a six-month stay using a VISA, must prove that they're indeed a national and declare their allegiance to a state via affidavit before an immigration officer for naturalization. This is one of the main benefits an Irrevocable Foreign Express Trust is registered with the probate court, superior court, or county recorder's office. Inside the Schedule of Minutes, the Settlor can declare its allegiance held by the trustee and recorded with the Clerk of Court. The term "clerk of court" means a naturalization court clerk, an oath swearing officer identical to an immigration officer. Once the Express Trust and its minutes are recorded, the Settlor/Applicant has proof to satisfy the Secretary of

State of its lawful requirements to apply for the U.S. Passport and receive its certificate of non-citizen national status without the need to receive a "green card." The Schedule of Minutes would also serve as the Supplemental Explanatory Statements as stated in the Acts or Conditions section of the DS-11. The Department of State reveals that no one is a U.S. citizen by birth but only through ignorance and misapplied information. Section 308 of the Immigration and Nationality Act states,

> Unless otherwise provided in section 301 of this title, the following shall be" nationals, but not citizens of the United States at birth:"

> (2) A person born outside the United States and its outlying possessions of parents both of whom are nationals, but not citizens, of the United States, and have had a residence in the United States, or one of its outlying possessions prior to the birth of such person;

The oath that the applicant must declare inside the Schedule of Minutes recorded with the Clerk of Court is found in Section 302 of Public Law 94-241, which pertains to any existing alleged U.S. citizen seeking to correct their status. It reads,

> Any person who becomes a citizen of the United States solely by virtue of the provisions in Section 301 may within six months after the effective date of that Section or within six months after

reaching the age of 18 years, whichever date is later, become a national but not a citizen of the United States by making a declaration under oath before any court established by the Constitution or laws of the United States or any other court of record in the Commonwealth in the form as follows, "I being duly sworn, hereby declare my intention to be a national but not a citizen of the United States."

When applying for a certificate of non-citizen national status, it is wise to apply for both the Passport Card and Passport Book. As laws in the United States become even more strenuous regarding Real I.D., having a passport card would resolve the need for a Real I.D. altogether. As a national, one will be able to travel anywhere within the United States of America, as well as having the ability to operate an automobile and have access to federal buildings without having to elect that one is a U.S. citizen within the Department of Motor Vehicles, using a State I.D. or Driver's License. Here is how to complete the entire DS-11 as a national but not a citizen of the United States:

(Note: The exact punctuation must be used, including information within brackets.)

Page 1 of 2

Box 1: Name Last – smith

Name First – john

Name Middle – doe

Box 2: Date of Birth – 09 | 11 | 2001

Box 3: Sex – M

Box 4: Place of Birth – pasadena california united states of america

Box 4: Place of Birth (if born in another country) – municipality of medellin, republic of colombia

Box 5: Social Security Number (SSN or ITIN) – 123-45-6789. (Note: Even though the social security number is the number attached to the ens egis, also known as a commercial avatar to do business in a fictitious system, the Department of State needs the number to update the U.S. citizens' status to a national successfully.

Box 5: Social Security Number (Note: if born outside the U.S. and the applicant never received an SSN/ITIN enter 9 zeros)

Box 6: E-mail – provide any e-mail to received notifications for approval or rejection of the application

Box 7: Primary Phone Number – enter a valid phone number if the Department of State needs to verify any information quickly.

Box 8: Mailing Address line 1 – in care of [1234] main street apt 777

Box 8: City – los angeles

Box 8: State – [ca]

Box 8: Zip Code – [00000]

Box 8: Country – [california usa]

Box 9: If any other names are used, such as maiden, previous marriage, or legal name change, provide here in all lower case.

**STOP! CONTINUE TO PAGE 2**

Page 2 of 2

Name of Applicant (Last, First & Middle) – smith, john doe

Date of Birth – 09 | 11 | 2001

Box 10: Parental Information (Mother: First & Middle) – jane susan

Box 10: Last Name (Mother at Birth) – robinson

Box 10: Date of Birth (Mother) – 03 | 01 | 1952

Box 10: Place of Birth (Mother; if born within the U.S.A.) – arkansas united states of america

Box 10: Place of Birth (Mother; if born outside the U.S.A. or outlying possessions) – bogota, republic of colombia

Box 10: Sex – F

Box 10: U.S. citizen? – Always Check No

Box 10: Parental Information (Father: First & Middle) – jack white

Box 10: Last Name (Father at Birth) – smith

Box 10: Date of Birth (Father) – 07 | 15 | 1949

Box 10: Place of Birth (Father; if born within the U.S.A.) – south dakota united states of america

Box 10: Place of Birth (Father; if born outside the U.S.A. or outlying possessions) – bogota, republic of colombia

Box 10: Sex – M

Box 10: U.S. citizen? – Always Check No

Box 11: If the applicant has ever been married, check yes and provide the spouse information always in lower case and check No to U.S. citizen.

Box 12: Skip

Box 13: Occupation – minister

Box 14: Employer or School – god (Elohim)

Box 15: Skip

Box 16: Skip

Box 17: Skip

Box 18: Skip

Box 19: Permanent Address [Per U.C.C. § 9-307. Location of Debtor (b)(1) A debtor who is an individual is located at the individual's principal residence; therefore, entering an address within the Internal Revenue District, such as house number, street name, and zip code, will re-enter the applicant back into the jurisdiction of the United States as a U.S. citizen again. Enter the address as Rural Free Delivery, a service that began in the United States in the late 19th century to deliver mail directly to rural farm families. Before the seven types of land use were established as residential, institutional, industrial, road greenbelt, roadside, park, and forest, it was known as rural farmland.] – in care of rural free delivery; NO APT/UNIT

Box 19: City – los angeles

Box 19: State – [ca]

Box 19: Zip Code – [00000]

Box 19: (Note: If the applicant is not from this country, the address must be a rural free delivery address within the united states of america to meet the requirement of INA 341(b)).

Box 20: Emergency Contact – enter the name of anyone within close contact, proving full name, phone, relation, and address in all lower case spelling with street number, State, and zip code in brackets. The zip should be all zeros as well.

Box 21. Have you ever applied for a U.S. Passport Book or Passport Card? – If yes, provide the full name in all lower case and the book or card or both numbers, including its issued date.

Referring back to page 1 of 2 – STOP! CONTINUE TO PAGE 2 section; the passport agent will complete this Section on behalf of the applicant upon receiving the satisfaction of identity, any State I.D., current valid U.S. Passport, Birth Certificate, VISA document, or Lawful Permanent Resident I.D. If the applicant is a national from overseas and currently has a valid VISA, it is optional to apply for a temporary state driver's license as a means to satisfy proof of identity before applying for U.S. Passport. Once the passport agent has received adequate identifying documentation, they will enter the identifying information and request the applicant's signature. The passport agent will act as a witness that the applicant is signing under penalty of perjury to the terms and conditions listed above the signature line. It is essential that the applicant read the terms and conditions carefully before signing and before the passport agent provide their seal of approval. There is an additional small detail the applicant must "update" inside of the terms and conditions to apply for a certificate of non-citizen national status properly. The contents are as follows:

I declare under penalty of perjury all of the following: 1) I am a citizen or non-citizen national of the United States and have not, since acquiring U.S. citizenship or nationality, performed any of the acts listed under "Acts or Conditions" on page four of the instructions of this application (unless explanatory statement is attached); 2) the statements made on the application are true and correct; 3) I have not knowingly and willfully made false statements or included false documents in support of this application; 4) the photograph attached to this application is a genuine, current photograph of me; and 5) I have read and understood the warning on page one of the instructions to the application form.

The subtle change that must occur is the crossing out of the word "national" in the terms and conditions, so that it reads, "I am a citizen or non-citizen of the United States." The wordplay is very cunning. Remember, a non-citizen national of the United States is the same as a U.S. citizen or U.S. national per Title 8 U.S. Code § 1101 – Definitions, section 22. As the applicant provides their signature on the required line before the passport agent, they must sign in this manner: smith, john doe, w/out the U.S. The final part of the application is drafting the Supplemental Explanatory Statements to attach to the application. The following is a word for word template that has been used with a 100% approval rate. Assume the applicant is a foreign national born in Colombia, currently living in South Florida. This explanatory statement works hand in hand with the Express Trust and its Schedule Minutes that will be detailed in the next chapter. In this template, the 1838 Florida Constitution is used, and should be replaced with the applicants pre-1933 state constitution pertaining to where they live. (Note: The explanatory statement will consist of 5 to 6 pages. Begin each page with a top-header in red lettering, as stated on the following page.)

THESE EXPLANATORY STATEMENTS ARE TO REMAIN WITH AND ATTACHED TO THE PASSPORT APPLICATION IN ORDER FOR THIS PASSPORT APPLICATION TO BE TRUE AND CORRECT UNDER PENALTY OF PERJURY UNDER THE LAWS OF THE UNITED STATES OF AMERICA.

## PASSPORT EXPLANATORY STATEMENTS

THESE EXPLANATORY STATEMENTS ARE DONE BASED UPON MY RELIGIOUS INSTRUCTIONS AND BELIEFS AND AS REQUIRED BY THE ACTS OR CONDITIONS LISTED IN THE INSTRUCTIONS ON PAGE FOUR

TAKE EQUITABLE NOTICE, of my unalienable Religious Instructions and Beliefs protected by the 1838 Florida Constitution – Article One – Declaration of Rights – Section Two to State and Declare my <u>Affidavit of Denial of U.S. [28 U.S. Code §</u> <u>3002 (15)(A)] Citizenship</u> pursuant to the Baby Act and pursuant to the 39th Congress, Session One – Chapter Thirty-One – Page 27 – Civil Rights Act of 1866 (enacted by the Senate and House Representatives of the United States of America in Congress assembled) and Declaration of being a <u>Moor Free Inhabitant and</u> <u>Native Colombian National "but NOT a citizen of the United States</u>

or United States national." The Constitution of United States of
America 1789 – Article IV – Section One, states, *"Full Faith and Credit
shall be given in each State to the public Acts, Records and judicial Proceedings
of every other State. And the Congress may by general Laws prescribe the
Manner in which such Acts, Records and Proceedings shall be proved, and the
Effect thereof,"* therefore the 1877 Georgia Constitution – Article One
– Bill of Rights – Section Four – Paragraph One, states, *"Laws of a
general nature shall have uniform operation throughout the State, and no
special law shall be enacted in any case for which provision has been made by
an existing general law. No general law affecting private rights, shall be varied
in any particular case, by special legislation, except with the free consent, in
writing of all persons to be affected thereby; and no person under legal disability
to contract, is capable of such consent,"* shall apply to my Explanatory
Statements.

THESE EXPLANATORY STATEMENTS ARE TO REMAIN
WITH AND ATTACHED TO THE PASSPORT
APPLICATION IN ORDER FOR THIS PASSPORT
APPLICATION TO BE TRUE AND CORRECT UNDER
PENALTY OF PERJURY UNDER THE LAWS OF THE
UNITED STATES OF AMERICA.

**TAKE  EQUITABLE  NOTICE,** **Each State
retains its Sovereignty, freedom and independence, and every
Power, Jurisdiction and right, which is not by this
confederation expressly delegated to the United States in**

**Congress assembled per Article II of the Articles of Confederation.**

I, Last Name, First Name Middle Name d/b/a FIRST NAME MIDDLE NAME LAST NAME, under Declaration of NAME EXPRESS TRUST Dtd 01/01/2020, hereby and forever, State, claim and declare I am not nor have I ever been a U.S. citizen or U.S. national.

I declare that my name is Last Name, First Name Middle Name d/b/a FIRST NAME MIDDLE NAME LAST NAME. *I am a Moor Free Inhabitant and Native Colombian National, but not a Citizen of the United States, domiciled in Florida.* (Note: if applicant is born in the U.S.A., the following statement applies) I declare that my name is Last Name, First Name Middle Name d/b/a FIRST NAME MIDDLE NAME LAST NAME. *I am a Moor Free Inhabitant and Native Floridian National, but not a Citizen of the United States, domiciled in Florida. (see copy 2016 G.P.O. style manual page 95)*

TAKE EQUITABLE NOTICE, I am NOT a Fourteenth Amendment Federal citizen (ratified in 1868) "Subject to the jurisdiction thereof." The U.S. State Department may recognize me as a Moor Aboriginal Colombian National but not a citizen of the United States. (Note: only if the applicant is formerly known as Hispanic, Latino, Black, Negro, American Indian, or African American…if any other nationality, provide it instead. For example, an Italian National or Israeli National or Dutch National.) In addition, my Right to a Certificate of Non-Citizen National Status and/or United States of America

THESE EXPLANATORY STATEMENTS ARE TO REMAIN WITH AND ATTACHED TO THE PASSPORT APPLICATION IN ORDER FOR THIS PASSPORT APPLICATION TO BE TRUE AND CORRECT UNDER PENALTY OF PERJURY UNDER THE LAWS OF THE UNITED STATES OF AMERICA.

Passport comes from my Natural Right being born in Medellin, Republic of Colombia; and my oath of allegiance taken before the Broward County, Florida, Clerk of Circuit & County Court (a sworn immigration officer), lawfully stated in Public Law 99-396 – August 27, 1986 100 STAT. 843; Section 16 (a) Section 341 of the Immigration and Nationality Act (8 U.S.C. 1452) is amended –

(b) A person who claims to be a national, but not a citizen, of the United States may apply to the Secretary of State for a certificate of non-citizen national status. Upon –

1) proof to the satisfaction of the Secretary of State that the applicant is a national, but not a citizen, of the United States, and

2) in the case of such a person born outside of the United States or its outlying possessions, taking and subscribing, before an immigration officer within the United States or its outlying possessions, to the oath of allegiance required

by this Act of a petitioner for naturalization, the individual shall be furnished by the Secretary of State with a <u>certificate of non-citizen national status</u>, but only if the individual is at the time within the United States or its outlying possessions. [See enclosed Declaration of Express Trust File No. 2020-1234567, Deed Book 62324, Filed & Recorded 03/03/2020 at 12:12pm, Clerk of Circuit & County Court, Broward County Florida, Honorable Brenda D. Forman, Pages #-# and Schedule A: Trustee Minutes 2-1234, Pages #-#, & Exhibit A – Certificate of Title No. 12345678 (English Translation attached) Dated eleventh day of September 2001, pages #-#], the same and "outside" of any corporate city municipality.

THESE EXPLANATORY STATEMENTS ARE TO REMAIN WITH AND ATTACHED TO THE PASSPORT APPLICATION IN ORDER FOR THIS PASSPORT APPLICATION TO BE TRUE AND CORRECT UNDER PENALTY OF PERJURY UNDER THE LAWS OF THE UNITED STATES OF AMERICA.

TAKE EQUITABLE NOTICE, that pursuant to 1877 Georgia Constitution (as ratified without subsequent amendments) ARTICLE ONE – BILL OF RIGHTS – SECTION FOUR:

Paragraph I. Laws of a general nature shall have uniform operation throughout the State, and no special law shall be enacted in any case, for which provision has been made by an existing general law. No general law affecting private rights, shall be varied in any particular case, by special legislation, except with the free consent, in writing of all persons to be affected thereby; and no person under legal disability to contract, is capable of such consent.

Paragraph II. Legislative acts in violation of this Constitution, or the Constitution of the United States, are void, and the Judiciary shall so declare them.

AND TAKE FURTHER NOTICE THAT

I, Last Name, First Name Middle Name, the Settlor, State that the NAME EXPRESS TRUST Dtd 01/01/2020 is the 1st lienholder of the fourteenth amendment person LAST NAME, FIRST NAME MIDDLE NAME corp. sole d/b/a FIRST NAME MIDDLE NAME LAST NAME, did not consent for me or my private property to being a fourteenth amendment citizen of the U.S. or STATE OF FLORIDA and any other State in writing or any other consent.

AND TAKE FURTHER NOTICE THAT THIS IS A CONTRACT, failure to answer and rebut this affidavit is acquiescence, allowing you 72 hours to answer; then this contract is law.

THESE EXPLANATORY STATEMENTS ARE TO REMAIN WITH AND ATTACHED TO THE PASSPORT APPLICATION IN ORDER FOR THIS PASSPORT APPLICATION TO BE TRUE AND CORRECT UNDER PENALTY OF PERJURY UNDER THE LAWS OF THE UNITED STATES OF AMERICA.

I, Last Name, First Name Middle Name, Declare and Let it be known by all immigration clerks and the Secretaries of State, Supreme Court Judge and Clerks for now, and forever *I am a Moor Aboriginal Colombian National* (Note:

enter other nationality here) *"but not a citizen of the United States or United States national,"* nor will ever be a U.S. citizen or U.S. national. You have three (3) days to bring forth your proof that I am.

## RESCISSION OF SIGNATURES

T A K E  N O T I C E  that I am not a statutory citizen and make no claim of statutory citizenship created by any State or Federal government. I hereby extinguish, rescind, revoke, cancel, abrogate, annul, nullify, discharge, and make void *ab initio* all signatures belonging to me, on all previously filed SS-5, Internal Revenue Service; W-4 Forms, W-2 Forms, USCIS Forms, Florida Application D.M.V. Forms, all Federal and State Income Tax Forms (if any) and all powers of attorney, real and/or implied, connected thereto on the grounds that my purported consent was voluntary and freely obtained, but was made through mistake, duress, fraud, and undue influence exercised by any or all governments (State or Federal) any agency and/or employers. Pursuant to Contract Law; "all previously signed Federal and State forms are, hereby, extinguished by this rescission."

Any alleged consent is null and void as it was given under duress, by mistake, and/or by fraud. Notwithstanding any information, which you may have to the contrary, any forms that have been filed, and any implied quasi-contracts that you may have with me, were filed illegally and unlawfully and are without force and/or effect.

THESE EXPLANATORY STATEMENTS ARE TO REMAIN WITH AND ATTACHED TO THE PASSPORT APPLICATION IN ORDER FOR THIS PASSPORT APPLICATION TO BE TRUE AND CORRECT UNDER PENALTY OF PERJURY UNDER THE LAWS OF THE UNITED STATES OF AMERICA.

I further revoke, rescind and make void ab initio all powers of attorney pertaining to me from any and all governmental, quasi, colorable agencies and/or Departments created under the authority of Article One, Section Eight,

Clause Seventeen, and/or Article Four, Section Three, Clause Two of the Constitution for the United States of America.

I preserve all of my unalienable Rights that are inherent from my Creator, at all times. This application is done based upon my

Religious Instructions and Beliefs under the NAME EXPRESS TRUST Dtd 01/01/2020, the Common Law jurisdiction of Florida (NOTE: your state/country), the Treaty of Marrakesh, the Treaty of Peace and Friendship, and the Constitution of the United States of America.

## <u>ACTS OR CONDITIONS</u>

"I have taken an oath and made an affirmation, formal declaration of allegiance to a foreign state and made a formal renunciation of nationality in the United States. Furthermore, I have not been convicted of a federal or State drug offense or convicted of a "sex tourism" crimes statute, and I am not the subject of an outstanding federal, State, or local warrant of arrest for a felony; a criminal court order forbidding my departure from the United States; a subpoena received from the United States in a matter involving federal prosecution for, or grand jury investigation of, a felony."

THESE EXPLANATORY STATEMENTS ARE TO REMAIN WITH AND ATTACHED TO THE PASSPORT APPLICATION IN ORDER FOR THIS PASSPORT APPLICATION TO BE TRUE AND CORRECT UNDER PENALTY OF PERJURY UNDER THE LAWS OF THE UNITED STATES OF AMERICA.

**Attached Exhibits:**

- Declaration of Express Trust

- Certificate of Title (Birth Certificate)

- Public Law 99-396, Aug. 27, 1986, 100 STAT. 837-847

(Note: if applicant is born in the U.S.A., include Copy of 2016 GPO Style Manual pages 1-4, 13 & 95)

(Note: if applicant is born outside the U.S.A., the jurat is as follows)

I, Last Name, First Name Middle Name, born in the land of Bogota, Republic of Colombia, South America, declare (or certify, verify or State) under penalty of perjury under the laws of the United States of America [28 U.S. Code § 1746(1)], that "I, Last Name, First Name Middle Name being duly sworn, hereby declare my intention to be a national but not a citizen of the United States" [Public Law 99-396 – AUG. 27, 1986, 100 STAT. 843, Section 16(b)(1)(2)] and the foregoing is true and correct.

(Note: if applicant is born in the U.S.A., the jurat is as follows)

I, Last Name, First Name Middle Name, born in the land of Florida united states of America, the territory of Broward, declare (or certify, verify or State) under penalty of perjury under the laws of the United States of America [28 U.S. Code § 1746(1)], that "I, Last Name, First Name Middle Name being duly sworn, hereby declare my intention to be a national but not a citizen of the United States" [Public Law 94-241 – March 24, 1976 – Article III. – 90 STAT. 266 – Section 302] and the foregoing is true and correct.

THESE EXPLANATORY STATEMENTS ARE TO REMAIN WITH AND ATTACHED TO THE PASSPORT APPLICATION IN ORDER FOR THIS PASSPORT APPLICATION TO BE TRUE AND CORRECT UNDER PENALTY OF PERJURY UNDER THE LAWS OF THE UNITED STATES OF AMERICA.

Executed this XX day of MONTH, 2021

Signed:_____

Last, First Middle without the U.S.

This concludes the supplemental explanatory statements! The last page includes a Certificate of Acknowledgment signed, sealed, and dated by a valid notary. The passport application, the explanatory statement, the attachments, and the proper identifying documents are needed to correct the applicant's commercial status. Once the applicant has received the U.S. Passport Card or Book, it is time to submit a F.O.I.A. (Freedom Of Information Act) request to the Department of State. The Privacy Act allows an applicant to obtain copies of their records, a minor child's, any person for whom they are legal guardians or anyone who has authorized them to obtain the records. The F.O.I.A. request would have the Department of State return a certified copy of each page of the passport application, which in turn is the actual "certificate of non-citizen national status." This certification is the actual document that would be provided with the corrected SS-5 form, mentioned in Chapter Two. The applicant needs to draft an affidavit providing the following information per travel.state.gov:

- Full name at birth and any name changes of the individual whose records are being requested, and if there are records for children or using an authorization, provide the full name as well.

- Date and place of birth of the individual whose records are requested.

- Mailing address.

- Daytime telephone number.

- E-mail address, if available.

- Date or estimated date of passport issuance.

- Passport number, if known, and any other information that will help the Dept. of State locate the records (preferably the passport application locator number)

- An exact copy of both sides of a valid government-issued photo identification, such as a driver's license, state I.D. or temporary driver's license

Sign and date F.O.I.A. Affidavit Request with the following statement:

I, Last Name, First Name Middle Name, declare under penalty of perjury, under the laws of the United States of America [28 U.S.C. § 1746(1)] that the foregoing is true and correct.

Provide a $50 Money Order made payable to U.S. Department of State and mail to:

- U.S. Department of State

- Office of Law Enforcement Liaison

- FOIA Officer

- 44132 Mercure Cir

- P.O. Box 1227

- Sterling, VA 20166

This method would resolve the hassles of receiving a lawful permanent resident card (green card) for aliens or foreign nationals and increase the number of persons in each State to have the right to vote for President and Vice President. The number of nationals increases, and the number of artificial persons such as U.S. citizens decreases. Common Law jurisdiction would usurp federal statutory legality.

# CHAPTER EIGHT

# The Temple & Trust

R ender therefore to Caesar the things that are Caesar's and to
God the things that are God's," as stated in the books of
Matthew 22:21, Mark 12:17, and Luke 20:25. The government
acknowledges and relies on biblical principles, recognizing that the
various treaties with the United States stem from the bible. Public
Law 97-280 – 97th Congress – October 4, 1982; Joint Resolution,
"Whereas the Bible is the rock on which our Republic rests," is a
crucial element to the treaties derived from the Old Testament.
When Yahusha stated, "Render unto Caesar what is Caesar's and unto

God what is God's," he was referring to covenant law, another word for contract law. Under Caesar's covenant is to be associated with its government's rules and regulations. Under God's covenant is to be in trust not just spiritually but in writing via declaration, with proper notice given to the ruling government. The bible is compiled of several treaties and decrees, which have influenced every country/state constitution in North America. The Apostle Paul, with inspiration from God, shares a paramount order given from God to the church in Rome, in Romans 13:1-7, reads,

> Let every soul be subject to the governing authorities. For there is no authority except from God, and the authorities that exist are appointed by God. Therefore whoever resists the authority resists the ordinance of God, and those who resist will bring judgment on themselves. For rulers are not a terror to good works, but to evil. Do you want to be unafraid of the authority? Do what is good, and you will have praise from the same. For he is God's minister to you for good. But if you do evil, be afraid; for he does not bear the sword in vain; for he is God's minister, an avenger to execute wrath on him who practices evil. Therefore you must be subject, not only because of wrath but also for conscience' sake. For because of this you also pay taxes, for they are God's ministers attending continually to this very thing. Render therefore to all their due: taxes to whom taxes are due, customs to whom customs, fear to whom fear, honor to whom honor.

*(New King James Version)*

Comparing this same verse with Matthews Bible 1537 edition, the word soul in the first verse of chapter 13 is the word sole, as in "corporate sole." A corporation sole is a legal entity comprised of a single "sole" incorporated office, occupied by a single "sole" natural person. In today's commercial system within the United States, every person needs a commercial avatar, also known as a legal person, such as the name associated with the social security number or social insurance number, to proceed with commerce worldwide. If one does not have an SSN, ITIN, or SIN (Social Insurance Number), then the passport from their respective country would suffice. Every single "sole" is occupied by a natural person, which is an Express Trust. God explains that the "sole" will either be held in a Foreign Trust under God's jurisdiction and registered within the ruling governments consuls, or the "sole" will be under the ruling government, known as the fourteenth amendment, Cestui Que Trust, a.k.a. a Domestic Trust, in other words, Caesar. Most corporation's sole are church-related, although some political offices of the U.K, Canada, and the United States are corporations sole. Allowing the Express Trust to be the beneficial owner of the "sole" and out of the United States jurisdiction would avoid judgment, receive praise from the ruling government, and avoid taxes. Following God's ordinances expressed in Romans 13:1-7, it is viewed as a good practice, which promotes so many benefits to neighboring communities and families financially. However, remaining as a U.S. citizen and leaving the "sole" within the United States jurisdiction is viewed as a practice of evil, followed by judgment and avenged by God's ministers, who today are the current leaders of the world. Some politicians know this role, and others may not. God speaks so heavily against usury and the charging of interest or taxes against one another throughout the Old Testament. However, if one chooses to ignore God's treaty laws, taxes and pillage are at their doorstep. The distinct detail to avoid usury/taxes is not to fall within a Domestic Trust definition.

> The term "domestic trust" means a trust in which a court within the United States is able to exercise primary supervision over the administration of the trust, and one or more U.S. persons have the authority to control all substantial decisions of the trust.
>
> *(IRC § 7701 Definitions)*

What does it mean to render unto God what is God's? Above all, it is love, joy, peace, longsuffering, kindness, goodness, faithfulness, gentleness, and self-control, as mentioned in Galatians 5:22. What exactly is the praise one would receive from the ruling government by following God's ordinances? It is written,

> "The thief does not come except to steal, and to kill, and to destroy. I have come that they may have life and that they may have it more <u>abundantly</u>."

*(John 10:10 New King James Version – Yahusha, the Son)*

Not only has the Son of God, Yahusha, come to give his life as the only sacrifice to reconcile man back to God as a remission of their sins but also to teach men the ways of righteousness and how to excel at commerce. The concept of corporation sole began for the orderly transfer of ecclesiastical property, serving to keep the title within the denomination or religious society. Yahusha very well knows the order of the ruling governments, and God has established access to wealth by utilizing the governments as God's ministers. The United States Treasury prints fiat currency and also mints lawful money via coin. The phrase, "This note is legal tender for all debts, public and private," is printed right on the currency, showing that there are two sides to money. The United States Financial system's private side is the United States Treasury Department, and the public side is the Internal Revenue Service. Through God's ordinances, the I.R.S. has a myriad collection of forms that can be utilized to access the wealth stored in everyone's ecclesiastical property (estate) via the "sole," by way of Yahusha. Readers of the bible are reminded,

"I am the way, the truth, and the life. No one comes to the Father except through <u>Me</u>."
*(John 14:6 New King James Version – Yahusha, the Son)*
Great is our <u>Lord</u> and mighty in power; His understanding is <u>infinite</u>.
*(Psalms 147:5 New King James Version)*

The word Lord in Psalms 147:5 is the word Adon in Hebrew, meaning sovereign, master, owner, or a reference to men. Adoni is an essential word to note when referring to the treaties associated with the United States. The I.R.S. has codified the words in the two scriptures above in their filing forms. There are many forms such as 1040, 1065, W-2, W-4, 1099-A, etc. It is interesting to see how the Internal Revenue Service comes to decide the naming of such forms and how it comes full circle in reference to a biblical treaty. The form to take note of regarding the commercial abundance that Yahusha and God have set aside for those that choose to partake in God's ways is the W-8BEN. Hebrew and Arabic are very similar in speech and writing, and the W-8BEN is Arabic and Greek lettering.

شِ is the Arabic word for God, which is Allah. The word is thought to be derived by contraction from al-ilah, which means "<u>the god</u>," and is linguistically related to El (Elohim) and Elah, the Hebrew and Aramaic words for God.

∞ is the Unicode mathematical symbol representing the concept of "infinity".

لَعِن is the Arabic and Hebrew word for "<u>Son of.</u>" In Arabic it is sometimes used as Bin or Ibn, so therefore when read altogether, the W-8BEN form is translated, "The way to <u>God</u> is through his <u>infinite son</u>!" The form is titled Certificate of Foreign Status of Beneficial Owner for United States Tax Withholding and Reporting (Individuals).

A trust includes a minimum of two people fulfilling three positions. The first position is the Settlor, which is the entity that establishes the trust to lawfully transfer control of an asset to the second position, known as a trustee, who manages it on behalf of the third position, beneficiary(s). This rule indeed comes from the mouth of Yahusha in the Book of Matthew.

> "Again, I say to you that if two of you agree on earth concerning anything that they ask, it will be done for them by My father. For where two or three are gathered in My name, I am there in the midst of them."
>
> *(Matthew 18:19-20 New King James Version – Yahusha, the Son)*

Another I.R.S. filing form worth reviewing, as it goes hand and hand with the W-8BEN form, is the W-9, Request for Taxpayer Identification Number and Certification. The W-9 is given to any entity the Express Trust will do business with, such as National Associations, Credit Unions, Insurance Companies, DMV, or any business seeking to enter into a contractual agreement that would result in the receiving of any I.R.S. Form 1099. The number 9 appears in scripture forty-nine times and symbolizes divine completeness or conveys the meaning of finality. Yahusha gave his life in the 9th hour, or at 3 PM, that all people of the world would have the free choice of reconciliation, including a tax-free life. The W-9 is a completion of the W-8BEN. The following is how to complete the W-9 form:

Box 1: Full name of the Express Trust

Box 2: Any business or other trade name the trust is also doing business in

Box 3: Federal tax classification = Trust/Estate

Box 4: To Be Discussed

Box 5 & 6: In care of mailing address within the United States

Part I: Employer Identification Number = 98 Number

Part II: Certification: Foreign trustee signature

To understand Box 4, the I.R.S. Manual must be analyzed to adequately provide the right Exempt payee code and Exemption from FATCA reporting code. In 21.7.13.2.4 – How an EIN is Assigned,

(3) 6/7 Million series EINs are reserved for Trusts, Estates, and Non-Profit/Exempt Organizations under the Tax Equity and Fiscal Responsibility Act (TEFRA). A 6/7 Million series EIN can be identified by the number 6 or 7 immediately following the dash (-).

After speaking on the telephone with an I.R.S. agent, the EIN 98 Prefix was issued. It should be noted that the number after the dash (-) is a six or a seven. According to section 3 of I.R.M. 21.7.13.2.4, if a six or seven follows the dash, it is recognized that all Estates, Trusts, and Non-Profits are exempt organizations under TEFRA. This is the exemption code that goes into Box 4 of the W-9, TEFRA! And all banks, trust companies, insurance companies, or other entities seeking to apply tax or charge fines/fees will undoubtedly file the Express Trust as an entity that cannot be taxed. Before the details on how the W-8BEN can be given, it is best to thoroughly review the treaties that the United States recognizes which makes the W-8BEN operate efficiently.

The Moors of the Mehomitan Nation (Morocco) was the first nation to recognize the United States. Most Moors and scholars believe that the first treaty to establish this relationship of commerce is the Treaty of Peace and Friendship in 1786 but it's real name is the Treaty of Marrakesh. This treaty is found nowhere on the Internet but only in the books of the Library of Congress in a special department. The treaty reads,

The following is the Treaty of Marrakesh:

1787 – In the name of God, the merciful. There exists strength and power only by God. From the Servant of God, Mohammed Ibn' Abd Allah – may God help him – to the President of the United States of America. Salvation be upon him who follows the Righteous Path. We received your letter in which you propose a peace treaty. (We are informing you that) our intention is also to maintain peaceful relations with you. We have also contacted Tunis and Tripoli regarding what you solicited from Our Majesty and all your requests will materialize, God willing. Written on the 15th Dhu al-Qa'da 1202 (July 18, 1787) the United States and Morocco share an uninterrupted period of friendship starting with Morocco being the first nation to recognize the independence of the United States and to have signed in 1787 a treaty of friendship and cooperation, the first of its kind concluded by the young republic. The American treaty of friendship with Morocco known as the "Treaty of

Marrakesh," was signed in 1786, and had been drafted by Benjamin Franklin, Thomas Jefferson and John Adams.

This was while Great Britain was turning its back on the young republic, ending its protection of all American trade ships sailing in the Mediterranean Sea. As a result, Americans were suffering heavy losses from the vicious pirate attacks in the area. Great Britain had even encouraged acts of piracy of vessels flying the American flag. With no friends in the region and no navy to protect its ships, the United States was left defenseless and, according to Thomas Jefferson, incapable of exporting almost one third of its wheat and one fourth of other items produced by the seven states of the union. Attempts made by the United States to solicit protection and support from France, however, failed since Britain had a stronger position than France in the area. Another attempt was made, and again failed, by turning to the Netherlands in 1782. On February 20, 1778, Sultan Sidi Muhammad bin Abdullah issued a declaration notifying all consuls and European merchants in Tangier, Sale, and Mogador that, "henceforth all vessels flying the American flag might freely enter the Moroccan ports and enjoy in them the same privileges and immunities with those of the other nations with whom Morocco maintains peace."

In response to the Moroccan Sultan's initiative, the United States Congress established a committee to write the draft of the agreement that took a few years to enact. When Benjamin

Franklin left Paris in 1785, Thomas Jefferson became the U.S. minister to France and Jefferson in Paris to form the final form of the "Treaty of Marrakesh" that ultimately was ratified on July 18, 1787.

Later, in 1820, the sultan gave further evidence of his friendship with America by presenting the United States with a palace in Tangier. The building is still used by the American consul in that city, and America is the only country to ever receive such an honor from the government of Morocco.

*(Treaties and Other International Acts of the United States of America, Washington: Government Printing Office, 1931)*

Notice the date of the Arabic Calendar (15th Dhu al-Qa'da I202) and the Gregorian Calendar's date (July 18, 1787). That is indeed the letter "I" 202 displayed in the image and not the number "1". In Arabic, the "I" refers to the era of Adoni, the year of our Lord and the Savior. Adon is defined as Lord and the suffix of "i" is defined as My, which completes the phrase My Lord. Many ancient texts used the "I" to establish the time period of Adoni also referred to as Anno Domini, which is Medieval Latin and means "in the year of the Lord." It is used to refer to the years after the birth of Yahusha but mistakenly interpreted "A.D." as "after death." Adoni was also commonly known as Iahoh (God of everlasting time) and Iahoh is the God who covenanted with Abram. Abram would eventually become Abraham and he planted a grove which invoked Iahoh as stated in Genesis

21:33. Iahoh influenced the era of I when it comes to dating systems. In many old documents filed with the United States, "I" ### referring to the year is everywhere. Within the International Court of Justice: YEAR 1952, August 27th 1952, CASE CONCERNING RIGHTS OF NATIONALS OF THE UNITED STATES OF AMERICA IN MOROCCO (FRANCE v. UNITED STATES OF AMERICA), reads,

> Consular jurisdiction in French Zone of Morocco as based on bilateral treaties, most-favored-nation clauses and multilateral treaties. – Meaning of "dispute" in Treaty of 1836 between Morocco and the United States;

This document is stating "In the year of our Lord" 952 or 836. This denotes that biblical times are not so distant from today, and the current year is not what it is! The quote above comes from a text written in French as well with the same dating system. In French, the phrase "In Morocco" translates "Au Maroc," derived from Latin out of Quebec, Louisiana. Quebec, Louisiana is a "country" in North America and a former French Empire colony. It was initially the name of the French colony consisting of Louisiana and the former province of Quebec, and it came to be after an independence movement in Quebec (aided by the French) seceded from British North America and managed even to take some land from Ontario to join the territory of Louisiana. This was one of Benjamin Franklin's descriptions when he mentioned all of the Americas and Europe were wholly swarthy and tawny people just a little over 200 years ago. An in-depth study of Adoni can be found in the document titled "The Mysteries of Adoni" by S.F. Dunlap, Deposited in the U.S. District Clerk's Office, Southern District of New York.

Followed by the Treaty of Marrakesh is the Treaty of Tunis and Tripoli. The Treaty of Tripoli substantiates the trust from paying any taxes on money earned while doing business in North America. The treaty was signed at Tripoli, 3 Ramada I, A.H. 1211 (November 4, 1796), initially written in Arabic.

There is a firm and perpetual Peace and friendship between the United States of America and the Bey and subjects of Tripoli of Barbary, made by the free consent of both parties, and guaranteed by the most potent Dey & regency of Algiers.

*(Article One)*

Should a vessel of either party be cast on the shore of the other, all-proper assistance shall be given to her and her people; no pillage shall be allowed; the property shall remain at the disposition of the owners, and the crew protected and succoured till they can be sent to their country.

*(Article Seven)*

The commerce between the United States and Tripoli, -the protection to be given to merchants, masters of vessels and seamen, - the reciprocal right of establishing consuls in each country, and the

Du'Vaul Dey

privileges, immunities and jurisdictions to be enjoyed by such consuls, are declared to be on the same footing with those of the most favoured nations respectively.

*(Article Nine)*

As the government of the United States of America is not in any sense founded on the Christian Religion, -as it has in itself no character of enmity against the laws, religion or tranquility of Musselmen, -and as the said States never have entered into any war or act of hostility against any Mehomitan nation, it is declared by the parties that no pretext arising from religious opinions shall ever produce an interruption of the harmony existing between the two countries.

*(Article Eleven)*

Article seven states, "No pillage shall be allowed," which is defined as to strip ruthlessly of money or goods by open violence as in war; plunder. This is the language, which will be used as one of the eleven steps to completing the I.R.S. Form W-8BEN. It is as follows,

Part I. Identification of Beneficial Owner

Box 1: Name of Individual who is beneficial owner –Express Trust Name

Box 2: Country of Citizenship – Mehomitan Nation

Box 3: Permanent Residence Address – Foreign Express Trust Address

Box 4: Mailing Address – U.S. Domestic Address

Box 5: SSN/ITIN (only for canceling a tax bill)

Box 6: Foreign Tax Identifying number – 98 Number

Box 7: Reference Number – Merchant Account Number

Box 8: Date of Birth (only for canceling a tax bill)

Part II. Claim of Tax Treaty Benefits

(Note: The underlined portion is the fill in the blank answers)

Line 9. I certify that the beneficial owner is a resident of TRIPOLI within the meaning of the income tax treaty between the United States and that country.

Line 10. Special rates and conditions (if applicable – see instructions): The beneficial owner is claiming the provisions of Article and paragraph ARTICLE 7, 9, & 11 of the treaty identified on line 9 above to claim a 0% rate of withholding on (specify type of income): i.e., Contractor Agreement, Mortgage: Principal & Interest, Earned Wages, Filing Application Fee, Court Filing Fee, etc.). Explain the additional conditions in the Article and paragraph the beneficial owner meets to be eligible for the rate of withholding: Per the Treaty of Marrakesh of 1786 and the Treaty of Tripoli of 1796: Article 7 states, "No pillage shall be allowed; the property shall remain at the disposition of the owners, and the crew protected and succoured till they can be sent to their country.

Part III. Certification

Signature of beneficial owner, Print name, Provide date – Foreign Trustee.

Whenever using the I.R.S. W-8BEN Form, it is always a professional gesture to provide a trust Office letter of introductory from the foreign trustee addressed to whoever receives the form, showcasing the Trust Office's intentions. The trustee has authorized the person of delivery to be an official Authorized Representative or Agent to administrate on its behalf. Using the W-9 and W-8BEN will completely eradicate any tax/usury any entity attempts forced onto the individual or business entity; however, to fully utilize these forms and the treaties; living in trust as God instructs in the book of Romans must be understood and performed. In the previous chapters, the Target Inc., employee, Christopher Wellington, completed the process of to avoid Federal, State, Social Security and Medicare withholding from his paychecks. Upon receiving a W-2, a tax bill would ultimately be established and Mr. Wellington would use the W-8BEN, proving his social security number in box 5 and also his unique I.R.S. reference number in box 7. This is the power of the Zero Percent and the process to cancel a tax bill with the inclusion of the non-U.C.C. Nine Billion Dollar lien, and a copy of the registered Declaration of Express Trust. An author named Carlton

Albert Weiss provides an excellent guide to the administration of an Express Trust under Common Law, functioning under the general law-merchant, titled "Weiss's Concise Trustee Handbook."

In a review of Mr. Weiss's writings, it must be understood that any trust, regardless of the many designations applied to them, is, in its most basic sense, a property interest held by one person (the trustee) at the request of another (the Settlor) for the benefit of a third party (the beneficiary). The classification applied to trust is based upon its mode of creation, in which it may be created either by an act of a party (express or implied) or by an act of the law.

> The court held that the Express Trust is a "contractual relationship based on trust form,"; and in Smith v. Morse, 2 Cal. 524, it was held that any law or procedure in its operation denying or obstructing contract rights impairs the contractual obligation and is, therefore, violative of Article I, Section 10 of the Constitution. Because the Express Trust is created by the exercise of the natural right to contract, which cannot be abridged, the agreement, when executed, becomes protected under federally enforceable right of contract law and not under laws passed by any of the several state legislatures.

*[Berry v. McCourt, 204 N.E.2d 235, 240 (1965)]*

The court made it clear that the Express Trust is not subject to legislative control. It went further to acknowledge the right-wise stance of the United States Supreme Court that the trust relationship comes under the realm of equity, based upon the common-law right of contract, and is not subject to legislative restrictions as are corporations and other organizations created by legislative authority. To clarify the equity and common-law distinctions, the basis for Express Trusts under the Common Law in this instance, is not that such organizations are creatures of Common Law, as distinguished from equity,

but that they are created under the Common Law of contracts and do not depend upon any statute.

*[Eliot v. Freeman, 220 U.S. 178 (1911)]*

The Declaration of Trust is the trust instrument that constitutes the trust. It has been noted in trust law that no technical expressions are required to create a valid declaration, so long as the words used to make clear the Settlor's intent to create the trust or confer, a benefit of some sort that would be best carried out utilizing a trust. A trust instrument doesn't necessarily need to be a declaration either, for a trust may be, and often is, formed out of a simple agreement or even a will. But with an Express Trust, the declaration has been preferred since the beginnings of trusts under England's Common Law, which otherwise shunned fictions of law. Moreover, the declaration, by its terms and provisions, serves to establish the entire contractual arrangement, including the identities and positions of the parties, the trust's name, jurisdiction and situs, and all particulars of administration, all of which the courts of equity will fully support by the principle that equity compels performance. The term natural person has been applied to Express Trust by courts of equity because of its administration, being carried out by men acting as natural persons. Under this application, the trust's right of contract is alienable, whereas its creditors' natural right of contract is not. Initially, the legal minds who perfected the Express Trust in America did so to accommodate the incredible obstacles in pr78ocuring special charters for corporations intended to deal in real estate, which trusts eventually came to be known as the "Massachusetts Land Trust."

> The trustee(s) of an Express Trust are protected under the Constitution as "citizens" throughout the continental United States. The trustee(s) under a will or declaration of an Express Trust are natural persons, "citizens" within the meaning of Article IV, Section 2 of the Constitution, and are therefore entitled to all the "privileges and immunities" of same.

> *(Paul v. Virginia, 75 U.S. 168 (1868)*

To all foreign nationals and nationals of the united States of America, the above case law just gave the solution to bypass extradition, or the need for various permissions of the USCIS. By becoming a trustee of an Express Trust that is appropriately registered within any united States of America court, and apply for the certificate of non-citizen national status via the U.S. Passport as previously mentioned. It is the power of trust within Common Law jurisdiction that provides real freedom. Thirty-three countries use the

English Common Law system such as Uganda, Tuvalu, Trinidad, and Tobago, Tonga, Singapore, St. Vincent, and the Grenadines, St. Kitts and Nevis, Pakistan, Northern Ireland, New Zealand, Nepal, Nauru, Myanmar, Kiribati, Jamaica, Israel, Ireland, India, Hong Kong, Grenada, Gibraltar, Fiji, England and Wales, Dominica, Cyprus, Cayman Islands, Canada (except Quebec), British Virgin Islands, Bhutan, Belize, Barbados, Bangladesh, Bahamas, Australia, Antigua, and Barbuda. Almost every other country is centered around a civil law system which is entirely statutory and excludes all trust law. The Napoleonic Code influences Spain, the Republic of the Congo, Bolivia, or Colombia based on the Chilean Civil Law. The Germanic Civil Law influences Croatia, and Lithuania is based on the Dutch Civil Law. The lack of education in these countries regarding trust law makes it very easy for the United States to obtain more fourteenth amendment citizens, which means more foreign nationals subjected to taxes and surrendering their nationality, becoming stateless. The United States is one of five permanent members who hold the highest voting power of the United Nations Security Council over China, France, Russia, and the United Kingdom.

Any trust may divide its trust property into shares and issue certificates. The power to issue certificates and bonds and employ an official seal has never been restricted to corporations. It is well-settled law that whatever else most corporations possess beyond their artificiality and right of suit in a corporate name is a mere incident or consequence of incorporation and not a "primary constituent."

Furthermore, the certificates have no determinable fair market value. Therefore, no gain or loss is recognized until the cost or other basis of the property disposed of has been recovered. In Commissioner of Internal Revenue v. Marshman, the court held that fair market value is determined by property received by the taxpayer, not the fair market value of the property transferred by the taxpayer into the trust. The certificates are considered not necessarily as chattels but as documentary evidence of ownership and intangible rights. In and of themselves, they are only personal property, not the actual interest or share itself. There are 100 units of beneficial interest and a separate total of 100 units of capital interest in the trust. The trustees determine the number of units (percentage of total interest) held by anyone beneficiary and may issue the full 100 units (100%) to a single beneficiary. One fascinating power the Express Trust can exercise is issuing bonds to obtain money for its endeavors. With bonds, because a bond is merely an obligation or promises to pay money or to do some act upon the occurrence of certain circumstances, the trust need only issue the bond according to the particular transaction, to back the performance of a particular contract, to raise capital from outside investors in the form of "IOU's," etc. Within the Florida Code – Business Organizations, Common-Law Declarations of Trust – Chapter 609 § 609.05, states,

> Qualification with Office of Financial Regulation. – Before any person may offer for sale, barter or sell any unit share, contract note, bond, mortgage, oil or mineral lease or other security of an

association doing business under what is known as a "declaration of trust" in this State, such person shall procure from the Office of Financial Regulation of the Financial Services Commission a permit to offer for sale and sell such securities, which permit shall be applied for and granted under the same conditions as like permits are applied for and granted to corporations.

The Express Trust can apply for a permit to issue bonds (IOUs) as an unregistered security, without the need of the Security and Exchange Commission (SEC). The unregistered security laws come from Rule 144A of the SEC, an exemption bypassing the requirements of Section Five of the Securities Act of 1933, which was amended for the sale of qualifying securities (promissory notes and bonds). This exemption applies to the sale of securities to qualified institutional buyers, who are commonly referred to as "QIBs." QIBs must be institutions and cannot be individuals – no matter how wealthy or sophisticated. Anyone besides an issuer may rely on Rule 144A. An issuer that intends to engage in multiple offerings may establish a "Rule 144A program." Rule 144A programs are programs established for offering securities (usually debt securities) on an ongoing or continuous basis to potential offerees. They are similar to "medium-term note programs," but they are unregistered, and the securities are sold only to QIBs. Originally, in 1990, the NASDAQ Stock Market offered a compliance review process that granted The Depository Trust Company (DTC) book-entry access to Rule 144A securities. That review was later abandoned as unnecessary. Moving forward, NASDAQ launched an Electronic Trading Platform for Rule 144A securities called PORTAL Rule 144A should not be confused with Rule 144 (public unregistered limited securities). At the same time, 144A pertains to unregistered private securities without limits.

The number 144 may be familiar to those of religious groups or to some who study eschatology. In the Book of Revelations, chapter 7:18, are the 144,000 servants of God. Twelve thousand servants or representatives are holding the plenipotentiary seats of financial power within the twelve tribes of Israel. These tribes are scattered across the earth but mostly the Americas, known as Yudah, Reuben, Gad, Asher, Naphtali, Manasseh, Simeon, Levi, Issachar, Zebulun, Joseph, and Benjamin or "Ben-yamin." By the proper use of the foreign Express Trust, under God's treaty laws, the trust can partake in the inheritance within the Tribes of Israel, using Rule 144A. When the Express Trust issues a bond or promissory note to a QIB, the instrument is sold or circulated, generating the funds, routed back to the trust account, and the trust does not pay the Interest or repayment of the Bond/Note. Instead, all fourteenth amendment citizens outside of God's ordinances are subject to Caesar's rendering.

Anyone (man or entity) capable of taking physical possession of the legal title to property can be a trustee. The number of trustees to serve in any one trust is not limited. Generally speaking, where there is more than one trustee concerning each other, they are referred to as co-trustees, and when collaborating as a collective body, they are referred to as the Board of Trustees. The powers of a trustee are divided into three categories such as general, special, and discretionary. The general is all those inherent in trustees *virtue officii*, i.e., ordinarily conferred by trust law; the special are all those conferred by the trust instrument, and the discretionary are all those arising out of the necessity of personal judgment (though broad discretion may also be conferred by law and as well as by trust instrument). It is well-settled law that under a declaration of trust, the trustees must have all the powers necessary to carry out the obligation of that private contract which they have assumed.

Some of the major differences between Express Trust and Corporations are as follows:

- Express Trust – Are governed under equity, and trust law is the most well-settled body of Law in America. Corporations – are governed under statutes, which are forever changing according to political agendas and schemes.

- Express Trust – Trustees, afforded more leverage and powers, are generally broader than corporate officers. Law provides that whatever any individual may lawfully do, trust can do. The sky (nature) is the limit. Corporations – Relatively have broad powers, such as with holding companies. But corporations may not do whatever any individual may lawfully do; they can only do what is legal. The statute (legislature) is the limit.

- Express Trust – Life-span of 20 to 25 years at a time to avoid rules against perpetuities. Death of a Settlor or trustee does not affect the life or affairs of the trust. A succession of power is quiet and private. Corporations – Life-span is a perpetual or certain number of years according to legislative requirements. All officer changes must be reported, which records are open for public review.

- Express Trust – Are not required to obtain business licenses whatsoever. Corporations – It is the very opposite.

- Express Trust – All Federal excise tax and state organization, and franchise taxes are legally avoided. Corporations – Federal excise tax is demanded except state taxes in some states. All corporations are taxed indirectly by way of inflation.

- Express Trust – The Trustees are not required to file reports with any entity and are accountable only to the beneficiary, governed strictly under equity principles. Corporations – They are required to file statements and reports quarterly.

These advantages and more have been and are still in action by some of the wealthiest individuals and families in America and abroad. But the widely perceived yet untraceable wealth of such individuals and families like the Rothchilds, the Rockefellers, the Kennedys, the

Forbes, the Vanderbilts, and many of the alleged American founding fathers, plus countless modern-day politicians, are strong circumstantial evidence of this. One may find many articles and information, as well as quotes, attesting to this.

When the trustee engages in trade or commerce on behalf of the trust, acting under general Common Law, the trust is within the jurisdiction over which the Bill of Rights' literal and absolute protections extend. They have no direct contact with the federal government. And, under the right of contract law protected under the Federal Constitution, the trustee may enter into the fourteenth amendment jurisdiction via contract, i.e., by willfully availing the trust of benefits like the quasi-corporate privilege/franchise of limited liability for the discharge of debts with Federal Reserve notes under H.J. Resolution 192. The many participants under this system, especially fourteenth amendment citizens from each state, form an unincorporated federation of state associations operating under interstate commerce as addressed in Article IV § three clauses two and reinforced by the landmark *Erie R. Co. v. Tompkins* decision. This is the basis for the federal government's, including state governments, the compulsion of persons to its public international law, commonly known as codes and statutes (state or federal), to regulate everything as a matter of commerce.

In Roman civil law, as a base-model for commerce regulation, was developed out of the necessity of the church to avoid political scrutiny for its handling of ever-increasing amounts of precious metals. It had become a "storehouse" for the money and property the people were persuaded to give in exchange for limited liability [in the form of tithing] (i.e., go directly to heaven instead of hell). As the people became more educated and saw what was really behind the power of religion [in generating wealth], the Roman Church fell under tremendous criticism. Which led to the development of a banking system to handle and control church wealth and take the critical focus [away from the church.]

The bank learned from the church about limited liability. Suppose they could get people to borrow money beyond their ability to pay back. In that case, they could get them to keep performing [paying interest in one form or another] on a debt (liability) without ever demanding it [the principal] back, thereby loaning out that same credit to more than one individual or company. This meant that the bank was limiting the borrower's liability. The borrower was not entirely responsible for the debt so long as the borrower continued to perform to paying the interest. In this banking method, real money (gold) became credit (paper money) by loaning to more than one person. Being involved in this sort of commerce was called "private commerce." With the church's control over wealth, this private commerce became standard practice in the world trade across the sea – private international or admiralty/maritime law became known as Roman civil law as it began to figure heavily in the politics of every city and country it touched through international commerce, governed by the Uniform Commercial Code.

In this law operation, all persons subject to its jurisdiction are regarded as vessels, having a distinct quasi-corporate, juridical personality, capable of suing and being sued in *rem*. Fourteenth amendment citizens of the United States, whether state or federal chartered corporations or metaphysical-chartered corporate-colored public person, are public vessels of the United States within the broad meaning of the Public Vessels Act and are regulated. The United States, as with the Roman Church, is the "ship of state." The Express Trust is a private vessel of the united States of America, navigating through the often hostile waters called interstate commerce.

In light of the Roman church influencing banks around the world to engage in private commerce, the Federal Reserve Bank of Chicago published their book called Modern Money Mechanics, with versions from 1961-1994 and most recently published in 1994; further describing the monetary system since the time of the creation of the Federal Reserve Bank. Who creates money? A question asked by so many and answered by the Federal bank itself.

Changes in quantity of money may originate with actions of the Federal Reserve System (the central bank), depository institutions (principally commercial banks), or the public. The major control, however, rests with the central bank. The actual process of money creation takes place primarily in banks. As noted earlier, checkable liabilities of banks are money. These liabilities are customers' accounts. They increase when customers deposit currency and checks and when the proceeds of loans made by the banks are credited to borrowers' accounts. In the absence of legal reserve requirements, banks can build up deposits by increasing loans and investments so long as they keep enough currency on hand to redeem whatever amounts the holders of deposits want to convert into currency. This unique attribute of the banking business was discovered many centuries ago. It started with goldsmiths. As early bankers, they initially provided safekeeping services, making a profit from vault storage fees for gold and coins deposited with them. People would redeem their "deposit receipts" whenever they needed gold or coins to purchase something, and physically take the gold or coins to the seller who, in turn, would deposit them for safekeeping, often with the same banker. Everyone soon found that it was a lot easier simply to use the deposit receipts directly as a means of payment. These receipts, which became known as notes, were acceptable as money since whoever held them could go to the banker and exchange them for metallic money. Then, bankers discovered that they could make loans merely by giving their promises to pay, or bank notes, to borrowers. In this way, banks began to create money. More notes could be issued than the gold and coin on hand because only a portion of the notes outstanding would be presented for payment at any one time. Enough metallic money had to be kept on hand, or course, to redeem whatever volume of notes was presented for payment. Transaction deposits are the modern counterpart of bank notes.

It was a small step from printing notes to making book entries crediting deposits of borrowers, which the borrowers in turn

could "spend" by writing checks, thereby "printing" their own money.

*(Federal Reserve Bank of Chicago – Modern Money Mechanics)*

As mentioned in Chapter Five: Eradicating Public Debt, money is created mainly within computer book entries instead of Federal Reserve notes being printed or actual coins being minted. To better understand the Federal Reserve Bank of Chicago's description of money creation, it is best to see it unfold in the court of law, straight from the bankers. In First National Bank of Montgomery v. Jerome Daly, in the Justice Court, State of Minnesota, County of Scott, Township of Credit River case; Jerome Daly was an attorney in Minnesota and also the defendant in an unlawful detainer action in the justice of the peace court where Martin V. Mahoney was the justice of the peace. In this case, the bank sought possession of the property it had already foreclosed the mortgage on. The Jury decided against the bank, all the while Daly did not prevail. In addition to learning the remedies of Express Trust, the case will reveal in great detail why the property reverted to the bank from an appeal and not to the defendant.

JUDGMENT AND DECREE

The above entitled action came on before the Court and Jury of 12 December 7, 1968 at 10:00 am. Plaintiff appeared by its President Lawrence V. Morgan and was represented by its Counsel, R. Mellby. Defendant appeared on his own behalf.

A Jury of Talesmen were called, impaneled and sworn to try the issues in the case. Lawrence V. Morgan was the only witness called for Plaintiff and Defendant testified as the only witness in his own behalf.

Plaintiff brought this as a Common Law action for the recovery of the possession of Lot 19 Fairview Beach, Scott County, Minn. Plaintiff claimed title to the Real Property in question by foreclosure of a Note and Mortgage Deed dated may 8, 1964 which Plaintiff claimed was in default at the time foreclosure proceedings were started.

Defendant appeared and answered that the Plaintiff created the money and credit upon its own books by bookkeeping entry as the consideration for the Note and Mortgage of May 8, 1964 and alleged failure of the consideration for the Mortgage Deed and alleged that the Sheriff's sale passed no title to plaintiff.

The issues tried to the Jury were whether there was a lawful consideration and whether defendant had waived his rights to complain about the consideration having paid on the Note for almost 3 years.

Morgan admitted that all of the money or credit which was used as a consideration was created upon their booked, that this was standard banking practice exercised by their bank in combination with the Federal Reserve Bank of Minneapolis, another private Bank, further that he knew of no United States Statute or Law that gave the Plaintiff the authority to do this. Plaintiff further claimed that defendant by using the ledger book created credit and by paying on the Note and Mortgage waived any right to complain about the Consideration and that the defendant was estopped from doing so.

At 12:15 on December 7, 1968 the Jury returned a unanimous verdict for the defendant.

Now therefore, by virtue of the authority vested in me pursuant to eh Declaration of Independence, the Northwest Ordinance of 1787, the Constitution of United States and the Constitution and the laws of the State of Minnesota not inconsistent therewith;

IT IS HEREBY ORDEred, ADJUDGED AND DECREED:

1. That the Plaintiff is not entitled to recover the possession of Lot 19, Fairview Beach, Scott County, Minnesota according to the Plat thereof on file in the Register of Deeds office.

2. That because of failure of a lawful consideration the Note and Mortgage dated May 8, 1964 are null and void.

3. That the Sheriff's sale of the above described premises held on June 26, 1967 is null and void, of no effect.

4. That the Plaintiff has not right title or interest in said premises or lien thereon as is above described.

5. That any provision in the Minnesota Constitution and any Minnesota Statute binding the jurisdiction of this court is repugnant to the Constitution of the United States and to the Bill of Rights of the Minnesota Constitution and is null and void and that this court has jurisdiction to render complete justice in this Cause.

The following memorandum and any supplementary memorandum made and filed by this court in support of this judgment is hereby made a part hereof by reference.

BY THE COURT

Dated December 9, 1968

Justice MARTIN V. MAHONEY

Credit River Township

Scott County, Minnesota

MEMORANDUM

The issues in this case were simple. There was no material dispute of the facts for the Jury to resolve.

Plaintiff admitted that it, in combination with the federal Reserve Bank of Minneapolis, which are for all practical purposes, because of their interlocking activity and practices, and both being Banking Institutions Incorporated under the Laws of the United States, are in the law to be treated as one and the same bank, did create the entire $14,000.00 in money or credit upon its own books by bookkeeping entry. That this was the Consideration used to support the Note dated May 8, 1964 and the Mortgage of the same date. The money and credit first came into existence when they created it. Mr. Morgan admitted that no United States Law Statute existed which gave him the right to do this. A Company v. Emma Mason, 44 Minn. 318, 46 N.W. 558. The Jury found that there was no consideration and I agree. Only God can create something of value out of nothing.

Even if defendant could be charged with waiver or estoppel as a matter of law this is no defense to the Plaintiff. The law leaves wrongdoers where it finds them. See sections 50, 51 and 52 of Am Jur 2nd "Actions" on page 584 – "no action will lie to recover on a claim based upon, or in any manner depending upon, a fraudulent, illegal, or immoral transaction or contract to which Plaintiff was a party."

Plaintiff's act of creating credit is not authorized by the Constitution and Laws of the United States, is unconstitutional and void, and is not a lawful consideration in the eyes of the law to support anything or upon which any lawful right can be built.

Nothing in the Constitution of the United States limits the jurisdiction of this court, which is one of original jurisdiction with right of trial by Jury guaranteed. This is a Common Law action. Minnesota cannot limit or impair the power of this court to render Complete Justice between the parties. Any provisions in the Constitution and laws of Minnesota which attempt to do so is repugnant to the Constitution of the United States and void. No question as to the Jurisdiction of this Court was raised by either party at the trial. Both parties were given complete liberty to submit any and all facts to the Jury, at least in so far as they saw fit.

No complaint was made by Plaintiff that Plaintiff did not receive a fair trial. From the admissions made by Mr. Morgan the path of duty was direct and clear for the Jury. Their Verdict could not reasonably been otherwise. justice was rendered completely and without denial, promptly and without delay, freely and without purchase, conformable to the laws in this Court on December 7, 1968.

BY THE COURT

Dated December 9, 1968

Justice MARTIN V. MAHONEY

Credit River Township

Scott County, Minnesota

It is revealed by the Justice of the Court that the arguments of the defendant were true given that the plaintiff could not produce any evidence that the bank did not create the money or credit from their bookkeeping as lawful consideration. The Justice of the Court also revealed that the defendant could not recover his property in a "Common Law action" because all Common law actions only have jurisdiction within a court of equity or chancery. The justice could not speak on a matter of equity while in a court of law (civil law) being that the arguments were in the realm of trust law and the defendant did not have an Express Trust as the owner of the property; registered with the court, giving the justice jurisdiction to even hear and speak on the matters of the Common Law. Had Daly correctly used a trust to fight this battle in equity court, First National Bank of Montgomery most likely would have never appeared in court but instead opt for settling out of court to escape the financial damages of equity and more importantly to escape the case becoming precedence.

All National Associations (banks or credit unions) engage in fraudulent mortgages by breaking the very laws that govern them, such as the National Currency Act of 1863. The banks break many sections of the act; however, three are worth examining, which the Express Trust can and should pursue in a court of equity to cancel the debt.

And be it further enacted, That it shall be unlawful for any officer acting under the provisions of this act to countersign or deliver to any such association, or to any company or person, any circulating notes contemplated by this act, except as hereinbefore provided, and in accordance with the true intent and meaning of this act; and any officer who shall violate the provisions of this section shall be deemed guilty of a high misdemeanor, and on conviction thereof shall be punished by fine not exceeding double the amount so countersigned and delivered, and imprisonment not exceeding fifteen years, at the discretion of the court in which he shall be tried.

*(Section 33 – National Currency Act of 1863)*

A countersign is defined as adding a signature to a document already signed by another person. All Presidents, CEOs, CFOs, Cashiers, or Secretaries countersign the received promissory notes or, better yet, the 1003 Mortgage Application before submitting to the Federal Reserve window for a deposit. In return, credits are applied to the banks bookkeeping to fund the loan. These applications come from all types of mortgages from fixed-rate, adjustable-rate, FHA, VA, USDA, Jumbo, Interest-only, Conventional, Conforming, Government-backed, and Reverse Mortgages. In other words, the note or the mortgage application is a check that the applicant signs with the social security number creating the money, distributed to the escrow closing table. The note is sold within open market operations and never to be seen again. According to Section 22 of the National Currency Act, only the comptroller can receive notes or bonds with countersigning duties. If the Express Trust were to request discovery in a court of equity, a certified copy of the front and back of the note displaying the bank officer's signature, with or without the comptroller's signature then the bank has violated section 33 of the act, facing severe penalties.

> And be it further enacted, That every association may take, reserve, receive, and charge on any loan, or discount made, or upon any note, bill of exchange, or other evidence of debt, such rate of interest or discount as is for the time the established rate of interest for delay in the payment of money, in the absence of contract between the parties, by the laws of several States in which the associations are respectively located, and no more: Provided, however, That interest may be reserved or taken, in advance, at the time of making the loan or discount, according to the usual rules of banking; and the knowingly taking, reserving, or charging of a rate of interest greater than that allowed by this section shall be held and adjudged a forfeiture of the debt or demand on which the same is taken, reserved, or charged; but the purchase, discount, or sale of a bill of exchange, drawn on actually existing values, and payable at another place than the place of such purchase, discount, or sale, at the current discount or premium, shall not be considered as taking, reserving, or charging interest.

(Section 46 – National Currency Act of 1863)

In 2003, of all new mortgages, 10.2 percent were interest-only, meaning the homeowner paid only the interest for the loan's initial period. In some areas of the united States of America where homes are expensive, these loans were prevalent in most California cities, Denver, Washington, Phoenix, and Seattle. Interest-only loans represented 40 percent or more of all mortgages issued in 2005. Traditionally, interest-only loans and adjustable-rate loans were used by people who expected to live in a house only a short time. Still, such loans have turned into "affordability products" as housing prices rose. The interest rate on the loans, while below that of conventional 30-year fixed-rate mortgages at the beginning, resets after 3, 5, 7, or 10 years, depending on the loan. Borrowers who took out loans in 2004 could find, for example, that their initial 4.25 percent loan increased to 6.25 percent or 7.25 percent in the following year. This is another violation of Section 46 of the National Currency Act. It is unlawful for a bank to provide such a loan where usury/interest can frequently change past the initial rate when the note was accepted. If the Express Trust were to bring this type of suit into a court of equity, the alleged debt would be adjudged as a forfeit.

> And be it further enacted, That all transfer of the notes, bonds, bills of exchange, and other evidences of debt owing to any association, or of deposits to its credit; all assignments of mortgages, sureties on real estate, or of judgments or decrees in its favor; all deposits of money, bullion, or other valuable thing

for its use, or for the use of any of its shareholders or creditors; and all payments of money to either, made after the commission of an act of insolvency, or in contemplation thereof, with a view to prevent the application of its assets in the manner prescribed by this act, or with a view to the preference of one creditor to another, except in payment of its circulating notes, shall be utterly null and void.

*(Section 49 – National Currency Act of 1863)*

Insolvency is defined as the inability to pay a debt or obligation. When referring to mortgages, it is within God's ordinances that his trust beneficiaries do not accept mortgages. Confirmed in Proverbs 22:26,

Be not one of those who shakes hands in a pledge, One of those who is surety for debts;

*(New King James Version)*

The word surety in Hebrew is Arab, meaning mortgage and the etymology of mortgage comes from the Old French word "morgage," literally meaning "dead pledge." Mort "dead" and gage "pledge" because mortgages are designed for constant refinancing on the property, which resets the amortization payment schedule in terms of term length. The alleged homeowner is under the impression they are making payments, principal, and interest towards homeownership upon final payment of the mortgage. In all actuality, the Deeds of Trust or Warranty Deeds clearly state that the alleged homeowner is making "leasehold payments" and "ground rents" as leasehold tenants. The State of Maryland provides ground rent detail. In the Greater-Baltimore area, ground rent is a periodic monetary payment by a tenant to a ground leaseholder who holds a reversionary interest in the property or "ground" underneath a home. Specific terms and conditions are contingent on the actual language of the ground lease. Still, such a lease often require payment from the lessee (homeowner) of between $50-$150 per year, commonly paid in semi-annual installments. In practical effect, a homeowner who is subject to a ground rent must make payment to a ground leaseholder for the right to dwell on the property. The property's absolute management and control remain with the leasehold tenant so long as the ground rent is paid *(Beehler v. Ijams, 72 Md. 193 (1890))*.

Consequently, the leasehold tenant has the authority to alter, remodel and reconstruct the property as he/she wills. The tenant must still ensure that their actions leave the reversioner's rent secure *(Crowe v. Wilson, 65 Md. 479, 484 (1886))*. The alleged homeowner is responsible for maintaining the land and any improvements on the land, including improvements made to the home itself *(Kolker v. Biggs, 203 Md. 137, 141 (1953))*. It is the alleged homeowner's "sole" responsibility to procure and make the payment on any utilities that service the property. In addition to the "Failure To Disclose Information" the banks' misleading statements within the note, states that the alleged homeowner will pay leasehold payments as tenants instead of payments toward proper ownership, would automatically position the alleged homeowner in a state of insolvency. In this case, the argument is self-explanatory, as the plaintiff cannot fulfill a promise to pay attached to a misleading Deed of Trust or Warranty Deed. Title 23 – Equity – Georgia Code § 23-2-52 – Misrepresentation as Legal Fraud, states,

> Misrepresentation of a material fact, made willfully to deceive or recklessly without knowledge and acted on by the opposite party or made innocently and mistakenly and acted on by the opposite party, constitutes legal fraud.

Furthermore, when the mortgage is sold or transferred to another creditor or lender atop the insolvency claim, it further provides a stronger case for violation of Section 49 of the National Currency Act, and the Express Trust would have the chancellor in equity court deem the evidence of debt null and void. The ground rents and leasehold payments are compiled inside the county property tax payment. If the tenant(s) do not pay the leaseholder, the county will foreclose the property despite the mortgage amount. Taxes trump mortgages and trust ownership trumps taxes because trust could never hold the status of a tenant in commons but only a natural person with fee simple title. In many counties, the actual ground leaseholder is listed within the property's legal description, referring to the ground underneath the property. For example,

‑ EXCEPTING ALL MINERALS, OIL, GAS AND OTHER HYDROCARBON SUBSTANCES BELOW A DEPTH OF 500 FEET WITHOUT RIGHT OF SURFACE ENTRY AS RESERVED BY CORPORATION OF THE PRESIDENT OF THE SAN BERNARDINO STAKE OF THE CHURCH OF JESUS CHRIST OF LATTER-DAY SAINTS, A CORPORATION SOLE, IN DOCUMENT RECORDED SEPTEMBER 22, 1983 AS INSTRUMENT NO. 19XXX7, OFFICIAL RECORDS.

Many patriots attempt to raise allegations of property trespassing against the banks and other corporations in courts "at law" and most assuredly always lose the case due to suing in the wrong capacity. Equity suits must rely on the use of a natural person, the Express Trust, and not as the individual, John Doe Smith. John Smith is a fourteenth amendment person who, according to section 5 of the amendment, Congress has the power to enforce the provisions of the amendment by appropriate legislation. That particular legislation is Section 4, which clearly states that no fourteenth amendment person can question the public debt's validity (mortgages, taxes, and loans). Understanding that most courts currently in business in America are, by the 1933 change in the operation of law, courts of limited jurisdiction, limited to cases involving subject-matter of the fourteenth amendment public trust, it becomes clear that whether they are distinguished as federal courts or state courts, such is a distinction without a fundamental difference they are inherently federal. To get at how such courts may obtain jurisdiction over an Express Trust or its trustee(s) in legal action, the nature of jurisdiction should be brief but sufficiently examined.

First, a court must have three essentials: jurisdiction to determine jurisdiction, jurisdiction over the subject-matter of the case (i.e., it must have the power/competence to decide the kind of controversy involved), and jurisdiction over the parties to the case; and any order, decree or judgment, other than dismissal, by such a court is void ab initio, having only the semblance or appearance of validity, and may be attached directly or collaterally and vacated at any time.

*See Morris v. Gilmer, 129 U.S. 315, 326-327 (1889). Once a judge has knowledge that subject-matter jurisdiction is lacking, he has no discretion but to dismiss the action, and failure to do so subjects the judge to personal liability.*

The Express Trust's jurisdiction can only be given to the court if the trust does not pass the court and control test. The control and court test are not met if one or more United States Persons does not have the authority to control all substantial decisions of the trust. No person has the power to veto any of the substantial decisions. This is why the Express Trust must have a sole foreign trustee at all times to maintain the trust as foreign from the United States. A guide to create a perfectly valid Express Trust instrument that can be registered within the probate court as a continuous open probate case in the Settlor's name or, depending on the state, within the county recorder's office will be reviewed on the following page. Every state/country is different from the next and it's laws recording Express Trust varies and will require in-depth study.

## DECLARATION OF TRUST
## Est. Month Day Year at Time

THIS INDENTURE ("Agreement") made this XX day of Month, Year serves as a Declaration of Express Trust and shall continue for a term of twenty-five (25) years from this day, between CHRISTOPHER ALEXANDER WELLINGTON herein known as the Settlor and Trust Protector, (the first party) and AHMED-EL BEN Sole Trustee, herein known as the First Trustee or Trustee, (the second party), under the name of HEINZ WOLFGANG EXPRESS TRUST d/b/a HEINZ WOLFGANG. With this contract, the Parties intend to create an Express Trust Organization for the benefit of the Trust Certificate Unit Holders and to identify, accumulate, purchase and hold any assets that become available and to provide for a prudent administration and distribution system administered by legal persons acting in a fiduciary capacity.

WITNESSETH: Whereas the Settlor, irrevocably assigns and conveys to the Trustee, in trust, specific properties as defined in The Trustee Minutes (X-1234), attached to this document in exchange for one hundred (100) units of Beneficial Interest, known hereto as

Trust Certificate Units (TCUs) to be held with this Indenture by the Trustees for the Beneficiaries also known as Members of HEINZ WOLFGANG EXPRESS TRUST d/b/a HEINZ WOLFGANG.

Trust: "Trust" includes an Express Trust, private or charitable, with additions thereto, wherever and however created.

Property: "Property" means anything that may be the subject of ownership and includes both real and personal property.

Person: "Person" means any natural person, individual, corporation, government or governmental subdivision or agency, business trust, estate, trust, partnership, limited liability company, association, or other entity.

Settlor: CHRISTOPHER ALEXANDER WELLINGTON – (defined) in law a **settlor** is a person who settles property in trust law for the benefit of beneficiaries. In some legal systems, a **settlor** is also referred to as a trustor or occasionally, a grantor or donor... A **settlor** may create a trust manifesting an intention to create it; grantor is the person who creates the trust.

Trust Protector: CHRISTOPHER ALEXANDER WELLINGTON or other authorized person in the future by settlor, – (defined) appointed under the trust instrument to direct, restrain, remove the trustee(s) or appoint a successor.

Trustee(s): AHMED-EL BEN – (defined) includes an original, additional, or successor **trustee**, whether or not appointed or confirmed by a court. A person or firm that holds or administers property or assets for the benefit of a third party and can be given the powers to make investment decisions for the Trust, or vote on the distribution of assets to the beneficiaries and/or has the power to hire persons whether an authorized person or not, including accountants, attorneys, auditors, investment advisers, appraisers or other agents even if they are associated or affiliated with the **trustee**, to advise or assist the **trustee** in the performance of administrative duties.

Beneficial Owner: HEINZ WOLFGANG herein known as the First Beneficiary and other beneficiaries to come in future (defined) **beneficial owner** is where specific property rights ("use and title") in equity belong to a person even though legal title of the property belongs to another person. This often relates where the legal title owner has implied trustee duties to the beneficial owner.

WHEREAS, the Trust Organization is authorized to exist and function through its Board of Trustees, comprised of the total active number of trustees who are legal persons holding fee simple title, not differentiating between legal and equitable, not as individuals, but collectively as the Board, according to the inalienable Common Law rights.

WHEREAS, the Trust shall be amendable, as described in the bylaws, and shall be irrevocable by the Settlor or by any other person or entity but said trustee can be fired by the Trust Protector and replace by new trustee appointed by the Trust Protector. It is the intention of the Settlor to make the Beneficiaries, an absolute gift of the Trust Certificate Units (TCUs), in which the Beneficiaries shall not have any vested interest, until the termination of this Trust and final distribution accumulated assets or any early distribution of the assets thereof. There shall be exactly 100 Trust Certificate Units (TCUs) available to the Beneficiaries.

WHEREAS, the Trust shall be administered, managed, governed and regulated in all respects applicable to Common Law jurisdiction of California, the Uniform Prudent Investors Act (UPIA), the Uniform Trustees Powers Act, Treaty of Marrakesh, Treaty of Tripoli, the Constitution of the United States of America and the Uniform Commercial Code (only when and if applicable and/or allowable to remain under the jurisdiction of the Common Law). The domicile of the Trust is within the Court of Equity, in California in the Republic of the United States of America as a last resort when everything else fails.

Last Name, First Name Middle Settlor/Trust Protector Date

Last Name, First Name Middle Sole Trustee Date

## DECLARATION OF TRUST

### Est. Month Day Year at Time

TRUSTEE MINUTES: X-1234

HEINZ WOLFGANG

(An Irrevocable Express Trust Organization)

Date: Weekday, Month Day, Year

The Settlor appoints Wellington, Christopher Alexander as the Trust Protector (first party) being present accepted the appointment and acceptance of Trust Property.

The Settlor appoints Ahmed-El Ben as the First Trustee or Trustee (second party) being present accepted the appointment and affixed their signature below.

Trustee called the meeting to order and affirmed that officially on Month Day, Year the Trust was established and all Personal Property, whether Tangible or Intangible and all "In Real Property" located in California or any other State, received now or in future, is held in Trust. The Sole Trustee's acceptance is listed on Schedule A and the Personal Property is listed on Schedule B.

Trustee approved the initial exchange of the specific property for one hundred (100) units of Beneficial Interest, known hereto as Trust Certificate Units (TCUs) to be held with this Indenture by the Trustees for the Beneficiaries also known as Members of HEINZ WOLFGANG EXPRESS TRUST d/b/a HEINZ WOLFGANG.

**The TRUSTEE shall:**

1. Keep minutes of all future business meetings and Board of Trustee meetings

2.  Act in the best interest of all Trust Certificate Unit Holders through prudent record keeping of certificate transfers and other business respecting the holders and this Express Trust.

Being no other business before the Board, the meeting was adjourned.

Principal place of Meeting: Dam 9, 1012 JS Amsterdam, Netherlands

This shall serve as our written acknowledgement and acceptance of the office as appointed herein this Weekday, Month Day, Year.

DECLARATION OF TRUST

Est. Month Day Year at Time

Schedule A: Trustee Minutes X-1234

Appointment of a Trustee

Minutes of Meeting of

HEINZ WOLFGANG

 (An Irrevocable Express Trust Organization)

"Time":

Date: Weekday, Month Day, Year

Persons Present: Settlor & Sole Trustee

Business Conducted: Appointment of Trusteeship

1. The Sole Trustee (second party) met with the Settlor and Trust Protector, Wellington, Christopher Alexander (first party) regarding his appointment as Sole Trustee of the HEINZ WOLFGANG EXPRESS TRUST d/b/a HEINZ WOLFGANG, an Irrevocable Express Trust Organization.

2. After discussion, it was mutually agreed that; Ahmed-El Ben would accept the appointment as Sole Trustee by contract.

3. The following action was taken as a result of that agreement. The acceptance agreement described herein on the "Schedule A: Trustee Minutes X-1234" was signed and these minutes were entered into the Trust records.

There being no further business to come before the Officers of the Trust, the meeting was adjourned at "Time."

Last Name, First Name Middle Name Sole Trustee Date

## DECLARATION OF TRUST

### Est. Month Day Year at Time

Schedule B: Trustee Minutes X-1234

Minutes of Meeting

Other Property Exchange – Non-Real Estate Assets

HEINZ WOLFGANG

(An Irrevocable Express Trust Organization)

At this meeting, the Board of Trustees of the HEINZ WOLFGANG EXPRESS TRUST, held in Los Angeles, California on this XX day of Month, Year, with the Sole Trustee being present, by unanimous accord, the following was affirmed and ratified, vis:

1.  All personal property, whether Tangible or Intangible located in California, received now or in the future is now held in trust.

2.  The Trustee has authorized the Authorized Representative to warehouse the Trust's non-Real Estate property wherever the Authorized Representative deems to be the safest and most convenient location to manage said property.

The Settlor, Wellington, Christopher Alexander (first party) by gift of the following said Personal Property to the Sole Trustee (second party) is now held in Trust for the beneficiaries:

a.  Fifty ounces of Au

b.  Two Hundred ounces of Ag

c.  35% XAU mining stock

d. Foreign Currency: Vietnam Dong and Iraqi Dinar (Central Bank of Iraq)

e. All accounts in the name CHRISTOPHER ALEXANDER Family of WELLINGTON ESTATE d/b/a CHRISTOPHER ALEXANDER WELLINGTON

There being no further business to come before the Officers of the Trust, the meeting was adjourned at "Time."

Last Name, First Name Middle Name Sole Trustee Date

This concludes the drafting of a functional Declaration of Trust. A proof of service signed under penalty of perjury under the laws of the united States of America (28 U.S.C. § 1746(1)) and a state-approved Notary Certificate of Acknowledgment would accompany the declaration as to its last two pages.

An adequately registered foreign Express Trust can give the trust access to top offshore bank accounts. Most offshore banks are closed to Americans. 95% of the best foreign banks have shut their doors to Americans because of the costly reporting now required by the I.R.S. The only way to get into the best banks is through the back door. The Foreign Account Tax Compliance Act now requires banks to spend hundreds of millions on computer generate annual reports that go to the I.R.S. Foreign banks have stricter compliance and U.S. reporting requirements than U.S. banks. The bottom line is no top tier foreign bank wants to do business with an American holding a U.S. Passport, at least not directly. The back door into these top offshore banks is a foreign trust. The national from the U.S.A., the settlor and owner of the assets in the structure, would then appoint the foreign trustee to protect the assets for the heirs' benefit. The trustee would then hire an investment advisor, usually based in Switzerland. This person has master accounts at the largest investment banks and can obtain access with scrutiny. The foreign trust can use its capital to buy a private placement life insurance policy or a High Cash Value Whole Life Insurance Policy on the settlor. Any gains inside the policy which is owned by the trust are tax-deferred until liquidated. If never closed, then the money passes to the beneficiaries tax-free.

In conclusion, the Express Trust is a powerful weapon that has promoted generational wealth and the ultimate protection against corporate discrimination and fraud upon trust property. At this particular time, the world has come subject to the ramifications of the world economic pandemic, known as the Corona Virus (COVID-19), which is currently undergoing new strands of mutation. The vaccine is not currently mandatory by the government for everyone to be inoculated; however, major corporations, such as United Airlines, are preparing to issue mandatory vaccination efforts to their employees. It will be the corporations, not the government, which will cause discomfort to everyday consumers when it comes to normal life activities. Many schools of thought believe the vaccine has yet to be tested long enough to be trusted. As of January 15, 2021, 181 people have died from taking the COVID-19 vaccination per the Vaccine Adverse Event Reporting System (VAERS). The VAERS reports describe outcomes ranging from "foaming at the mouth" to massive heart attacks." A Miami obstetrician, Dr. Gregory Michael, suffered from a hemorrhagic stroke after receiving Pfizer/BioNtech's COVID vaccine. He died two weeks later. Pfizer stated that it didn't believe there were any direct connections to the vaccine; however, data regarding deaths are emerging from Israel, Norway, Portugal, Sweden, and Switzerland with fatal outcomes. Another public figure, Henry Louis Aaron, nicknamed "Hammer" or "Hammerin' Hank," was an American professional baseball right fielder who played 23 seasons in Major League Baseball. Aaron himself surpassed Babe Ruth as he closed in on the 714 career home runs record. He had received the COVID-19 vaccination on January 5, 2021, at the Morehouse School of Medicine in Atlanta, Georgia. He and several other "African American" public figures, including activist Joe Beasley, Andrew Young, and Louis Sullivan, did so to demonstrate the vaccine's safety and encourage other Black Americans (i.e., Moors) to do the same. Aaron died just weeks later, on January 22, 2021, at 86, conveniently listed as natural causes. Pharma and Federal agencies are attributing the majority of these cases to "coincidence." Amid this devastating news, Congress members have passed legislation for mandatory vaccinations to all children who attend public and secondary schools. This legislation is coming from the 116th Congress, 1st Session, H.R. 2527 on May 3, 2019, for a State or political subdivision to be eligible to receive "grants," not for the well-being of the children. The bill is as follows,

Be it enacted by the Senate and House of Representatives of the United States of America in Congress assembled,

SECTION 1. SHORT TITLE.

This Act may be cited as the "Vaccinate All Children Act of 2019."

SEC. 2. REQUIRING STUDENTS AT PUBLIC ELEMENTARY AND SECONDARY SCHOOLS TO BE VACCINATED.

1. Requirement. – Section 317 of the Public Health Service Act (42 U.S.C. 247b) is amended by adding at the end of the following:

(n) Requiring Students at Public Elementary and Secondary Schools To Be Vaccinated. –

"(1) REQUIREMENT. – For a State or a political subdivision or other public entity of a State to be eligible to receive a grant under this section, the applicant shall demonstrate to the Secretary's satisfaction that, subject to paragraphs (2) and (3), the State requires each student enrolled in one of the State's public elementary schools or public secondary schools to be vaccinated in accordance with the recommendations of the Advisory Committee on Immunization Practices.

All this to say, if it ever comes to the point of mandatory vaccination, the Express Trust provides a veil of protection. If such a one chose not to receive the COVID-19 vaccine due to uncertainties; no State or corporation may violate a private contract such as the Declaration of Trust. The Express Trust would sue any corporation in equity court, should any corporation bring about discrimination with claims such as,

"The equity under trust or contract for value is superior to that of a mere volunteer;"

*(Georgia Code § 23-1-13)*

"When one of two innocent persons must suffer by the act of a third person, he who put it in the power of the third person to inflict the injury shall bear the loss;"

*(Georgia Code § 23-1-14)*

"No National emergency or Executive Order, including but not limited to The Act of October 6th, 1917, as amended [12 U.S.C. Sec, 95a] March 9, 1933, shall nullify any of the Constitutional Protections of this "Trust Estate." "No Emergency justifies a violation of any constitutional provision." 16 Am Jur 2nd Ed.71, 72 "The prohibitions of the federal constitution are designed to apply to all branches of the national government and cannot be nullified by the executive and senate combined;"

*(Reid v. Covert, ant, U.S. 1,1-Ed 2nd 1148 (1951))*

"Actual fraud consists of any kind of artifice by which another is deceived. Constructive fraud consists of any act of omission or commission, contrary to legal or equitable duty, trust, or confidence justly reposed, which is contrary to good conscience and operates to the injury of another;"

*(Georgia Code § 23-2-51(b))*

Preserving and keeping the wealth earned and held in Express Trust should be entrusted to the Sole Trustee to deposit into the foreign bank account, whether offshore or within the united States of America. The trustee may open any business checking account, financial account, trust account, etc., which he/she is authorized by the declaration to open, but he/she must keep in mind that by doing so, the trust will participate directly in that unincorporated interstate banking association with all its limited-liability consequences. There is only one type of account that avoids those consequences, which is the non-interest bearing account. The trustee can ask the banker to select this option when setting up the account. When utilized in conjunction with the following banking practices, the trust and the trustee will remain out of public policy –

- Never contract for any credit cards, lines of credit, or C.D.s and if the trust has already obtained them, rescind and cancel the contracts;

- Open a non-interest bearing checking account to avoid the "privileges and immunities" associated with interest;

- Maintain the minimum required balance at all times;

- Use the trust account solely for depositing checks or money orders when transacting business;

- Never send or allow checks to be sent across state lines without a DBA in that state;

- Instead of writing checks, use postal money orders or the bank's corporate certified checks or corporate money orders when sending interstate payments; and

- Use a bonded or non-bonded agent to establish the account on behalf of the trustee.

As mentioned before, domestic banks within the United States backed by the F.D.I.C., cannot do business with any foreign tax identifying number which does not have an SSN/ITIN in correlation with it. Therefore, another Trust EIN will need to be obtained in the trust's name. Using Mr. Wellington as the example, the following essential steps should be applied via the online EIN application for his trust affairs.

- 1. Identity: Select "Trust"

- 1. Identity: Select "Irrevocable Trust"

- 2. Authenticate: Enter "Full birth name and social security number as the responsible party"

- 2. Authenticate: Again Enter "Full birth name as the co-trustee"

- 3. Address: Enter "Full private mailing address"

- 4. Details: Enter "HEINZ WOLFGANG EXPRESS TRUST as the Legal Trust Name, followed by the county and state of place of business and month and year trust was established."

- 4. Details: Select "No as there are no employees"

- 5. EIN Confirmation: Select "Receive Letter Online"

The new Trust EIN should have a 6/7 Million Series following the dash which means the entity is tax exempt under TEFRA laws. When opening a non-interest bearing trust account, the I.R.S. Form W-9 should be given to the bank manager with TEFRA provided in both sections of box 4. Just as the estate utilizes a corporate seal, the trust should have its own seal attached to the Declaration of Trust and the Trust Certification. The Declaration of Trust is more a private document kept in a safe place but the Trust Certification mirrors key information from the declaration and can be disbursed within the public. It should be given to the bank to open the non-interest bearing trust account. Most banks will attempt to convert the Express Trust from a Common Law jurisdiction to the United States jurisdiction by not accepting the Trust Certification and using the banks internal forms. In the event of this occurring, simply copy the written language from the declaration and certification to the banks internal form stating,

"WHEREAS, the Trust Organization is authorized to exist and function through its Board of Trustees, comprised of the total active number of trustees who are legal persons holding fee simple title, not differentiating between legal and equitable, not as individuals, but collectively as the Board, according to the inalienable Common Law rights."

Corporate seal selection for a trust can be anything, however selecting a familiar insigne that the U.S. government would recognize is ideal. Only two insigne's would suffice as a recognizable seal. They are the exact seals the various Sheriff departments use under Moroccan treaty law; the Seal of David or the Seal of Solomon. Analyzing the Sheriff's badge of the County of San Bernardino and the badge of the County of Riverside will reveal which trust the two county Sheriff's are subjected to. Riverside County is under the Seal of David and San Bernardino County is under the Seal of Solomon. The Express Trust must do the same. Further evidence and research of the Sheriff's governed authority can be found in Morocco (General Act of Algeciras), signed April 7, 1906. Chapter 1, page 467, reads,

## Declaration relative to the organization of the police

Article 1. The conference summoned by His Majesty the Sultan to pronounce on the measures necessary to organize the police declares that the following provisions should be made;

Article 2. The police shall be under the sovereign authority of His Majesty the Sultan. It shall be recruited by the Maghzen from Moorish Mohamedans, commanded by Moorish Kaids, and distributed in the eight ports open to commerce.

Article 3. In order to aid the Sultan in the organization of this police, Spanish officers and noncommissioned officers as instructors, and French officers and noncommissioned officers as instructors, shall be placed at His disposal by their respective Governments, which shall submit their designation to the approval of His Shereefian Majesty.

*(34 Stat. 2905; Treaty Series 456)*

Every State, County, Province, City, Town or any municipal police force is under that municipality's Shereefian Majesty, who is submitted unto the Sultan, which explains the specific seal types worn over the Sheriff's heart in uniform. The Sheriff is likened to the President of his/her respective county.

The trust account serves as a close access account to preserve any financial assets from any future financial crisis or depressions by enrolling the trust account EIN under the foreign 98 tax identifying number using I.R.S. Form 8832.

Last but not least, due attention must be paid to the Internal Revenue Service, for they are the lawful, legal entity, duly authorized to collect association dues (income taxes) from fourteenth amendment citizens and other persons volunteering and availing themselves of the "privileges and immunities" regarding non-payment of debts in the system implanted under former H.J. Res, 12 U.S.C. § 95a, and 15 U.S.C., Ch. 41, §1602(c)(d)(e). It may come as a shock; the I.R.S. also refunds foreign trust all of their business expenses related to all forms of indirect inflation, taxes or interest applied to payments through the tax year. The process of filing taxes under the foreign Express Trust to receive its annual business expenses as a payment to the trust from the Internal Revenue Service may be delivered in another writing in the near future. It is always advised to seek the counsel of a tax professional for any filing with any entity type.

The only way to thrive in the twenty-first century North America is to "own nothing but control everything." And though any trustee is the legal owner of the property in trust, the trustee(s) of Express Trusts do not experience the incidents of personal ownership due to properly limited liability via trust instrument and the utter shrewdness of the trustee(s). Under the Express Trust, the trustee is clothed in a veil impenetrable but from within. This suit of armor is the trust instrument, which molds the trustee in all of their good-faith dealings on behalf of the trust, all without the excessive weight of inquisitorial legislation. When one is a trustee, he is in a fiduciary position looked upon with respect for the position's integrity. Usually, there are three prominent positions (settlor, trustee, and beneficiary) fulfilled by at least two persons in trust. The settlor can be the trustee, trust protector but never the beneficiary, fulfilling all three prominent positions. The trustee can be a beneficiary and trust protector but never the settlor, also fulfilling all three prominent positions. However, private Express Trust has utilized the term "sole" to acquire a position while escaping the judgment of a "sham trust," meanwhile surpassing the United States court and control test. For example, Mr. Wellington can be the settlor, trust protector, co-trustee, and "sole" beneficiary. A sole beneficiary is an entity designated to receive all of the assets associated with the trust. As long as the foreign trustee has accepted the position of "sole" trustee and not fulfilling any positions as a beneficiary, Mr. Wellington can perform limited duties as a co-trustee delegated to him by the sole trustee. For a sole beneficiary to exist, Mr. Wellington must include other beneficiaries within the trust. These very rules are substantiated by biblical treaty law that fully protects the trust in honor and allows it to be the only Zero Percent tax bracket strategy that does not rely on ever-changing tax-cut codes and statutes or retirement. The Express Trust under foreign jurisdiction within equity or chancery court will provide asset and family protection, rightful claim to one's estates (inheritance), actual ownership and control of land and property, and generational wealth.

The Americas are a part of the Mehomitan Nation (Morocco; ancient Egypt) with descendible inheritance for all who choose to operate in God's ordinances within the biblical treaty expressed by trust instrumentation. About Moroccan-American history relations, dating back to the late eighteenth century, the Sultan Sidi Muhammad Ben Abdellah issued a declaration in December 1777, asking the Americans to conclude with his majesty (Great Britain) a treaty of peace and friendship. President Joe Biden, former Vice-President under President Barrack Obama, stated this fact at the Global Entrepreneurship Summit in Marrakech, Morocco, on November 20, 2014. Surprisingly, the decree has its roots with ancient Egypt and the Great Pharaoh alongside his governor Joseph, as written in the book of Genesis in the bible, for the sole purpose of developing the inheritance held within all the Tribes of Israel, here in the Americas. To connect the dots between the United States and ancient Egypt, an imperative article is reviewed within the Moroccan World News, titled Sidi Mohamed Ben Abdellah's Diplomatic Initiatives towards the U.S., written on March 20, 2012. The title Sultan and Pharaoh are semantically related, with the title Sultan being derived from Old French Souldan or Soudan. Before reading the article, keep in mind the previous understanding of Quebec Louisiana, a "country" in North America and a former French Empire colony, with territories covering a vast majority of North America and some lands in Ontario to the Great Lakes of Canada. The article reads,

> One main direct reason behind the sultan's interest in the Americans can be traced back to early 1766, when the Sultan released a 'fatwa' concerning the exportation of wheat to Europeans through the port of Fdala, which the sultan built for that particular purpose. The sultan allowed his people to sell their crops, especially wheat, to Europeans, who in turn, bought and shipped large amounts of wheat and food supplies abroad. In this context, the exportation of wheat increased between 1770 and 1774 towards Portugal, Spain and France. In 1774, 100.000 quintal (quintar) of wheat was exported to Spain and almost the same quantity was exported to France. Indeed, the exportation of wheat to Europe affected the whole country especially after successive years of drought. The rain did not fall for over seven years from 1776 to 1783, and the swarms of locust came from the south and completely destroyed crops. The country knew serious food crisis due to the plague of locusts and drought. The prices of wheat increased rapidly, and poor people were unable to buy enough amounts. According to the French consul Louis de Chenier in one of his letters, the reserves of wheat decreased in stores and its price increased three times in 1775. Louis de Chenier describes the chaotic situation of Morocco in detail. He describes the effects of a series of famines, which brought about

infectious diseases, plagues of locusts and successive years of drought. The locusts ravaged the empire of Morocco, especially after the year 1778. In 1779, the quantity of young locusts eaten up the whole country, and nothing that is green on earth could escape the voracity of these insects. The consequences of swarms of locusts and successive years of drought were so fatal. The lands produced no harvest, and the people began to feel a dearth. Their cattle died with hunger. People perished of indigestible food and want. Fathers sold their children, and husbands bestowed their wives in marriage. The sultan's exportation of wheat and food supplies to Europeans worsened the situation of the country and made the crisis more serious. The export of wheat to the Sultan's need for firearms, suggesting that when S. Muhammad had sufficient weaponry, he no longer allowed the sale of grain. In fact, the sultan stopped exporting wheat and food supplies to Europe because he realized the serious food crisis that the whole country was enduring. He released a 'fatwa' through which he forbade exporting wheat to Europeans. Then, he issued a declaration on December 20, 1777, announcing that all Europeans and American vessels could freely import wheat to Morocco. The sultan declared that all vessels importing food supplies from Europe and especially America would not pay taxes or tributes in his ports. The sultan Sidi Muhammad III was neither looking for the friendship of the Americans nor to recognize their independence in 1777. But, he was rather trying to get support from Americans and Europeans to overcome the food crisis of the country, just as the Americans were looking for support from France to get their independence. Moreover, the sultan renewed the maritime trade through establishing diplomatic relations with Americans and Europeans. For this purpose, he encouraged the presence of American and European vessels in coastal cities. He built new cities with big ports and big ships and frigates to fight corsairs. The sultan rebuilt the port of Anfa in 1760, the port of Mogador in 1765, expelled the Portuguese from the port of Brija. He also regained the control over the port of Agadir.

The Sultan (Pharaoh) endured a harsh dearth (famine) and is expressed in great detail in the book of Genesis 41:28-36, which reads,

This is the thing which I (Joseph) have spoken to Pharaoh. God has shown Pharaoh what He is about to do. Indeed seven years of great plenty will come throughout all the land of Egypt; but after them seven years of famine will arise, and all the plenty will be forgotten in the land of Egypt; and the famine will deplete the land. So the plenty will not be known in the land because of the famine following, for it will be very severe. And the dream was repeated to Pharaoh twice because the thing is established by God, and God will shortly bring it to pass. Now therefore, let Pharaoh select a discerning and wise man, and set him over the land of Egypt. Let Pharaoh do this, and let him appoint officers over the land, to collect one-fifth of the produce of the land of Egypt in the seven plentiful years. And let them gather all the food of those good years that are coming, and store up grain under the authority of Pharaoh, and let them keep food in the cities. Then that food shall be as a reserve for the land for the seven years of famine which shall be in the land of Egypt, that the land may not perish during the famine.

Verse 39-42, Then Pharaoh said to Joseph, "Inasmuch as God has shown you all this, there is no one as discerning and wise as you. You shall be over my house, and all my people shall be ruled according to your word; only in regard to the throne will I be greater than you. And Pharaoh said to Joseph, "See, I have set you over all of the land of Egypt." Then Pharaoh took his signet ring off his hand and put it on Joseph's hand; and he clothed him in garments of fine linen and put a gold chain around his neck.

Verse 46-49, Joseph was thirty years old when he stood before Pharaoh king of Egypt. And Joseph went out from the presence of Pharaoh, and went throughout all the land of Egypt. Now in the seven plentiful years the ground brought forth abundantly. So he gathered up all the food of the seven years which were in the land of Egypt, and laid up the food in the cities; he laid up every city the food of the fields which surrounded them. Joseph gathered very much grain, as the sand of the sea, until he stopped counting for it was immeasurable.

Verse 53-57, Then the seven years of plenty which were in the land of Egypt ended, and the seven years of famine began to come, as Joseph has said. The famine was in all lands, but in all the land of Egypt there was bread. So when all the land of Egypt was famished, the people cried to Pharaoh for bread. Then Pharaoh said to all the Egyptians, "Go to Joseph; whatever he says to you, do." The famine was over all the face of the earth, and Joseph opened all the storehouses and sold to the Egyptians. And the famine became sever in the land of Egypt. So all the countries came to Joseph in Egypt to buy grain, because the famine was severe in all lands.

Pharaoh's governor, Joseph, was the foremost diplomat for all countries of all the earth to receive grain in exchange for lawful money on behalf of Pharaoh (Sultan) to survive the upcoming seven-year famine (dearth) and drought, that Joseph interpreted based on the vision given to Pharaoh by God. Joseph's position would eventually lead to his eleven brothers (of the Tribes of Israel), including his father Jacob, to settle in Egypt's best lots (parishes), known as Goshen. Genesis 46:4-6 states that Jacob, alongside all his descendants, all goods and livestock went down into the land of Egypt from the land of Canaan. The word "down" in verse 4 is the Hebrew word "yarad," literally meaning to go downwards, or conventionally to a lower region, going south. The land of Canaan is what is known today as the land of Canada, and directly below it is North America, formerly known as ancient Egypt. Joseph enters the seven-year famine and begins to collect tribute as a means for seed, time, and harvest to all those under the jurisdiction of Pharaoh stated in Genesis 47:23-26, which reads,

> Then Joseph said to the people, "Indeed I have brought you and your land this day for Pharaoh. Look, here is seed for you, and you shall sow the land. And it shall come to pass in the harvest that you shall give one-fifth to Pharaoh. Four-fifths shall be your own, as seed for the field and for your food, for those of your households and as food for your little ones. So they said, "You have saved our lives; lets us find favor in the sight of my lord, and we will be Pharaoh's servants." And Joseph made it a law over the land of Egypt to this day, that Pharaoh should have on-fifth, except for the land of the priests only, which did not become Pharaoh's.

The famine under the rule of Sultan (Pharaoh) described in Morocco (ancient Egypt; the Americas) began in 1776 full of starvation, disease, drylands, and no harvesting of crops throughout all the earth, and ended in 1783, precisely seven years. This seven-year span from 1776 to 1783 is significant to highlight when piecing the timeline together. In remembrance of the Treaty of Marrakesh, it is written that,

On February 20, 1778, the Pharaoh issued a declaration notifying all consuls and European merchants in Tangier, Sale, and Mogador that, "henceforth all vessels flying the American flag might freely enter the Moroccan (ancient Egypt; the Americas) ports and enjoy in them the same privileges and immunities with those of the other nations with whom Morocco maintains "peace." In response to the Pharaoh's initiative, the United States Congress established a committee to write the draft of the agreement that took a few years to enact.

*(Treaty of Marrakesh, 1202 (1787))*

The seven-year famine is why the enactment of the U.S. Congress committee "took a few years" to be established. All countries and consuls of the earth were undergoing the magnifications of the drought and severe famines. The Treaty of Marrakesh, referred to as the Treaty of Peace and Friendship, the first document of its kind, was finally drafted by Ben-Yamin Franklin in Paris of 1785, to be signed in 1786, a ratification date of July 18, 1787. While Joseph of the Mehomitan Nation (ancient Egypt; the Americas) established a one-fifth tax on all countries, storing up goods and wheat; led to Pharaoh (Sultan) allying with the United States, one year after the beginning of the severe famine, to protect its dominions from the piracy of Great Britain. The United States and other dominions were exempt from the one-fifth tax tribute, demanded by the Sultan and reinforced by Joseph. The Treaty of Marrakesh further clarifies,

> This was while Great Britain was turning its back on the young republic, ending its protection of all American trade ships sailing in the Mediterranean Sea. As a result, Americans were suffering heavy losses from the vicious pirate attacks in the area. Great Britain (Brutish Moors) had even encouraged acts of piracy of vessels flying the American flag. With no friends in the region and no navy to protect its ships, the United States left defenseless, and according to Thomas Jefferson, incapable of exporting almost "one-third" of its wheat and "one-fourth" of other items produced by the seven states of the union.

Such recognition and aid from Morocco to the United States in 1777 is why so many other public figures, including President Joe Biden, acknowledged Morocco (ancient Egypt; the Americas). Further confirmed in the Marrakesh Treaty,

> The United States and Morocco being the first nation to recognize the independence of the United States and to have signed in 1787 a treaty of friendship and cooperation, the first of its kind concluded by the young republic.

It's interesting to note the following treaties, spawning from the Marrakesh Treaty with a ratification date of (Arabic 1202) 1787, are available to the public; however, the Treaty of Marrakesh is a guarded document and only obtained from the various libraries of the United States Congress. The purpose of this hidden document is first to conceal the accurate calendar timeline. Not knowing the exact current year can distort real history! And second, to disconnect people from the powerful message of the bible, which is in sync with most recent events. If the actual timeline is obscured or rearranged, then a lack of connection with biblical events is the only outcome. Events that have allegedly happened thousands upon thousands of years ago would automatically deposit a non-essential state of perception when in all actuality, those events took place just over two centuries ago. The Marrakesh Treaty initially implemented in (Arabic 1200) 1785, states the Arabic year of ratification to be 1202 (the era of Adoni/Iahoh), to which is the English translated ratification date of 1787, and the following document is the Treaty of Peace of Friendship with Morocco on June 23, 1786 (Arabic 1201).

One of the deceiving tactics of providing an English Gregorian calendar date to the Arabic dating system can be seen within the document known as the Magna Carta of 1215. It would have the reader believe it is dated the year 1215, 806 years ago, when in actuality, the documents maritime strength relies on the initial 1786 (Arabic 1201) Treaty with Morocco. Therefore, it is not the year 1215 but instead Arabic 1215 (the English Gregorian year 1800), just fifteen years from Marrakesh's initial Treaty. The Magna Carta is an extension of the Treaty with Morocco, which is an extension of the Treaty of Marrakesh. Section 41 of the Magna Carta states,

> All merchants may enter or leave England unharmed and without fear, and may stay or travel within it, by land or water, for purposes of trade, free from all illegal exactions, in accordance with ancient and lawful customs. This, however, does not apply in time of war to merchants from a country that is at war with us. Any such merchants found in our country at the outbreak of war shall be detained without injury to their persons or property, until we or our chief justice have discovered how our own merchants are being treated in the country at war with us. If our merchants are safe they shall be safe too.

A similar decree is found in section 18, of the Treaty with Morocco,

> All goods shall be weighed and examined before they are sent on board, and to avoid all detention of Vessels, no examination shall afterwards be made, unless it shall first be proved, that contraband Goods have been sent on Board, in which Case the Persons who took the contraband Goods on board shall be punished according to the Usage and Custom of the Country and no other Person whatever shall be injured, nor shall the Ship or Cargo incur any Penalty or damage whatever.

Marrakesh's Treaty's final extension to take reference of is The Royal Proclamation, with the alleged date October 7, 1763, being twenty-two years ahead of the Marrakesh Treaty. It is easy to discern the government's deceptive tactic in hiding the "first document," which spawned all the others. The Royal Proclamation begins,

> Whereas We have taken into our Royal Consideration the extensive and valuable Acquisitions in America, secured to our Crown by the late Definitive Treaty of Peace, concluded at Paris; the 10$^{th}$ Day of February last (1763);

There is the lie in plain sight. The "Definitive Treaty of Peace" is not the Treaty of Peace and Friendship beginning in 1763 but the Treaty of Marrakesh, also known as the Treaty of Peace and Friendship, the first document of its kind originating in 1785. The date of 1763, associated with the Proclamation, is completely forged. The Proclamation continues as the following,

> And being desirous that all Our loving Subjects, as well of our Kingdom as of our Colonies in America, may avail themselves with all convenient Speed, of the great Benefits and Advantages which must accrue therefrom to their Commerce, Manufactures, and Navigation, We have thought fit, with the Advice of our Privy Council. To issue this our Royal Proclamation, hereby to publish and declare to all our loving Subjects, that we have, with the Advice of our Said Privy Council, granted our Letters Patent, under our Guest Seal of Great Britain, to erect, within the

Countries and Islands ceded and confirmed to Us by the said Treaty, Four distinct and separate Governments, styled and called by the names of Quebec, East Florida, West Florida and Grenada, and limited and bounded as follows, viz.

The ninth paragraph of the Royal Proclamation utilizes the principles of the biblical laws. It reads,

And Whereas, We are desirous, upon all occasions, to testify our Royal Sense and Approbation of the Conduct and bravery of the Officers and Soldiers of our Armies, and to reward the same, We do hereby command and impower our Governors of our said Three new Colonies, and all other our Governors of our several Provinces on the Continent of North America, to grant without Fee or Reward, to such reduced Officers as have served in North America during the late War, and to such Private Soldiers as have been or shall be disbanded in America, and are actually residing there, and shall personally apply for the same, the following Quantities of Lands, subject, at the Expiration of Ten Years, to the same Quit-Rents as other Lands are subject to in the Province within which they are granted, as also subject to the same Conditions of Cultivation and Improvement; viz

To every Person having the Rank of a Field Officer – 5,000 Acres.

To every Captain – 3,000 Acres.

To every Subaltern or Staff Officer – 2,000 Acres.

To every Non-Commission Officer – 200 Acres.

**To every Private Man – 50 Acres.**

Those that have served in the army would be rewarded a couple of thousand acres as a reward; however, every "private man" would get 50 acres. A national who has corrected their commercial status, obtaining a non-citizen national status certificate, would be classified as a private man, also known as a natural person in trust. A Non-Commission Officer (NCO) and a Private Soldier (Pte) are the same. Non-Commissioned Officers is a military officer who has not earned a commission. NCOs usually obtain their position of authority by promotion through the enlisted ranks. NCOs also includes most or all enlisted personnel, which are of the lower ranks of an officer. A private soldier is a soldier of the lowest rank in an army or the marines. To further solidify, a private person means any natural person or artificial person, including a corporation, partnership, trust, or other entity other than a Governmental Unit.

According to God's ordinances, God demands lots (acres) of land to all private men within God's trust, listed in Numbers 33:54,

And you shall divide the land by lot as an inheritance among your families; to the larger you shall give a larger inheritance, and to the smaller you shall give a smaller inheritance; there everyone's inheritance shall be whatever falls to him by lot. You shall inherit according to the tribes of your fathers.

*(New King James Version)*

Then the Lord spoke to Moses, saying, Command the children of Israel, and say to them: 'When you come into the land of Canaan, this is the land that shall fall to you as an inheritance – the land of Canaan to its boundaries.

*(Numbers 34:1-2 New King James Version)*

Canada is the ancient land of Canaan and is with Morocco's (ancient Egypt, the Americas) dominions (Great Britain). Canada is provided in the Articles of Confederation, which helped establish the united States of America corporation after the Articles of Association. Section 11, which reads,

Canada acceding to this confederation, and adjoining the measures of the United States, shall be admitted into, and entitled to all the advantages of this Union, but no other colony shall be admitted into the same, unless such admission be agreed to by nine States.

(Article XI.)

The Canadian Corporation is listed with the Securities and Exchange Commission (S.E.C.) in New York, New York, alongside the Depository Trust Corporation, with a C.I.K. No. 0000230098, Reporting File No. 033-05368 and SIC Code 8888, meaning a foreign government to the republic united States of America. The governor Joseph and his eleven brothers who established the twelve Tribes of Israel in the land of modern Canada and in the Americas have paved the way towards the establishment of the 12,000 seat representatives from each tribe; holding plenipotentiary power within the S.E.C. rules of Rule 144A, leading to the estate inheritance stored in trust for anyone to claim. The treaties that shaped the Americas were initially written in Arabic, synonymous with Latin or the Old French language. Sultan and Pharaoh are from the Old French Souldan or Soudan; Hebrew is from the Old French Ebreu from Latin Hebraeus and Aramaic (Semitic) ebhrai, corresponding to ibhri "an Israelite;" Quebec is derived from the Old French word Quebecois, and Canada is the Latinized form of the word "village" in an Iroquoian language. Pharaoh can also be attributed to Amir, meaning a high title of nobility or office, used in some Muslim countries or otherwise known as Mehomitan Nations. Governor is from the Old French governeor meaning prince or ruler, and the Modern French gouverneur, directly from the Latin gubernatorem.

There is so much more that can be discussed, but one thing for sure, the world is still in biblical times, and due to reconstructed history, many are unaware. Still, many wealthy families who utilize biblical treaty law are very much aware. These families fully understand that this commercial system must utilize the ens legis in the public while the Express Trust owns and controls it in the private. The ens legis is likened to the legal public fiction, known as Thomas Anderson, to which Neo (the trust) utilized to enter in and out of the public and private side of the Matrix. Very much like the private people of Zion, unable to enter into the public side of the Matrix, there are individuals that are not in the public system and only operate within private markets. To immediately reach the Zero Percent tax bracket and obtain wealth, one must declare their true nationality as a national but not a citizen of the United States and entirely operate in the truth of the Express Trust.

# Acknowledgments

First and foremost, praises and thanks to the God, the Almighty, the Alpha and Omega, for His showers of blessings throughout my research work to complete the research successfully.

I would like to express my deep and sincere gratitude to my research mentor and grand master teacher in the world of history, private process and commerce, Jonah Bey. His dynamism, vision, sincerity and motivation to uplift fallen humanity, have deeply inspired me to write this book with the intention of carrying on the vision. He has taught me the methodology to carry out the research and to present the research works as clearly as possible. I also would like to give an honorable mention to Dr. Frederick K. Price Jr., head Pastor of Crenshaw Christian Center in Los Angeles, California, Horace Butler, Ron LeGrand and the late Frank Pastore of the Frank Pastore Show on KKLA, 99.5 FM. Price has been an extreme role model in my life displaying righteous traits in seeking to be a good man, friend, all around writer, historian and teacher of the word of God. His father now with the Lord of Lords, has influenced him and I along with others in the community of faith. I would like to thank Mr. Butler for his avid research with geography and historical artifacts described in his book, "When Rocks Cry Out." Ron LeGrand is a well-known real estate titan and I most certainly appreciate his teachings and devotions to help others acquire success. Although Frank Pastore is no longer with us but his powerful teachings as a radio talk show host in the world of politics and apologetics have influenced me to question everything and only believe the evidence thereof. I am extremely grateful for what these three role models have offered me. I also extend my heartfelt thanks to my family and immediate friends for their acceptance and patience in allowing me to share this in-depth, life changing information.

I am extremely grateful to my mother for her love, prayers, motivational support and the many sacrifices devoted to my education and preparing me for my future, in following her footsteps in the field of law. I am very much thankful to my father for his devotion in my life displaying that no matter what comes, God will always be by your side through the good and the bad. And finally, my thanks go to all the people who have supported me to complete the research work directly or indirectly.

Du'Vaul Dey

CPSIA information can be obtained
at www.ICGtesting.com
Printed in the USA
LVHW020753160822
726054LV00008B/118